SEARCH AND RESCUE DOGS

The remarkable story of search and rescue dogs
– from the mountains to the shore

Bob Sharp & Bill Jennison

Foreword by Malcolm Grindrod

[signatures]

HAYLOFT PUBLISHING LTD
KIRKBY STEPHEN

First published by Hayloft 2012

Hayloft Publishing Ltd, South Stainmore,
Kirkby Stephen, Cumbria, CA17 4DJ

tel: 017683 41568
email: books@hayloft.eu
web: www.hayloft.eu

Copyright © Bob Sharp and Bill Jennison, 2012

ISBN 1 904524 75 3

Designed, printed and bound in the EU.

Papers used by Hayloft are natural, recyclable products made from wood grown in sustainable forest. The manufacturing processes conform to the environmental regulations of the country of origin.

Illustrations and design: © Judy Whiteside
Cover photograph: © Peter Sandground

*To search and rescue dogs
past, present and future.*

Contents

'The search dog, by virtue of its highly developed sense of smell combined with its intensive preparatory training, becomes a vital cog in the machinery of mountain rescue providing an added dimension to the search facilities. And so, despite its position as a well-loved member of the family, the dog can only be viewed as another item of specialised equipment – like the stretcher, rope, radio or searchlight.'

Pete Durst 1982

Preface

As members of the same mountain rescue team, we often discussed the activities of the Search and Rescue Dog Association (SARDA). On one occasion, we joined a number of team members from across the UK, who had gathered for a SARDA assessment course. Those that passed would become part of a select group of qualified dog handlers whose lifestyle would change significantly — on call 24 hours every day without a break, often searching for missing people in poor weather at night time and in challenging and unfamiliar terrain. Why, we pondered, would experienced team members take on such challenges in addition to their normal mountain rescue work? We also reflected on how the whole business of training dogs and handlers has developed over the past half century.

It occurred to us that many substantial changes had taken place since the notion of using dogs to search for missing walkers was first mooted: training techniques, search management, breeds of dogs used in searching, the formalisation of national associations and the key role search dogs play within the emergency service framework. It also struck us that very little about these matters had been documented. In fact, it seemed quite extraordinary that the unique and vital contribution dog teams make to the search and rescue effort in the UK had never been fully documented, described and publicised.

The initial developments back in the 1960s were described by Ernest Dudley in *Rangi – Highland Rescue Dog,* now a classic in the field of mountaineering literature. His book reveals how the use of dogs to search for missing persons grew from one person's idea (the celebrated mountaineer Hamish MacInnes) to the involvement and interest of a few like-minded people and the emergence of a formal organisation — the Search and Rescue Dog Association. There have been a number of other publications, typically stories about particular dogs, but never a complete look at the whole picture. On this basis, we felt it fitting to combine our respective experiences, put pen to paper and fill the gap in provision.

We have written this book to fulfill a number of aims and appeal to a wide variety of people, not just those involved in search and rescue. Most important, it brings together a number of relevant subjects such as how dogs are trained to search, how dog teams are assessed, canine intelligence and sense of smell, the wider place of dogs in society, and how they work in collaboration with other emergency services. In combining these and other subjects, the book provides an up-to-date and complete reference source for all those either currently working with dogs or planning to become involved. Throughout, we focus on genuine incidents and record the feelings and views of people who are directly involved with dogs and rescue work — dog handlers, assessors, casualties, rescuers and dogsbodies. Many of these people have made a seminal contribution across the years and we feel very privileged to have worked with them and to record the impact of their work. Notably, we also record the 'thoughts' and experiences of a few dogs along the way!

We know the book will appeal to those involved in mountain rescue as well as the wider mountaineering fraternity but also, knowing the popularity of dogs as pets and the expanding use of working dogs into all aspects of our lives, we feel there will be wide interest from those involved in the training of dogs and the dog-loving public at large.

Bob Sharp
& Bill Jennison

Foreword

When Bob Sharp and Bill Jennison asked me to write the foreword for *Search and Rescue Dogs*, my mind went back over my 40 years training SARDA dogs. So many memories!

As a new handler, going out on a search, you're full of mixed emotions. To save a life would be fantastic, but will your dog indicate when it finds a casualty — especially if you've been out working on a search all night? 'Trust your dog,' they say. 'A well trained dog won't let you down. Remember, you're a well-trained team'. You've been told this many times, but there's so much at stake. Life is so precious.

Then comes your first good find. Confidence is restored. You know that you and your dog are an asset to any well run search. Those early days proved to me, beyond doubt, that dog and handler really are a team — you work and train and learn together. And that close relationship was reinforced many times during my career in mountain rescue.

Dogs have a sense of smell many times better than our own and *Search and Rescue Dogs* explains how humans capitalise on this. The history of search dogs is well documented, even as far back as the First World War when dogs were used to locate victims of collapsed buildings.

Search dog handlers now have better clothing, better footwear and better equipment — GPS devices, mobile phones, radios — but a dog still goes out in its birthday suit, covering the ground with a speed and efficiency no human could ever dream of. I've watched dogs work onto a scent on hundreds of occasions and been amazed at the distance a dog can pick up on a human scent.

I was interested to read other dog handlers' tales of actual searches, in a wide variety of situations. Even a few from the dogs themselves! It's not just about the walkers and climbers who get lost or injured in the mountains. Elderly people and children fail to return home, often in heavily populated areas.

The section about helicopters took me back to early one morning, with my friend, Dave Riley, and his dog, and an all night search for a group of young lads. Dave's dog found the boys who were soon being winched up into a hovering Sea King. When the time came for us to be winched, down came a double strop and up we went, each holding our dog tight in our arms. Trouble was, six or seven metres up, our dogs began to fight! Clinging on for dear life to two struggling dogs, the pair of us finally arrived at the helicopter, Dave 'wearing' his dog on his head like a 'Davy Crocket' hat!

'Search and Rescue Dogs' describes the remarkable relationship between dogs and humans, work and play, from ancient times, through the twentieth century to Hamish MacInnes and the beginnings of SARDA — dwelling briefly on just how much dogs have influenced popular culture — then on via health matters, training and assessment to the search and rescue dogs we know today. It's a fascinating read.

As a search dog handler with six graded dogs to my name, there's one thing I know for sure: there's nothing finer than training your four-legged friend to save human life. You couldn't ask for more — and, once you've read this book, you'll begin to understand why.

Malcolm Grindrod

1 In the beginning

'Without encouragement she is off into the corrie we have come to search. Orna's tail is high. She's having a ball. It is then, just as the first rays of sun creep over the ridge to our east, it occurs to me that if I had a tail I would be wagging it too because there isn't anything in the world I would rather be doing. And it was all Hamish MacInnes's fault.' Tom Gilchrist (SARDA Scotland)

'A man's best friend is his dog'. So they say. But what is it about these four-legged bundles of sheer, unadulterated energy, that so inspires? Beyond a seemingly endless capacity for doe-eyed, unconditional love? More than likely — we think — it's down to their incredible versatility and the many and varied ways dogs have helped us over the centuries.

They've helped us hunt and track, guard and haul, entertain and search. They've even helped us heal, but it's so much more than that. Dogs are remarkably good at the practical stuff and, as any dog owner knows, they can give affection, love and friendship in abundance. Which makes them one of the most popular pets across the world — an estimated eight million in the UK alone — with over one million dogs born worldwide, every day of the year!

This special relationship, between humans and dogs, has inspired hundreds of sayings and idioms — quite unlike any other animal. The extraordinary versatility with which dogs and humans interact lies, essentially, in the way dogs have been selectively bred across many centuries to serve particular needs. A wide variety of different breeds have evolved and developed to serve specific, practical purposes, although most dogs are also companionable in nature.

But one thing is certain about dogs: there's no doubting their practical value to man, and this is no less so in the world of search and rescue.

The association between men and dogs goes back a very long way. In Homer's Ancient Greek story, The Odyssey, Argos was a hound that waited patiently for over twenty years for his master Odysseus to return home. Most people thought Odysseus dead but, when he returned disguised as a beggar, Argos knew him immediately.

Cerberus was the three-headed dog that guarded the gates of Hell, and boasted a mane of live snakes and a dragon's tail. The ancient Greeks greatly revered dogs and had a particular relationship with them, advising one to 'always pat your dog's head after he catches a hare and say 'Well done' for, like men of generous spirit, they love praise'.

Several Greek gods are portrayed alongside greyhounds and other breeds. Dogs were used in warfare by the Greek generals, many bred specifically for their hunting and guarding capabilities. The Greeks classified dogs according to their function, such as hunting or guarding a herd or estate, and advocated they should always be purchased to suit their intended use. For protecting farms and cattle, for example, dogs should be 'big, and have a loud bark in order to intimidate intruders.'

FACING PAGE: CATHERINE AND HAMISH MACINNES WITH RANGI © SANDY SEABROOK.
RIGHT: CERBERUS, THE THREE-HEADED DOG THAT GUARDED THE GATES OF HELL © MARTIN MALCHEV, DREAMSTIME.COM.

Dogs used by shepherds should be white, to avoid mistaking them for wolves, and be 'long and slim, but also strong and fast, so they can repel wolves or pursue one that had taken its prey.'

Over time, individual breeds came to be recognised for their physical characteristics and capabilities. Thus, Laconian Hounds were considered ideal for hunting hare and other wild animals, but also as guard dogs for watching over homes and livestock.

The ceramics of ancient Iran, and the tombs of the Pharaohs in Egypt, show pictures of dogs, and dog mummies have been found with those of the Pharaohs inside pyramids. After the Roman city of Pompeii was destroyed by volcanic eruption, a dog was found in the debris, spread-eagled over a dead child, appearing to have lost its life trying to protect the child.

There are early references in literature to tracking techniques, and to dogs using airborne smells to chase their quarry. Bloodhounds — originally bred to hunt deer and wild boar — were often used to track people including, legend has it, Robert the Bruce and William Wallace, as far back as the thirteenth and fourteenth centuries.

In the sixteenth century, they were used to track thieves and poachers, notably the Border Reivers in the Scottish Borders. Bloodhounds helped locate runaway slaves before the American Civil War in the nineteenth century and, more recently, the Oscar-winning film *Oh Brother Where Art Thou* depicted bloodhounds tracking escaped criminals.

The breed most popularly associated with dogs helping those in distress is the St Bernard. These large working dogs are a gentle breed which, over the years, has come to be associated with first aid, emergency rescue and safety. Their story centres on the Great St Bernard Pass. The oldest of the passes running through the Western Alps, this road links Italy and Switzerland and rises to a height of over 2,400 metres. The monastery at the summit was founded in 1049 by Saint Bernard of Menthon and served as a refuge for travellers. It's estimated around 20,000 travellers used the pass every year and the monks were often called to assist those who were lost or avalanched.

Around 300 years ago, 'St Bernards' (as they came to be known) began to accompany the monks on their rescue missions. The breed's keen sense of direction, their ability to negotiate deep snow, and their worth as guides in bad weather conditions, were invaluable traits. Reports from the time indicated that dogs were sometimes able to locate missing persons, even when they were completely covered by snow. The dogs are credited with saving the lives of many lost travellers and even avalanche victims.

The popular myth is that St Bernards carry small casks of brandy around their necks for medicinal purposes. Nowadays it is widely known that giving alcohol to anyone suffering from hypothermia is very bad medical practice. Alcohol has a vasodilatory effect which leads to further loss in body temperature. It is now assumed the barrels worn by the dogs probably contained first aid supplies, which would account for the cross inscribed on each barrel.

The most famous St Bernard was Barry, who reportedly saved somewhere between 40 and 100 lives. Amongst his rescue adventures is the story of a young boy found stranded on an icy ledge during a heavy snowfall. It wasn't possible for anyone to climb the icy ledge but Barry, braving all adversity, crawled inch by inch to the injured boy and began to lick the boy's face, causing him to wake up.

With the young boy's arms wrapped around his strong neck, Barry pulled him carefully from the ledge and carried him to safety. This heroic dog lived from 1800 to 1814 and, to this day, the largest dog at the hospice is always called Barry in his honour. A monument in the Cimetière des Chiens bears the legend: 'Il sauva la vie à 40 personnes. Il fut tué par le 41ème' meaning he saved the lives of forty people, but died while attempting to save the forty-first. Barry's body is preserved in the Natural History Museum in Berne.

And so, the St Bernard became the patron saint of mountaineers but, whilst they were probably the first dogs used in mountain rescue, they were not an influencing factor in the formation of the search and rescue dog organisations we know today.

There are numerous instances of dogs used in times of war. In the Middle Ages, suitably armoured Great Danes were used to defend supply caravans. In the mid-eighteenth century, Frederick the Great used Russian dogs as messengers in the Seven Years War. The Americans established a bloodhound 'Canine Corps' during the Seminole (Indian) War of 1835, using the dogs to track Indians and runaway slaves. Early in the nineteenth century, Napoleon posted dogs — mainly poodles — as sentries at the gates of Alexandria in Egypt to warn his troops of attack. In the 1960s, over 400 military-trained dogs were used as sentries, scouts and trackers to deter Vietcong attacks on military installations. And, during the Gulf War, over 1000 highly trained German Shepherds were used by the French forces to guard and protect troops, supplies and aircraft.

During the First World War, dogs were trained and used by the Red Cross to locate injured personnel on the battlefield at night and during lulls in the fighting. They were trained to 'find' by using the airborne scent from a human body. The dogs carried a 'bringsel' clipped to their collar. When the dog located an injured soldier, it would return to its handler with the bringsel in its mouth indicating that the dog had found a soldier. This particular method was used because it was thought barking might frighten or distress the injured soldier. The bringsel is still used today by the Norwegian search and rescue services.

A fascinating tale, towards the end of the war, tells of a search in heavy snow conditions. A rescue team member's dog showed continued interest in a particular location, which had already been investigated. After some time, the dog began to bark and, when the location was re-examined with probes, the buried person was found alive. This specific incident led a Swiss dog-training expert to train four Alsatians (German Shepherds) to search for avalanche victims. The dogs were subsequently presented to the Swiss Army for operational work.

During the Second World War, dogs were used with great success in the London Blitz to locate people buried in buildings, again by the use of airborne scent. Most were Alsatians, trained by the police, although others were owned by private individuals or the London Fire Brigade.

One particular dog called Rip made a huge impact on the search effort. Rip was a mongrel, made homeless when the Luftwaffe attacked East London in 1940. He managed to survive the bombing but was left to roam the streets, foraging for scraps to keep alive. One day an Air Raid Precaution Warden called Mr King came across the dog foraging for food. Mr King tossed him titbits in the hope he would go away, but this brief gesture led to a partnership which endured for the duration of the war. Rip became the unit's first mascot then, crucially, the service's first sniffer dog. He had a talent for locating people buried in bomb debris, mostly around the docks area — a prime target during the Blitz.

Mr King noted that it wasn't necessary to train Rip — in fact, it proved impossible to stop him. Despite the dangers, Rip worked courageously through the explosions of the bombing raids, braved fire and smoke with apparent disdain, and was completely unfazed by the scream of the air raid sirens. The first sign someone was trapped in the rubble was a twitching and sniffing of his sensitive nose. So keen was he to follow it through, he would dig at the fallen bricks and masonry like a Jack Russell looking for a rabbit. During the Blitz he is credited with finding and rescuing more than a hundred victims of German bombings and, according to Mr King, Rip was never off duty. After black-out, the dog accompanied Mr King on his nightly tour of street shelters, always accepting food from grateful people he met.

In July 1945, his unusual valour earned him the PDSA Dickin Medal for Gallantry — the animal equivalent of the Victoria Cross. When Rip died, he became the first of a

GREYFRIARS BOBBY

John Gray was a police officer in Edinburgh in the mid-19th century. As a condition of his service, he acquired a watch dog – Bobby, his faithful Skye Terrier – and the two became inseparable, even after death.

In 1858, Gray was buried in Old Greyfriars churchyard in Edinburgh. For the next fourteen years, Bobby kept constant watch and guard over the grave until his own death in 1872, only leaving his post for food. It's said he did this regularly at one o'clock each day, when he would walk to the entrance to the graveyard to be fed his mid-day meal by waiting visitors.

Because Bobby was no longer licensed and didn't wear a collar, he was at risk of being put down by the local authorities. However, the Lord Provost of Edinburgh — a dog lover and Director for the Scottish Society for the Prevention of Cruelty to Animals — decided to pay Bobby's licence and had a collar made with the brass inscription:

'Greyfriars Bobby from the Lord Provost 186 — licensed.'

In time, Bobby too was buried in Greyfriars churchyard, about 70 metres from John Gray's grave. Shortly after his death, the President of the Royal Society for the Prevention of Cruelty to Animals — who had visited Bobby when he was alive and been deeply moved by his story — gained permission from the City Council to erect a granite fountain with a statue of Bobby on top. William Brody, a celebrated artist of the time, sculptured the statue, which was unveiled without ceremony a year after Bobby's death. A red granite stone, erected by the Dog Aid Society of Scotland, now marks Bobby's grave. The inscription reads:

'Greyfriars Bobby — died 14th January 1872 — aged 16 years. Let his loyalty and devotion be a lesson to us all. Unveiled by HRH The Duke of Gloucester CCVO on the 13th May 1981.'

Sited on the pavement near the churchyard, Bobby's memorial is a popular attraction for visitors to Edinburgh.

INSET: GREYFRIARS BOBBY © ELIFRANSSENS, DREAMSTIME.COM

TOP: RIP HELPS AN AIR RAID PRECAUTIONS WARDEN SEARCH AMONGST RUBBLE AND DEBRIS FOLLOWING AN AIR RAID IN POPLAR. THE WARDEN SIGNALS FOR HELP FROM HIS COLLEAGUES TO SEARCH THE SPOT INDICATED BY RIP © THE PDSA.

CENTRE: THE DICKIN MEDAL, AWARDED FOR CONSPICUOUS GALLANTRY OR DEVOTION TO DUTY WHILE SERVING IN MILITARY CONFLICT, WAS INSTITUTED IN 1943 IN THE UK BY MARIA DICKIN (WHO FOUNDED THE PDSA) TO HONOUR THE WORK OF ANIMALS IN WAR © THE PDSA.

ABOVE: TREO THE BLACK LABRADOR, MOST RECENT RECIPIENT OF THE DICKIN MEDAL FOR HIS WORK IN AFGHANISTAN © THE PDSA.

FACING PAGE: HAMISH MACINNES IN HIS WORKSHOP © HAMISH MACINNES.

succession of 'supreme animal heroes' to be buried in the PDSA cemetery in Ilford, Essex. The headstone inscription reads: 'Rip, D.M., 'We also serve' — for the dog whose body lies here played his part in the Battle of Britain.'

It was partly due to Rip's outstanding efforts that local authorities — notably the police — later decided to formally train dogs to trace missing persons. The Dickin Medal, incidentally, was named after Maria Dickin who founded the PDSA. It has been awarded to 63 animals in total: 27 dogs, three horses, one cat — and 32 Second World War messenger pigeons! The latest award was to Treo, a Black Labrador, for his work searching for roadside bombs in Afghanistan in 2010.

After the Second World War, the Swiss Alpine Club reviewed its existing method for finding the victims of avalanches. This involved a system of inserting a long rod into the snow in the hope of feeling it strike a body. Probing was carried out using a line-out of personnel inserting the probes at predetermined intervals. The system is still used in Scotland but it is very slow and, whilst being very thorough, gives a very limited chance of finding victims alive.

The Swiss Alpine Club considered the previous use of dogs in rescue work, focusing especially on the dog's natural scenting ability to find people buried under debris, and decided to train dogs for avalanche work, to assist their own rescue network. This proved highly successful and, significantly, was the inspiration for the formal training of mountain search and rescue dogs in the UK. But it was the determination and drive of one man in particular that brought that inspiration home to these shores.

Hamish MacInnes takes the initiative

Hamish MacInnes was born in Gatehouse of Fleet, Dumfries and Galloway in 1930. He moved to Glencoe in 1959 where he has lived ever since. It is no exaggeration to say he has been a mountaineering legend for well over half a century. He has a prodigious record of achievements as a mountaineer, rescuer, author and consultant and is widely recognised as one of the great British mountaineers. In particular, his contribution to mountain rescue is without parallel.

In 1948 he was required to complete a two-year spell in National Service. Up until the end of 1960, all men in the UK aged between 18 and 41 years were required by law to spend two years in military service. Following the Second World War, National Service was undertaken in peacetime situations but national servicemen were often used in full military operations. Many were stationed abroad for a period of time.

Hamish completed his National Service from 1948 to 1950 and it was fortuitous that he spent most of his time in the Austrian Tyrol, where he became friends with mountain guide Hans Spielman. Hans owned two dogs that had been used to search for people caught in avalanches. By all accounts, his dogs weren't specially trained for rescue work and searches were somewhat haphazard affairs, but the seeds of an idea were sown.

On completion of his National Service, and return to Scotland, Hamish pursued his new-found interest in using dogs to locate people lost in the mountains. He was aware of reports that dogs had been used to help find climbers lost or avalanched in the Highlands but they had been mainly shepherds' dogs — because they were the only ones in the locality, and they possessed an aptitude for finding lost sheep.

The years following Hamish's return to Scotland marked significant changes in society. The austerity of the war years was beginning to decline and a new sense of mobility and freedom saw many people taking advantage of the outdoors for leisure pursuits. The Cairngorms and Glencoe were opened up for skiing and the long winter season meant people could ski and climb from the end of November through to mid-May. Inevitably, as winter sports increased in popularity, there was an increasing number of accidents, with people caught in sudden blizzards, bad weather and avalanches. Civilian mountain rescue had yet to be fully established but calls for help (around 50 each year in 1960) never went unanswered. Police officers and local people, shepherds, gamekeepers, farmers and foresters (with little or no proper training, and often ill-equipped with no searchlights, ice axes or crampons, or even climbing ropes) were called out to assist people in distress, sometimes at risk to their own lives. Early search parties were largely dependent on people with local knowledge, gained through their work on the hills. Their only equipment was perhaps a stick or crook and a telescope, their only means of communicating with each other a shout, whistle, or wave of a handkerchief.

Hamish was convinced this situation could be improved. He felt sure that if dogs were used, trained along the lines Hans Spielman had demonstrated, they would be capable of covering search areas in much less time than a man. In this way, rescue operations could be executed more quickly so the whole process of searching for missing people could be carried out with greater success.

Ever the innovator, Hamish began to train his own dog, Tiki. Early in 1960 he had been given Tiki, a seven months' old Alsatian, by some friends in Glasgow. She proved to be affectionate, obedient and a first class watchdog but, more important, she was intelligent and showed a natural willingness to learn. She seemed to have all the potential to become a first rate search and rescue dog. However, a few months after taking ownership, Tiki fell ill with cancer. Hamish and his wife Catherine were devastated. It looked as if, not only were they about to lose a loved companion, but Hamish's ambitions to train her as a search and rescue dog would never be realised. The prognosis looked bleak, but Hamish convinced Catherine they should get another dog and train it as they had trained Tiki over the past year.

Unknown to Hamish and Catherine, an advertisement to sell a young Alsatian had been placed in the *Greenock Advertiser*. The puppy had been bought as a pet for the owner's children, but they soon learned they'd made a mistake. The children lost interest, there was nowhere for the dog to run, it was given little exercise and received no obedience training. The advertisement attracted no attention so the owners decided to have the dog put down. However, the veterinary surgeon convinced them that, as the dog was so good looking and physically very strong, he should be given a reprieve. So a second advertisement was placed in the local press.

Again, fortune was to play a part in Hamish's involvement with search and rescue dogs. His sister, who lived in Greenock, noticed the advertisement and, knowing her brother was looking for a dog, contacted him with the news. His response was to call his wife, who was working as a locum GP in nearby Dunoon. Catherine decided to pop in and see the dog on her way back home to Glencoe.

She was impressed by the dog's appearance. Its coat was black and silver instead of the normal black and tan and it seemed in good physical condition, but it was quite apathetic, having had no exercise for many weeks. Catherine was concerned the dog's living conditions might have had a serious psychological effect: would it ever learn to be a useful search dog? Nevertheless, she agreed to take it and, following a fraught journey during which the dog was constantly sick, she reached Glencoe and home.

Almost immediately, Hamish began to train his new dog, which they called Rangi. Obedience training was high on the list of priorities and he found it helped to work Tiki and his new dog together. The change in Rangi's environment from the cramped flat in Greenock to the fresh open space of Glencoe had an immediate and significant effect. His strength and fitness grew daily and he soon learned to outpace Tiki. He was a slower learner than Tiki and teaching him to sit, lie down, retrieve and stay took many weeks of training, but he had a physical quality that endeared him to Hamish. Steep, rough terrain and long days on the hill in bad weather had little effect on his energy or enthusiasm. Hamish was sure he could count on Rangi to keep going long after he himself was exhausted.

In the summer of 1961, Hamish left Scotland to climb in the Caucasus Mountains as a member of a Scottish-Russian climbing expedition. One of his climbing colleagues, George Ritchie, agreed with Hamish that there was merit in establishing some kind of search and rescue dog team. Hamish had mixed feelings, as an initial attempt by him to use dogs for searching proved unsuccessful. On this occasion he had acquired a pair of Tibetan Mastiffs to help him track down the famed Yeti on his Abominable Snowman Expedition. George Ritchie encouraged him that he was likely to be more successful with Tiki and Rangi. So, on his return, Hamish set about devising a structured method for training his dogs.

His technique started with simple retrieval skills where he would throw an object for the dog to retrieve. He made a point of always shouting 'Search!' as the command for the dog to retrieve. He varied the direction of throw and, in time, increased both the search area and difficulty of the terrain. He also used different objects and always threw them out of the dog's sight.

Hamish's ideas about the usefulness of a search and rescue dog team were picked up by a number of influential and interested people. In October 1963, two people paid him a visit: a mountain rescue expert from Norway and Jack Arthur, who was chairman of the Scottish branch of the British Red Cross. They watched Hamish's

dogs in action and the Norwegian visitor asked Hamish what 'grade' were his dogs. Somewhat taken aback, Hamish admitted he hadn't understood the question. The visitor said he was referring to the gradings given to dogs that had undertaken training for avalanche rescue work. Hamish didn't know things were so well-established abroad and wondered if he could become involved in some way. Taken with Hamish's enthusiasm and commitment, Jack Arthur managed to secure funding from the British Red Cross for Hamish to attend an avalanche dog training course at Thrubsee, Engelberg in Switzerland, later that year. Funding also came from the cigarette manufacturer Player's, as well as the Swiss Rescue Service.

Hamish was the first British person to attend such a course and, although he couldn't take his own dogs, owing to quarantine regulations, he joined people from a number of other European countries with whom he worked in a variety of new and different training situations. The group included police officers, ski instructors, mountain guides, hotel workers, bar staff and others from a wide variety of occupational backgrounds. All of these, like Hamish, were volunteers who shared a common interest in helping save people caught in avalanches. Throughout the course, emphasis was placed on using dogs to find people buried under the snow. 'Victims' were buried at varying depths and then required to wait for the dog to find them. Hamish was surprised how quickly dogs found buried people, even when the dog had no prior training, and when the search area was extended to several hundred square metres. He noted how, in many cases, the dog went straight to the

victim's location without undertaking a broad search to begin with. Little did he know that many of the search and rescue ideas used by the Swiss had been borrowed from the British, who had used dogs to locate people buried in bombed-out buildings during World War Two.

It became clear to Hamish that training a dog is as much about training the handler. To work the dog to best advantage, the handler had to be fully conversant with the nature of snow and avalanche formation, weather conditions and general rescue procedures, as well as understanding the conditions under which a dog can be used most effectively. Great store was placed on the 'understanding' between handler and dog. The handler should always have confidence in their dog's ability to pick up a scent, even if their own hunches differ. Hamish was also introduced to the importance of assessment and the classification system used to grade dogs at different levels of expertise.

Following the course, Hamish continued to train his dogs in difficult and challenging mountain terrain. Several others learned of his efforts and came to visit him, intrigued to know whether their own dog could also be trained. One of these was Sandy Seabrook.

Sandy was an army sergeant stationed on Dartmoor. He was interested in rescue work and had already established the Devon Cave Rescue Organisation with a friend (and was later to establish the Lomond Mountain Rescue Team in Scotland). Early in 1964, Sandy and his friend had driven to Glencoe for a weekend's climbing. They decided to camp on the hills and, during the first night out, Sandy's dog Judy, an Alsatian, went

ABOVE: THE FIRST COURSE IN GLENCOE. FROM LEFT TO RIGHT — KENNY MACKENZIE WITH FRAN, SANDY SEABROOK WITH RORY, WILLIE ELIOT WITH CORRIE, AND CATHERINE MACINNES WITH RANGI AND TIKI © HAMISH MACINNES.   FACING PAGE: SANDY SEABROOK'S DOG, RORY © SANDY SEABROOK.

missing. The two men searched for two days to no avail, eventually returning to barracks without the dog. Before their departure, they told local shepherds and the police about the dog but, after two weeks without news, they gave up hope.

Then Sandy received a phone call from Hamish MacInnes. He and a party had been camping in the same area as Sandy two weeks earlier and, as they huddled around a campfire, they heard a 'ghostly howl'. They went to investigate and found Sandy's dog, looking somewhat sorry for itself having not eaten for almost two weeks. Overjoyed with the find, Sandy drove up to Glencoe immediately to collect his dog from Hamish and it was at this meeting that Sandy raised the idea of a training course using dogs for rescue work.

Later that year, Kenny Mackenzie, who was the police officer in Kinlochleven, took the opportunity to watch Hamish training Rangi and Tiki. He was fascinated by the way the three worked together and wondered if his own dog Fran, also an Alsatian, could be trained. Kenny explained that his dog was very self-willed, but energetic and intelligent. Hamish was sure the dog could be trained, as long as it was done in the right manner — with patience, know-how and affection.

Hamish's neighbours Walter and Willie Elliot, who were shepherds living further down the glen, questioned whether their two Border Collies might become good search and rescue dogs. The Elliot brothers and their father were not unaccustomed to rescue work in Glencoe, having been involved in searching and rescuing climbers and walkers for many years. Hamish thought the collies might be trainable but was concerned about their

long coats, which would 'ball up' quickly as they ran through snow. Unlike Alsatians, which have thick, short-haired coats, the balling-up problem with collies would not only impede their progress but also reduce

body temperature. However, he felt collies would be fine in conditions when the weather was more favourable and the ground not covered in snow.

Others expressing a keen interest in Hamish's work included Mike Hammond, who ran a climbing school in Ballachulish, and Tom Mackenzie, a forester from Aviemore. Mike had a long-haired Pyrenean puppy, which he had begun to train, and Tom had an Alsatian bitch. Tom paid a visit to Hamish and was so enthused by what he saw that he started to train his own dog immediately he returned home.

The first training course

As 1964 progressed, Hamish became more and more certain the time was right to bring together the growing interests of the many people who were training their dogs for search and rescue, and to formalise all he had learned about training dogs and handlers.

So, with strong support from his wife Catherine and his friends, he decided to build on his Engelberg experience and run a bespoke course in Glencoe.

The start date was 14 December and the course was planned to run for five days. It was advertised far and wide and attracted local people as well as others from further away, including the Chief Constable of Argyll Constabulary. Handlers on the course included people from Scotland, England and Wales. In addition, and with one eye on publicity, Hamish invited members of the media, including BBC and newspaper reporters.

Each day of the programme included both daytime and evening sessions and, as with the Swiss course, each dog was assessed and graded as they were in Switzerland. Successful dogs were graded into one of three categories. Grade A was for novice dogs that would be permitted to take part in daytime searches. Grade B was for more experienced dogs and, if the handler was a competent all-year-round mountaineer, the letter M was appended. Grade C was for qualified dogs and handlers who had actually made a find during a call-out and had also attended a course in Glencoe to demonstrate their ability to locate in snow conditions. Hamish felt that assessment was a critical part of the training regime: it not only demonstrated the intense and progressive nature of training, but also gave it credibility and official recognition.

A key feature of assessment, established right from the start, was its ongoing nature. Dogs and their handlers would be assessed but would need to be reassessed on a regular basis as a way of maintaining exacting standards. Hamish was aware that, whilst some of the aspects he had borrowed from the Swiss experience were highly relevant to Scottish conditions, there were also differences. Search and rescue dogs in Switzerland were trained primarily to locate people caught in avalanches. Whilst there was an avalanche risk in Scotland, Hamish felt dogs could also be put to great use to locate walkers and climbers lost in poor weather. In this regard dogs would need to be trained in all weather conditions — not

ABOVE: KENNY MACKENZIE'S DOG, FRAN © HAMISH MACINNES. FACING PAGE: KENNY MACKENZIE WITH HIS DOG FRAN AND CATHERINE MACINNES © HAMISH MACINNES.

just when the ground was snow-covered — and trained to search large areas of terrain, both open and mountainside. Search dogs and their handlers should, therefore, be much more versatile in the kinds of assignment they were required to undertake.

The first course proved popular and was highly successful. Only a small number of people were involved including Catherine MacInnes, Walter Elliot, Kenny Mackenzie and Sandy Seabrook. Sandy was the only person from outside Scotland to attend the pilot course and, at the subsequent formal course a year later, he and his dog Rory became the first ever team in England to become qualified with SARDA. The course convinced everyone there that dogs could be used effectively to locate people missing or buried in snow. It also showed, particularly to the police authorities, that dogs are an additional and unique resource to support the existing emergency services in the search for missing persons. But the course revealed something else: that, if the training and assessment of dogs was to continue and develop, it needed suitable coordination. It seemed logical that a formal organisation should be created to oversee the work.

And so, in May 1965, Hamish called a meeting at his house, to include his wife Catherine, Kenny Mackenzie, Walter and Willie Elliot. By the meeting's end they had agreed to set up a dedicated organisation, its two prime aims to further the development of search and rescue dogs in Britain, and to raise funds to help pay for the cost of training and rescue work. It would be entirely voluntary, raising funds through its own efforts. The intention was to develop a national association, and

arrange an annual course, based in Scotland, to help train and reassess dogs that had been working during the year.

Membership was open, not only to climbers, but to anyone with an interest in training dogs for search and rescue. Anyone who lived and worked in the mountains — gamekeepers, police officers, military personnel, foresters, shepherds — who was a competent mountaineer could apply. Hamish invited a number of well-

known people to serve as patrons. Sir Vivian Fuchs, a well-known explorer and climber at the time, agreed to be the honorary president and others, including Lord Hunt, agreed to be patrons of the association. Hamish himself took on the role of secretary; Catherine was the medical adviser and Willie Elliot the treasurer.

SARDA — the Search and Rescue Dog Association — had finally come into being.

SARDA comes of age

'Shouting to Rangi, he plunged on. He saw him now, his mouth wide open, his tongue lolling out. He was looking up at his master and there was an expression in his almond eyes which Hamish had rarely seen before. Those eyes, fiery and unblinking were trying to convey something'. Ernest Dudley

By 1965, the world was changing fast: history in the making. As the 'Swinging Sixties' rocked the world, Britain saw the death penalty abolished and a Liverpool band of musical mopheads set young girls' hearts on fire; the Vietnam War had just begun and *Tom & Jerry* ran amok across our TV screens. Diverse, exciting, memorable times. Few, though, would then have been aware of search and rescue dogs, much less the launch of a national association.

From the outset, SARDA was a 'British' association, even though its roots were in Scotland. Within a year, Hamish had contacted every police force in the country about the potential of using dogs to search. Which prompted a rapid increase in people wishing to become involved, keen to see if their own dog could be trained and used for search and rescue work.

So much so that, by 1971, the British association had become so large it was decided to split into three sections — Scotland, England and Wales — with each branch taking responsibility for its own training programme and fundraising. In the space of just a few years, SARDA had grown into a credible and versatile body, comprising handlers from a wide variety of backgrounds and occupations, using dogs of many breeds, and operating across many parts of the UK, from the Scottish Highlands to the rolling landscapes of Dartmoor.

Today, the public is much more aware of the use of dogs by the emergency services and their role in helping locate missing people. Members of the press in particular are keen to seize upon a rescue involving dogs. In fact, if a serious mountain incident involves the use of either a helicopter or dog — even better, both — it inevitably receives massive public attention!

Public knowledge about the work of the emergency and rescue services has been enhanced through the many TV series focusing on the emergency services. *Send in the Dogs*, for example, described — often quite graphically — the use of police dogs in all kinds of criminal work such as drug detection and offender apprehension. *Extraordinary Dogs* documents the work of rescue dogs around the world, focusing on their healing and curative powers as well as their capacity to track, search and work for man.

Any organisation which plays a valuable role in society grows and changes over time. As more people become involved, the operation develops and diversifies, its role more widely established. And SARDA is no exception.

SARDA is now recognised as the umbrella organisation for air scenting search and rescue dogs in the UK. From its small, focused beginning, the number of dog handlers has increased, the organisation has grown and developed into several constituent associations, training and assessment procedures have become sophisticated, and funding and sponsorship deals are in place. But, most important, search and rescue dogs and their handlers now play a crucial role in the overall operational framework of mountain search and rescue in the UK. Year on year, they are responsible for helping locate countless missing people and saving the lives of many others. Indeed, SARDA dog teams across the UK are involved in well

FACING PAGE: HAMISH MACINNES'S FORMER HOUSE IN GLENCOE — THE 'THREE SISTERS OF GLENCOE' RISING IN THE BACKGROUND: FROM LEFT TO RIGHT, THE FLANK OF BEINN FHADA, GEARR AONACH AND AONACH DUBH. THE GLEN BETWEEN THE FIRST AND SECOND 'SISTER' IS THE LOST VALLEY © BOB SHARP.

CLOCKWISE FROM TOP LEFT: 1974 COURSE IN GLENCOE; CASS MAKES A FIND; ROGER SMITH UNDERGOING THE STOCK TEST WITH MAGNUS; PC KENNY MACKENZIE OF INVERNESS MRT WITH SUMBA AND JIM COYLE OF COCKERMOUTH MRT WITH ROCK (IMAGES COURTESY OF SARDA ENGLAND).

over 500 searches each year — and counting.

So, what does SARDA do?

Essentially, in pursuit of its ultimate purpose — the search and rescue of missing persons — it performs three roles: training, assessment and the deployment of search and rescue dogs. Fundamentally, it doesn't matter where those persons may be missing — the way dogs are trained, and the principles involved in the search process, are largely independent of the terrain. Dogs and their handlers are able to search on hills and mountains, moorlands and rural areas, through forests and woodland, alongside waterways and shorelines. Some are trained to search over water to locate drowned casualties, others are trained in the special techniques required in civil disasters such as earthquakes, collapsed buildings and flooding.

Training consumes a vast amount of time. It demands total commitment and continues beyond qualification, throughout the operational life of the dog, because there's no guarantee key skills won't fade away. Every aspect needs reinforcing, practising and refining. Most handlers train every week of the year and frequently during the week. Then there are the weekend exercises and week-long annual courses, over and above mountain rescue team training for the handler. It takes an extraordinary level of dedication and persistence to train a dog to assessment standard and this huge commitment cuts across all four seasons, whatever the weather.

When it comes to assessment, although each association has its own distinctive criteria and skill categories, through which dog teams must pass on their way to qualification, all the associations involve assessors from their sister associations in the assessment process. So, for example, a SARDA Scotland assessment might include assessors from Ireland, England, Southern Scotland and the Lakes. It's an efficient, not to say extremely sociable, way of keeping operational standards high and maintaining parity across the associations. Assessment is rigorous and demanding and, along with training, it's an ongoing process.

Key to the early assessment of any search dog, because they have to work in open country, is the stock test. The majority of the associations continue to reassess their dogs every year for their safety in the presence of livestock. Whilst the test is carried out with the dog in the company of sheep, it would be removed from the call-out list for showing an unhealthy interest in other animals such as sheep, cattle, deer or even rabbits. It is critical that farm animals, and other animals encountered on the mountains, are not worried by dogs, and that dogs are not distracted from their work by other animals.

Once qualified, dog teams go onto the call-out list for a period — between two to three years — before reassessment. Failure at this stage may mean a return to lower categories or removal from the list entirely.

Each association also has its own system for alerting handlers when there is a call for help but the response is always rapid. Handlers can be on their way to the search location within minutes. Invariably, dog teams work in conjunction with other agencies, which may include local mountain rescue teams, helicopter flights and police forces. Dog handlers must be ready to travel long distances and be away from home for many hours, which means they must be prepared to look after their own needs in terms of food and drink, clothing and equipment, as well as those of their dog.

To a degree, the distinct geographical differences between the associations dictate the level of work, and the nature of their searches. But there are common threads, not least their shared interest in finding people!

Perhaps most importantly, each is a registered charity which brings its own defining characteristics. To achieve charitable status, any organisation must meet a number of criteria: they must be voluntary in nature, non-profit making and encompass aims seen to be philanthropic, social or charitable. In other words, they have to serve the public interest — clearly central to the work of SARDA. According to the Charities Act (2006) SARDA meets this requirement in a number of ways: 'the advancement of health or the saving of lives', 'the relief of those in need, by reason of ill-health or other disadvantage' and 'the promotion of the efficiency of the police, rescue or ambulance services.'

A distinct advantage of charitable status is that funds raised are not liable to income tax. Which means public generosity in the form of donations and bequests is used fully to help the cause. So those who give money to help SARDA know that every penny benefits the charity — and businesses with a philanthropic nature are more inclined to support organisations with charitable status.

Then there is the principle of self-funding. With an average annual expenditure heading towards £20,000, each association must work hard to raise income. The bulk is spent on the cost of accommodation for the assessments and training weekends but there are insurance, equipment and administration costs to meet. In a good year, income might just exceed expenditure. Considering the amount of kit required — avalanche transceiver, radios, dog jacket, winching harness, first aid kit, neck collar, torches, waterproof clothing, rucksack, GPS receiver — it's not surprising the total cost of providing for a single dog team can be in excess of £4000.

In most instances, costs have spiralled since the early years. In the mid-1970s, the cost of running a training course was around £700, now it might be in the thousands. Radios, however, are a different matter. When a revised frequency bandplan was first run out across the UK, to improve communication between the various emergency agencies, there were some concerns about radio provision. Whilst it was desirable for all dog handlers to have their own radio, given the extreme circumstances they might be working in, radios were difficult to get hold of and relatively expensive at around £500. Decades on, the price is relatively unchanged and they are staple kit for the majority of mountain rescue team members.

The need to self-fund was recognised very early in Scotland, prompting the sale of bespoke postcards. Back in the 1960s, postcards were still a popular means of communication. These simple black and white cards, printed by *The Oban Times*, depicted scenes of dogs and handlers in action and listed the various patrons of the day including Lord Elphinstone, Lord Wakefield, Sir Charles MacLean, Sir Francis Walker and Sir Vivian Fuchs.

But times change — collecting cans and public donations can only accrue so much. And, although Scottish mountain rescue teams do receive £300k of government funding each year — part of which is top-sliced for SARDA Scotland and SARDA Southern Scotland — their cousins south of Hadrian's Wall have not been so fortunate. That said, in August 2011, the Government announced that they would be making a grant to mountain rescue teams across England, Wales, Scotland and Northern Ireland of £200,000, to be divided between the teams. This will be repeated annually for four years 'subject to proper use of the grant' (the money must be spent on equipment) and also subject to available funding. As team members, dog handlers will benefit from the grant in the same way as their team colleagues and yet, appreciated though the funding will be, the sum represents a benefit of less than £2,000 per team, so there is still much to find. Income from fundraising events, legacies and donations is essential.

Every association benefits from sponsorship by a wide variety of companies, individuals and professional agencies. In Scotland, the Order of St John and the Mountain Rescue Committee of Scotland, provide financial support. Burns Pet Nutrition provides free food for graded search dogs, together with an annual cash donation for Scotland, England and Lakes handlers. In Southern Scotland, Eukanuba supply food for all graded dogs.

Specialised companies such as Rosker and Ruffwear provide lighted search coats, collars, leads and collapsible dog bowls.

In England, a variety of fundraising strategies have been employed over the years — including the collection of Green Shield stamps until their withdrawal in 1991 (enabling, on one occasion, the provision of a Henri Lloyd waterproof suit, a Whillans rucksack and a woollen pullover to each member). Páramo and Montane help with discounted clothing to handlers and Satmap Systems offer discounted GPS receivers.

Digital mapping companies such as Mapyx Quo and ViewRanger supply free mapping and software so, of course, dog handlers benefit from this too. These systems use mobile phone technology to show the area a team member is searching and tracks exactly where they are in real time. On their return to base, the search manager can download the tracks from their phones, plot them on the laptop and print out a copy for the police.

A variety of local sponsors also help raise funds, providing toys for training and helping with pet accommodation. In the Lake District the 'Friends of SARDA Lakes', endorsed by TV personality Julia Bradbury, helps provide a regular income.

Funding is equally challenging in Ireland, coming mainly through public donations, an annual street collection and a small grant from the Irish Government. In recent times, the Northern Ireland Mountain Cave and Cliff Rescue Coordinating Committee (NIMCCRCC) extended its capital grant to include SARDA and this has gone part way to purchase a team vehicle and GPS radios for training and call-outs.

The lowland teams may not suffer the sizeable running costs of their mountain-based cousins but, even so, these can exceed the £2000 mark each year. So the drive to fundraise remains the same, as do

TOP: GETTING READY FOR AN EXERCISE IN ASSYNT, 1974. KENNY MACKENZIE'S CAR IS IN THE FOREGROUND WITH HIS DOG SIMBA. ROGER SMITH AND HIS WIFE, PLUS HIS TWO DOGS, ARE FAR RIGHT. NOTE THE OLD BEDFORD LORRY LIVERIED UP AS SARDA SCOTLAND.

ABOVE: 1974 COURSE IN GLENCOE — BIDEAN NAM BIAN.

'This photograph was taken in the early1970s. The vehicle was purchased from old MOD stock. At the time it was a communications vehicle but was reclassified by SARDA Scotland as an ambulance. The vehicle was based in Fort William and used regularly by Lochaber MRT for incidents on Ben Nevis. A team member was the usual driver – he was responsible for its maintenance and would also drive it to the scene of any SARDA operations where it served as both a search management base and a bunkhouse for overnight incidents. Its presence on rescues was a good advertisement for SARDA although, as the vehicle aged, SARDA arranged for its disposal and it was never replaced.' Kenny MacKenzie

the mechanics. In the Isle of Man, individual members have generated a number of small-scale sponsorship deals resulting in free dog food and reduced ferry costs, even clothing, equipment and travel expenses when training with SARDA Wales but they have yet to attract a major sponsor, which would provide some stability to the finances. The lowland teams of England also rely on donations, from a wide variety of individuals, businesses, charitable trusts and professional agencies, to supplement the day-to-day fundraising efforts of the members. Pets At Home also provides some assistance. Lowland Search Dogs are currently sponsored by Rough Gear, an outdoor adventure store, and individual units have negotiated other sponsorship deals with local and national companies such as Eukanuba, CSJ, Burns Pet Nutrition and Satmap.

Although all this helps immensely, wherever they are based, the handlers themselves inevitably make their own huge contribution to their overall costs — the heaviest investment unquestionably through the first few years of training, when a place on the call-out list is still a distant, hard-earned dream.

The voluntary ethic has been central to mountain rescue from its beginning and shows no sign of diminishing any time soon. As with all rescue team members, dog handlers and their dogs are ready to respond 24 hours a day, 365 days a year. Handlers come from a variety of different backgrounds and occupations. Some are retired, but the majority work at day jobs and, more often than not, have families at home. Whatever the circumstances, their expertise and time is given freely and without question. They may be called to search in urban, rural or mountainous areas, in their own area or further afield, often travelling hundreds of miles to assist. Far from just a hobby, caring for their dog, training and rescue work is a central part of a handler's life. In fact, more than that: it's a way of life, and a rather costly one at that.

With a few exceptions — in the case of 'non-mountain' dogs — SARDA members must be active members of their local mountain rescue team, or have at least two years current or recent mountain rescue experience of another UK team, so they understand the context and procedures underpinning search and rescue in the mountain environment. It helps too that they have the skills and fitness required to work, often alone and for long periods of time, in poor weather and in challenging and sometimes hazardous terrain. They must be recommended by their own team leader in regard to their mountain capability and also demonstrate their ability to navigate in the most extreme weather conditions.

In the main, these common threads in aim and organisation grew from within the UK, reflecting local needs and resources, and society in general although, every so often, an event of earth-shattering proportions occurs, in whose wake the future changes, in ways not immediately appreciated. Lockerbie was one of these and its impact on SARDA was immense.

Prior to December 1988, when PanAm Flight 103 ploughed its deathly furrow through the quiet Scottish town of Lockerbie, the police only considered search dogs as a 'mountain' resource but their involvement in this incident changed that perspective. Many SARDA members were called to help in the immediate aftermath. Handlers from across the UK travelled to Lockerbie to assist. Such a major disaster represented a steep learning curve for everyone concerned, prompting much discussion about the type of work a dog team could do. It was a significant moment: the start of diversification in capability. Police forces began to request the use of dog teams more frequently in the search for missing persons, not just in the hills and rural areas, or for those known to be deceased. It set the scene for a wider involvement in searches for people missing from care homes, and civil contingency operations such as flooding.

The structure of SARDA in the UK

Despite the common threads, each of the associations has its own distinct characteristics and they are each quite individual. Over 45 busy years, the ground-breaking, single organisation inspired by Hamish MacInnes and a few like-minded friends, has taken on a life of its own. Given the geographical spread of its parts, it was perhaps inevitable SARDA would ultimately divide, first into its constituent countries then even further, into more regional sections and yet there remains an overarching organisation, looking after the needs of search dogs and their handlers, across the UK and Ireland. This is the National Search and Rescue Dog Association (NSARDA). The timeline for the development and structure of the various associations can be found in Appendix 1, page 232.

NSARDA evolved from an ad hoc group of representatives from the individual associations whose remit was to decide how to share money given to SARDA by the sponsors of the day, Pal Dog Foods, and to arrange assessments. The more formal body evolved to give the various police authorities a single point of reference so that, when they needed a dog team, they could be assured of an appropriate response. Established in 1979 (and finally constituted nineteen years later), NSARDA fulfils four roles. It provides a single voice for its constituent associations, raises public awareness of search and rescue dogs, helps raise and maintain the capabilities and standards of all types of search dogs in the UK, and fosters responsible dog ownership.

Membership currently comprises SARDA England, Wales, South Wales, Southern Scotland, Ireland, Ireland North and the Isle of Man. SARDA Scotland and SARDA

Lakes — renamed Lake District Mountain Rescue Search Dogs Association (LDMRSDA) in 2011 — are not members, but SARDA Lakes was involved with the initial development of training standards. Two other groups have recently joined — NSARDA CanTech and Anglia. Both comprise lowland dog teams and have helped with the development of national lowland search dog standards. At the time of writing, NSARDA represents more than 90 qualified search dogs across the UK, although the number of dogs varies constantly as dogs are retired or injured, and others become newly qualified.

Over the years, NSARDA has developed a set of working standards and nationally agreed criteria which search dogs in the member associations work towards in a step-like manner through training. Dog teams must achieve each stage before they proceed to the next one. Only when they have passed through every stage do they become qualified and go onto the call-out list of their own association. There are now national criteria not just for mountain and wilderness search dogs, but also for lowland search dogs, trailing dogs, building search dogs and drowned victim search dogs. A memorandum of understanding, drawn up with Lowland Search Dogs, reflects the broad philosophy, post-Lockerbie, that the use of dogs in lowland environments is every bit as important as their more traditional use in the mountain environment.

The same philosophy has seen the association supporting a variety of beneficial developments — most recently in scent discrimination training for dogs and handlers and, significantly, its work with the Welsh Assembly on animal welfare and the banning of electric collars.

The electric collar is designed to force a dog into submission, if it behaves improperly, by delivering a shock of electricity to the dog's neck. Thanks to NSARDA — and with support from the RSPCA and The Kennel Club — Wales is now the first part of the UK to outlaw the use of collars, with a heavy fine for anyone who breaks the law.

The association sits on the Animal and Behaviour Training Council, working on behalf of all types of animal trainers and also plays a leading part in the specialist group, Search and Rescue, which empowers both trainers and handlers to correctly train their dog. This will eventually lead to a formal qualification in dog training which is nationally recognised and available to any handler who wishes to work towards approved national standards. The course was set up through Compass Education, a distance learning provider offering courses in animal behaviour and training. Handlers who wish to undertake courses are sponsored by NSARDA.

The organisation may not have the same expenditure as the individual associations, but still has costs to meet. Representatives from each of the constituent associations meet formally twice a year, at various locations across the UK to aid those who have to travel long distances. NSARDA funds attendance at meetings, supports specialist courses (such as the Drowned Victim Search Dogs course in Ireland) and provides financial support for those who wish to attend relevant courses and conferences here in the UK and overseas. Learning from, and working with, dog handlers from other countries, is seen as vital — indeed, Hamish MacInnes's experience of dog training in Switzerland was early proof of the value of international exchange.

Besides supporting the search dogs and their handlers, NSARDA also helps all those agencies that work alongside them — the police, mountain rescue teams and civil contingency boards — to recognise the standards dogs achieve prior to qualification. Work is ongoing to encourage all police, fire and rescue services to use qualified search dogs.

But, what of the individual associations? Despite the common threads, how did they sub-divide and how do they differ?

SARDA Scotland remained a single association until 1983, when it divided into two sections — Highland and Southern — still under the banner of SARDA Scotland and, in 1984, SARDA Southern changed its name to SARDA Southern Scotland. The Highland Line, running from Inverness to Fort William, marked a natural geographical division between the north and south of the country, but also reflected developing differences in the way dogs and their handlers were trained and assessed. SARDA Highland later reverted to using the title 'SARDA Scotland' in 1999.

Members of SARDA Scotland live throughout Scotland, but primarily in the Highlands, and members of Southern Scotland live primarily in the Central and Borders regions. Operationally, members of both work together in perhaps a quarter of all their call-outs — sometimes travelling great distances to do so.

New members attend an introductory training weekend then, after a further three weekends, their potential as a search dog and handler is assessed. If successful at this stage, they must commit to 75% of training weekends up to qualifying as a full dog team.

Training weekends take place every four weeks or so, focusing on the different stages of training as well as specialised areas such as helicopter and pyrotechnics familiarisation, and avalanche work. An annual assessment course in Glencoe, at the end of March comprises a livestock test for potential novice search dogs, followed by three full days of search activities in three different areas for potential novice and novice dogs aiming to reach the next grade and, depending on availability and weather conditions, time is also spent in the other disciplines.

On average there are around 25 fully graded search dogs available on call with SARDA Scotland, the vast majority of them Border Collies. Over the years, the number of incidents has increased significantly — currently around 80 a year — and, because of the geographical size of Scotland, only one or two handlers tend to attend each call. Most involve missing walkers or climbers, but around 50% are searches for vulnerable people, including children and adults missing in urban or semi-rural environments.

SARDA Scotland periodically awards the Madras College Trophy in recognition of the 'best' novice dog at assessment. This unique award takes the form of a silver salver, originally given to the association in the early 1970s to recognise the find by a dog team of one of the college's students, missing in the Scottish mountains. The trophy was first awarded three years later to Roger Smith and his Yellow Labrador, Magnus. According to a local newspaper at the time: 'Magnus, a lively Yellow Labrador from Nairn, won top novice search and rescue award in Glencoe

yesterday. The handler, Roger Smith, put Magnus through his paces during a three day course run by the Scottish Search and Rescue Dog Association. Magnus, bought nearly eighteen months ago for £15 from a breeder in Fife, will probably join either the Cairngorm or Inverness mountain rescue team. Roger and his wife wanted Magnus mainly as a pet, but with a view to possible training as a rescue dog. A silver salver was presented to dog and master by a physical education teacher from Madras College St Andrews where the pupils raised nearly £600 for Glencoe Mountain Rescue Team and the dog team.'

To date, the salver has been awarded an equal number of times to Border Collie and German Shepherd teams. More recently, Mike Walker and his collie Druim, received the award in 2010.

For some time after the split between north and south, the two associations remained close, sharing the same charity number and holding a joint bank account. In fact, handlers could be members of both. Although the boundary line was accepted as the Highland Boundary Fault, this was far from set in stone, with members from each branch occasionally tasked to work in the other's area. Today, this distinction is largely irrelevant because the first point of contact for the police to summon search dogs is through the police force areas.

SARDA Southern Scotland counts around ten dog teams on its call-out list, with a number in training, across a wide spread of teams, including Galloway, Moffat, Tweed Valley, Ochils, Lomond, Killin, Tayside, Arran and Oban. With incidents averaging 70 a year, handlers may be called to assist in parts of Scotland further

north such as Glencoe and the Cairngorms, as well as parts of northern England, including the Lake District. A much higher percentage (around 75%) of their call-outs involve missing person searches for the old or vulnerable. Some years ago, the association enjoyed a spell in the media spotlight when member James Coles was gifted the *Blue Peter* dog, Corrie, via the show's presenter at the time, Matt Baker. Corrie already has a number of finds to her credit.

Training is held at different locations across the whole of Southern Scotland — the Pentland Hills, Trossachs, Angus Glens, Cairngorms, Galloway, Borders, Rannoch, Crianlarich and Loch Lomond — where these include sessions with SAR helicopters, mainly from the RNAS Gannet, and the Loch Lomond rescue boat. Surprisingly, many dogs take to helicopter winching with no problems but few enjoy travelling at 40 knots across a loch in a rib!

When it comes to assessment, the Southern Scotland grading system varies slightly, with the dogs graded on a scale of 1 to 5. Grade 3 dogs are deemed to be fully qualified and placed on the call-out list. Dog teams are then expected to upgrade within five to eighteen months. By grade 5, a dog team is expected to have the experience to work with far greater efficiency within the search area, and would be expected to assume responsibility for all the dogs from Southern Scotland during an incident. Grade 4 was introduced to give handlers an additional incentive to demonstrate improvement in their working efficiency following initial qualification.

Grades 1 and 2 are internally assessed. Grade 1 requires a dog team to demonstrate its ability to carry out the find sequence in different locations. Grade 2 requires the team to work small areas culminating in a find. Grades 3, 4 and 5 are assessed at the official assessment weekends in the presence of internal and external assessors. On these occasions, dog teams are required to complete five searches covering an area of up to one square kilometre with at least one body (but typically two) present. Grade 5 dogs are reassessed every two years although, if the dog and handler has attended 70% of training and no concerns have been raised by colleagues within the association, reassessment is waived for an extra year.

South of Hadrian's Wall, following its formation in 1971 SARDA England sought to establish itself as a formal and independent association with its initial courses — first at Thirlspot in the Lake District and, later that year, in the Peak District. Attendance was open to virtually anyone and the entry criteria were simple: if a dog showed signs of being able to hunt and scent a body, it was given an opportunity to train. Several breeds were considered for training including collies, German Shepherds, labradors and even Irish Setters. Members of Keswick MRT tested the handlers' mountaineering skills, including an overnight stay on the hills. Today, of course, all handlers are required to possess all the appropriate mountaineering skills before they join the association.

From the start, the idea was to develop communication between members of local mountain rescue teams as well as those more distant. It was felt a better knowledge of handlers in adjacent geographical areas would be beneficial at times of large scale incidents, when teams from different areas would be required to coordinate their efforts. Throughout the 1970s, the number of handlers in England gradually rose, from around 20 to 30, with members drawn from teams in the Lakes, Peak District, the North East, the Pennines and Dartmoor.

Despite the universal challenge of funding, one enterprising handler, Geoff Reid was the inspiration behind the bespoke fluorescent orange dog jacket, screen-printed with a large red cross and the word 'RESCUE', which set the scene for the jackets in use today. Geoff was a police officer with Cumbria Constabulary. Courtesy of a Winston Churchill Travelling Fellowship, he visited a number of European countries to explore more fully how they went about search and rescue work. Along the way, he noticed that many working dogs wore marked cloth coats so, on his return, he arranged for the manufacturer of police 'Accident Scene' jackets to design and produce bespoke jackets for the SARDA dogs.

Initially, SARDA England dogs were graded in three groups: A, B and C. Grade B was actually the highest level of competency, with Grade C awarded only for 'meritorious' service — such as when a dog made a find — and Grade A further divided into ten numerical categories. This arrangement continued for a few years but proved cumbersome to apply in practice. There was also a widely held view that standards needed to be raised, not just to lift the credibility of the organisation but also its operational capability. As a result, the grading system was simplified to Initial Search Dog and Full Search Dog, the system that continues to the present day.

As the significance of events at Lockerbie influenced the use of search dogs across the country, their deployment on searches in England increased dramatically — from around 20% to 85% of all those undertaken. By the late-1980s, the average number of call-outs in a year was 50, about half of which were searches in the Lake District. There were some remarkable finds during this period and this helped firmly establish dog teams as an indispensable resource.

Training in England changed dramatically through the 1970s and '80s. Initially, only a single course was organised but this increased to two, then four and five each year. Training now rotates between different parts of the country, to accommodate members travelling long distances, and national training courses are held most months of the year in locations as diverse as Dartmoor, the Yorkshire Dales, the Peak District and Northumberland. Regular local training also takes place every week and regional courses are being trialled in an attempt to accommodate land access and travel issues. Twice-yearly assessment courses take place in January, in the Lake District, and November in South Wales.

SARDA England handlers cover the whole of England with the exception of the Lakes. In practice, they tend to be called primarily to the mountain regions of England whilst the lowland associations cover non-mountainous areas such as Kent and Anglia. There are approximately 32 qualified dog teams and around a dozen in training, from all the key mountain areas of England — South West, North East, Peak District, Mid Pennines and the Yorkshire Dales. In common with their counterparts in Scotland and Wales, dogs and their handlers cover not only their local area but also travel across England, and sometimes other parts of the UK, to assist with searches. The number of call-outs varies from year to year but the average in the five years up to 2010, was around 140.

In 1992, dog handlers in the Lake District decided to form their own association: SARDA Lakes. The geographical area of operation is the catchment area defined by the Lake District Search and Mountain Rescue Association (LDSAMRA). Essentially, this is the county of Cumbria, which is bounded by the Scottish border to the north, the western edge of the Pennines to the east and the north Yorkshire Dales to the south but, from time to time, handlers work outside this area in support of other dog teams in Dumfries and Galloway, the north east of England, Yorkshire Dales and the mid-Pennines.

All Lakes handlers are full members of one of the ten mountain rescue teams in the Lake District: Cockermouth, Coniston, Duddon and Furness, Kendal, Keswick, Kirkby Stephen, Langdale Ambleside, Patterdale, Penrith and Wasdale. Many are highly experienced in mountain rescue, some of them involved in the work of SARDA for over 40 years. There are hopes of their numbers doubling, despite the limited pool of around 400 rescue team members in the area — albeit something of a challenge. In exceptional situations, probationary team members are accepted as trainee dog handlers, but under no circumstances is anyone accepted who is not a member of one of the ten rescue teams. Like the individual teams, the association is affiliated to LDSAMRA but, like SARDA Scotland, not to NSARDA.

Much of the Lake District is high ground above 600 metres, including numerous mountains, cliffs and crags, so handlers must be competent mountaineers, skilled in first aid and survival in the mountain environment. There are around thirteen graded dog teams on the call-out list, with a number in various stages of training and several waiting in the wings. Around three Lakes dog teams qualify each year, which helps to ensure a constant service to the public. Those who aspire to the task are advised to spend at least six months 'bodying' for other trainees before they commit to training. It is also suggested aspiring trainees take advice from existing members before actually buying a dog. Whilst the large majority of Lakes dogs are collies, there are other breeds at work, including German Shepherd, labrador and lurcher.

Besides their monthly training weekend, and informal weekly training — on Tuesdays and Thursdays for dogs in the north and south of the area respectively — handlers attend a one week avalanche training course in Scotland every March. Frequently, a one day seminar at the November monthly course is followed by a night exercise. The monthly courses are planned a year in advance, covering three stages, each overseen by a training coordinator.

Stage 1 includes a pre-registration introductory assessment, including basic obedience, followed by training to establish the find sequence. Stage 2 introduces area searching, building the dog team's experience in different terrain with increasing challenges over longer periods of time until they are considered ready to be formally assessed. Stage 3 is the assessment phase. Dogs and handlers who aspire to go on the call-out list are assessed over a minimum of eight training days, two of which must span consecutive days. These assessments include a forest search, line search and night search. The Lakes operates a system of continuous assessment for all graded dogs, so weekend training also includes a 'look-see' assessment of one or two graded dogs. Notably, the association only has one grade of search dog — there is no 'novice-graded dog' system as in some associations.

In the ten years up to 2010, the number of call-outs rose from 27 to 72, with an average of around 60 each year. In 2011, SARDA Lakes changed its name to Lake District Mountain Rescue Search Dogs (LDMRSD).

In the west of the UK, meanwhile, SARDA Wales — formed in the initial country-wise split in 1971 — had already started to train dogs for search and rescue as early as 1968. At that time, the association covered the whole of Wales but, following the establishment of SARDA South Wales, its area of operation was altered. Today, Wales dog teams are frequently called to search for walkers missing in the mountains of Snowdonia National Park, as well as people missing in coastal and inland urban and rural areas, and on Anglesey. They also cover parts of Cheshire, and members have been tasked occasionally to locations in the Midlands. In 1986 a dog team went to the earthquake disaster in El Salvador and, since then, dog teams have travelled to assist other rescue teams in Ireland on major searches — truly cosmopolitan!

A distinguishing feature of SARDA Wales is the importance the association attaches to both air-scenting and trailing dogs. Unlike the other associations, it is actively involved in training for both kinds of work, helping develop the lowland and trailing standards which are now adopted by NSARDA and used by other associations across the country.

The initial work on trailing began in 2003 when Gwen Patmore started to train her Chocolate Labrador, Rolf. She, Andy Dunn and Iain Nicholson developed the first procedures for training and assessment and, by 2008, the standards they established had been formally adopted by NSARDA. Throughout this period, Tom Middlemas was a significant influence in helping shape the various training and assessment procedures. The essential difference between these dogs and their mountain rescue fellows is that, whilst air-scenting dogs search for airborne human scent particles — from any human being — they do not look for specific people missing in an area. In contrast, trailing dogs discriminate scent between different people. They are given an article of the missing person's clothing and then hunt for a trail that matches that scent. Trailing dogs can significantly reduce the time spent searching for, say Alzheimer's patients or people intent to self harm, where their 'point last seen' (PLS) is known and a 'scent' article such as a piece of clothing is available.

Training happens every second weekend of the month, with weekly evening sessions over the summer period, and assessment courses in March and December. The majority of handlers are members of one of the established mountain rescue teams — Llanberis, Ogwen Valley, Aberglaslyn or North East Wales — or the RAF Mountain Rescue Service, but aspiring handlers needn't necessarily be involved in mountain rescue. In 1996, the association decided to accept and train people from a non-mountain rescue background such as the coastguard service. All these handlers are committed hillwalkers, some as qualified mountain leaders. Nevertheless, they must meet a number of relevant criteria. For example, they must show they are competent navigators and possess a relevant first aid qualification. Further, they must attend a number of short courses related to search and rescue work, including protocols for dealing with deceased persons. They qualify for 'lowland search dog' status, which means their operational work is confined to moorland, forest or urban areas. However, depending on their mountain experience and qualifications, they may well be involved in searches in serious mountain terrain.

Members attend around 80 incidents each year, typically searching for children missing from home and adults reported missing from care homes or hospitals, but there are also calls to search for overdue hillwalkers and climbers. Members of both SARDA Wales and South Wales work together for training and assessment purposes and, depending on the nature and location of the incident, assist each other on call-outs, sometimes alongside SARDA England.

As the pace of technology has changed the nature of the hillwalking experience, so has the association invested a great deal of time and expertise in developing its operational capability with GPS receivers. Since 1999, all qualified handlers have used GPS receivers but, in 2006, Richard Beech — together with a local company — developed a bespoke search jacket with an integral GPS unit, to be worn by dogs. The first design was based on a standard dog jacket with a sewn pouch to hold the GPS unit. This was trialled for a year then modified on the basis of feedback received. Today, all qualified dogs wear a jacket that is tailored for breathability, strength and comfort, its central feature a load-bearing mesh and bell loop to facilitate helicopter winching. An integrated pocket holds the GPS unit, and reflective trim strips enhance visibility at night. The system provides a highly accurate review of the areas searched by dog teams once back at base as well as live GPS tracking of the exact movements of dog and handler, whilst they are out searching.

In Wales, as in Scotland, the mountain geography between north and south came to bear on the organisation and a separate association, SARDA South Wales, took shape in 2002. Its key upland areas are the Brecon Beacons and Black Mountains, which lie to the north of Swansea and Cardiff, in three police areas — South Wales, Gwent and Dyfed Powys — although handlers respond to call-outs anywhere in South Wales and beyond if required. In recent years, dog teams have been called to search for missing people as far west as Fishguard on the west coast, Swansea in the south and Symonds Yat in the east. The large majority of calls are to search for vulnerable people missing in urban or semi-rural environments although each year includes a small number of searches in serious mountain terrain. Training is often supplemented by trips to the Lakes, North Wales, Dartmoor and Scotland to bring depth of experience across a variety of terrain. The annual tally of searches varies considerably but currently runs at around 40 each year.

Membership is restricted to those who

are full members of one of the four mountain rescue teams in South Wales — Brecon, Western Beacons, Longtown and Central Beacons. Unlike other associations, where the 'time-served' criteria for SARDA membership is two years, aspiring handlers are required to have been a member of one of the four teams for at least twelve months. There are five qualified mountain rescue dog teams, six trainee search dogs and two trainee trailing dogs, mostly Border Collies.

Across the Irish Sea, the use of dogs for search and rescue in Northern Ireland was the initiative of one man, Neil Powell. A member of the Mourne Mountain Rescue Team at the time, he began to train his own dog — a German Shepherd called Kim — in the mid-1970s. Unaware of the existence of SARDA, and the developments taking place in Scotland, he thought it might be a good idea to train a dog to help speed up searches for missing people. When he later learned what was happening in Scotland, he was invited to train there and subsequently received a great deal of help from both Hamish MacInnes and Kenny MacKenzie. The Northern Ireland Mountain Rescue Coordinating Committee (NIMRCC) sponsored his trips to Scotland and Neil eventually qualified Kim with SARDA Scotland in 1979.

Initially, those involved in training dogs for search and rescue in Ireland referred to their organisation as 'SARDA Northern Ireland'. Formally established in 1979, it adopted the label 'Northern Ireland' rather than 'Ireland' simply because funding and other support was given by the NIMRCC. With growing awareness and interest from across the island, training developed beyond Northern Ireland and, in 1987, the name was changed to SARDA Ireland, to better reflect the growing geographical spread of handlers. By the mid-1990s, difficulties in maintaining a single structure, with members spread across such a large area, led to a division. SARDA Ireland North became a separate entity.

SARDA Ireland and Ireland North perform the same function within mountain rescue as their colleagues in Great Britain. There is no formal boundary line between them, but Ireland North tends to operate north of a line between Newcastle in the east, and Sligo in the west — essentially, this includes Northern Ireland and the county of Donegal to the west. SARDA Ireland operates to the south of this line, which is primarily the Republic of Ireland.

With call-outs numbering around a dozen each year, dog teams are mobilised through the Gardai, the Irish Coast Guard or the Irish Mountain Rescue Association and can be tasked anywhere in Ireland — be it mountain, moorland, suburban, lowland or coastal — although handlers tend to work within a few hours of their homes.

Both groups count a number of mountain search dogs on their call-out lists, whilst Ireland North can also call on collapsed structure search dogs and a drowned victim search dog. And they too are venturing into the field of trailing dogs. The mountain rescue dogs have been involved in searches in both Northern Ireland and the Republic of Ireland. Meanwhile, the collapsed structure dogs are declared assets within the Northern Ireland Fire and Rescue Service and have assisted in numerous searches in Northern Ireland and Wales, and even further afield in the earthquakes of Algeria, Pakistan and Turkey.

To train a dog to search collapsed structures, a handler must be approved by the Northern Ireland Fire and Rescue Service and undertake their urban search training programme. To search for drowned victims, they must previously have had a qualified air-scenting dog. Training for international and collapsed structure work also takes place periodically with members of British International Rescue Dogs in North Wales.

There have been some newsworthy characters over the years. One dog, Dylan, was awarded the PDSA's Gold Medal for 'displaying outstanding gallantry and devotion to duty' when he located four students lost in the mountains of Mourne in 1999. Another dog, Cracker, received the same award for his contribution in the Turkish earthquake of 1999. Cracker's owner remarked that conditions at the time were appalling: the air temperature exceeded 35 degrees and everything was covered in a fine dust. Cracker's airways became clogged with dust and it was lucky a stream was found in which he could be cooled and washed down. He continued searching for lost children and was eventually awarded not only the PDSA Gold Medal, but also the UK Canine Global Heroes Award of 2004.

SARDA Ireland hosts around half a dozen national training weekends, between September and late May each year, in different locations around the country, from the Commeraghs in County Waterford to the mountainous areas of County Galway and Wicklow, and The Burren in County Clare. Members from all over the country meet and train together at these two-day events. Between training weekends, members train weekly in their own areas and are also encouraged to travel to training events outside Ireland such as the annual Lakes avalanche course in the Cairngorms. Joint training exercises between dog teams in SARDA Ireland and its sister organisations in Great Britain ensure everyone is familiar with each other's capabilities.

A structured training and assessment programme covers all the search dog disciplines — air scenting, trailing, drowned victim, collapsed building — and, when handlers have successfully completed the first two levels of the programme and are deemed ready, they undertake a pre-assessment test prior to Novice assessment. Full Search Dog status can be attained a year on and dog teams are reassessed every three years. For practical and financial reasons, all the assessments take place in Northern Ireland, with the support of impartial external assessors.

SARDA Isle of Man took shape in 2004, thanks to the efforts of former Metropolitan police officer Matt Creer. Matt had some experience working with the Metropolitan Police Dog Unit and, when he moved to the Isle of Man as a probation officer, he considered the need for a search and rescue dog unit on the island. Realising he couldn't pursue his ideas alone, he contacted SARDA Lakes, who responded with crucial support and even gave Matt a dog that was undergoing training — Border Collie pup, Lola. Another interested handler quickly joined Matt and both continued training, first with the help of handlers from the Lakes and then SARDA Wales. Lola qualified as a novice dog in 2006 and immediately went on the call-out list. Her first find quickly followed and she qualified as a full search dog in 2007.

Jim MacGregor had previously worked with Matt as a 'dogsbody' — one of a dedicated bunch who support aspiring trainees and fully graded dog handlers by hiding in all manner of places in the hills, pretending to be injured or lost (see chapter seven for more about the work of dogsbodies). Jim qualified with his collie, Star, in 2007 achieving full dog status in 2009. All of these assessments were carried out with support from SARDA Wales. The success in qualifying the first two dogs gave enormous substance and credibility to the Isle of Man search dogs as an association.

Links with SARDA Wales continue to be extremely strong. The adoption of the working and assessment standards developed by SARDA Wales represents one of the biggest changes for the association to date, providing a single, clear set of standards and working procedures rather than a hybrid of systems borrowed from different organisations. As a full member of NSARDA, the Isle of Man also benefits from the expertise and support of many other handlers across the UK.

Handlers train twice a week, typically on a Tuesday evening and Sunday morning, in a variety of areas: coastal settings, buildings, forestry, urban and upland areas. The dogs are observed by an external handler once a year and must requalify every three years. There are plans to train dogs for mountain search and rescue, and for at least one handler to become an assessor. Handlers also train with other emergency services on the island such as the Fire and Rescue Service, Coastguard and Civil Defence.

Recent times have seen the administrative structure change from a three-member committee, to a separate executive committee supported by a nine-member committee, with a group of around 30 dogsbodies supporting training — which allows the handlers to concentrate on training dogs.

Despite the inevitable teething problems which beset any new organisation, the Isle of Man hopes to increase the number of dogs from their initial two so that complete 24/7 coverage can be offered, as well as back-up should a dog be injured or unavailable. Membership here is different from the other associations, in that handlers must belong to one of the island's emergency services — Police, Fire, Coastguard or Civil Defence. The association attends only a small number of incidents each year — about one a month — and these are mainly lowland incidents involving searches for children and adults missing from care homes or hospitals. Whilst most searches take place in coastal, urban and farmland areas however, handlers also train to search high ground (which rises to over 600 metres in the northern part of the island) in order to be prepared should the occasion arise.

The lowland associations develop

Given that so many calls to dog teams across the UK are to search for vulnerable people missing in urban and semi-urban settings, it's not surprising that enthusiasts living in the more lowland areas have sought to establish their own search dog capability and three groups have developed in the past ten or so years, in the flatter parts of England — NSARDA CanTech, NSARDA Anglia and Lowland Search Dogs. Their membership may be small in number by comparison with the more established organisations, but they are highly committed, exceptionally well organised and prepared to learn from the existing associations.

Anglia and CanTech enjoyed a similar period of gestation to becoming the first low terrain search dog units to have their standards accepted by NSARDA. Prior to that, of course, NSARDA had dealt solely with mountain search dog groups.

The group that would become NSARDA CanTech undertook its first operational search in 1997, for Lincolnshire Police. In July 1999, with input from International Rescue, the British Canine Technical Unit (BCTU) was born, with about thirty members concentrated in Kent and Lincolnshire. In time, BCTU adopted the abbreviated name CanTech and, in 2001, changed its name to CanTech Volunteer Search Dogs. Full membership of NSARDA

came in 2007 and, three years later, the unit was renamed NSARDA CanTech to differentiate it as a lowland unit.

Although membership initially comprised handlers from Lincolnshire, Essex, Leicestershire, South Yorkshire and Norfolk, today the majority of its members live within its operational area of Kent. All operational members of CanTech are also members of their local ALSAR unit, Kent Search and Rescue (KSAR) and some are qualified as team leaders or advanced search technicians.

NSARDA CanTech trains every other Sunday throughout the year. Each training day is geared towards dogs, handlers and 'supports', relevant to the level of their training. The handler is the team leader and focuses on working the dog whilst the support member assists with matters such as navigation, communications and first aid delivery when required. Each year the unit organises at least one operational exercise and a separate training weekend and, in common with all the SARDA groups, members are encouraged to travel around the country to train with other associations, whilst those qualified also act as external assessors. This spirit of collaboration also extends to other search and rescue organisations and emergency services.

Stock tests and assessments are organised as and when required and

CanTech assesses handlers and their dogs to NSARDA standards and dog team supports to standards devised by its own members. This is shared with the local ALSAR unit and used to train and assess search technicians should they be required to deploy with a dog team. Prospective members attend an induction day before being invited to attend four training days. A decision is then taken, based on their potential to train further. If successful, they become a probationary member and remain so until they qualify either as a dog handler or support.

CanTech supplies dog teams to KSAR who are called on primarily by Kent Police and the Coastguard, as well as other emergency services and the local authority. Over the last three years, the number of call-outs has averaged 37 per year with at least one dog team deployed to every search in Kent since 2009. Members not deployed with their dog sometimes join members of the KSAR foot team.

A variety of breeds are used including collies, labradors, Springer Spaniels and hovawarts although other breeds are considered if deemed appropriate for search work. Early in 2011, Jo Kenny and her Border Collie Bryn was presented with the Endal Medal at the London Pet Show to recognise her progress from Battersea Dogs Home rescue dog, to qualification as an air scenting search dog, and almost immediate success in finding a despondent person.

Further north, in East Anglia, Kevin Waterson was inspired to pursue the use of search dogs in a more lowland environment after seeing them in action in Snowdonia, with the Ogwen Valley Mountain Rescue Organisation (OVMRO), rescuing a party of walkers trapped on the hill. As had others before, it occurred to him that, with a little tweaking of some of the techniques, these dogs could be successfully used in searching for people suffering from such things as Alzheimer's and depression, and those who get lost or confused. So, in 1997, he began the process of setting up what he hoped would become SARDA Lowland. The following April, he met with the Chief Inspector of Operations for Suffolk Constabulary to initiate the idea of using search dogs and a search and rescue team in the search for vulnerable missing people.

Following an initial reluctance on the part of SARDA to accept his fledgling organisation, in 2000, SARDA Wales invited Kevin to a weekend training session to observe their training methods. Later that year — thanks to a good deal of positive help and encouragement from Lyndon Jones in particular — 'Lowland Search Dogs' was coined as a working title, the ultimate intention to adopt 'SARDA Lowland'. In the event, this plan was confounded when the Lowland Search Dogs (LS Dogs) took the name in 2002, so the East Anglia group changed its working title to 'Search Dogs Suffolk'.

By this time they were working very closely with SARDA, and in particular with Harold Burrows and SARDA Wales. As it gradually became evident they were following the NSARDA guidelines and training methods, so the new group gained the respect of the national body. Despite the many name changes forced upon them, the singularly most important point was that their dog training followed and adhered to NSARDA standards. And so, in 2006, almost ten years after Kevin Waterson's tentative approach to Suffolk Constabulary, 'NSARDA Anglia' had their first assessments, with two dogs gaining their Novice grading.

The association covers the counties of East Anglia consisting primarily of Suffolk, Norfolk, Essex and Cambridgeshire, incorporating a diversity of terrain including Thetford Forest, the largest man-made forest in the country, open prairie-style field, dense brambles, marshes and an extensive coastline. Historically they have opted for the gun dog breeds such as labradors and Springer Spaniels, although there are currently a number of German Shepherds in training.

Training follows the strict format that all the SARDA teams adhere to, but it soon became evident a 'lowland standard' was needed. It wasn't just the different demands of the terrain and environment to consider — there were issues encountered in the lowland areas not realised by those in the mountains. NSARDA Anglia was instrumental in helping form the NSARDA Lowland Standard, which would not compromise the original SARDA standard, but would be more appropriate to these areas.

Although police dogs tend to be used in the first instance in this environment, frequently the job is handed to the lowland search dog handlers as a more efficient resource, with the police maintaining contact with operations via Airwave radio. Suffolk Constabulary's dog trainer has attended training sessions to ratify the quality of training on behalf of the force, and the lead Police Search Adviser (POLSA) for missing persons has also attended training, to observe both Anglia's training methods and their management of search dog teams. Only afterwards did the visiting POLSA inform them of his previous occupation as RAF dog handler! Fortunately, he was hugely impressed by the professionalism of the training, and the dog team in general.

Grading uses the same simple system of Novice and Fully Qualified as SARDA. Formal training is provided twice a month with individuals doing their homework in between times. The sessions are tailored to best progress the development of each individual dog and handler, based on a simulated 'live' search for the qualified dogs and, at every training session, a qualified dog will be picked out at random and put through a full assessment. All handlers keep a record of their training and a copy is kept separately to monitor their performance — particularly helpful when training the new dogs in remembering the stage they've reached. With this aid, specific scenarios are tailored to suit each dog and handler in question to overcome any difficulties they may be encountering.

Assessments run between late April and late October, when it is arguably more difficult to search due to the dense vegetation giving good ground cover to hide the bodies, the wind being light to non-existent and the distinct possibility of heat disturbing the scent. Two external assessors, together with two local

Fire and rescue

CANINE CRIME FIGHTING DUO

Central Scotland Fire and Rescue Service owns two accelerant detector dogs – Jay, a seven-year-old Border Collie and Mitch, a five-year-old Springer Spaniel. Jay and Mitch are the only such dogs in use in Scotland, although accelerant detector dogs have been used to spot deliberate fires south of the border for around ten years.

Handled and cared for by Trevor Lynch, a retained fire officer based at Larbert in Clackmannanshire, the dogs live with Trevor as family pets and travel throughout Scotland to work on fire scenes. Jay was originally going to be trained as a search and rescue dog but, after reading about the use of fire dogs in England, Trevor persuaded his employers to follow suit. Mitch was a rescued dog whose owners gave him up when he was just four months old.

Together, they have been reported as a 'canine crime fighting duo', dedicated to catching criminals who use fire as a weapon. To date, they've been 100% successful in sniffing out the use of petrol and other accelerants in deliberate fires in Scotland. Accelerants are

hydrocarbon-based fuels, such as petrol, diesel fuel, turpentine and butane. They are also known as ignitable liquids. Trevor says that if accelerants are present, then his dogs will find them. Their sense of smell is so acute they can tell in seconds whether a flammable substance was used at a fire incident. They indicate to Trevor by 'freezing' close to the source. They can also pinpoint the location of the accelerant and, because they are so small and nimble, they can gain access to areas that firefighters would find impossible. Their use extends from burned-out buildings to charred corpses. Already, their efforts have resulted in huge savings in time and money on forensic testing and detective workload.

In one incident, the dogs' efforts

helped to convict a murderer. Following the discovery in woods of a badly burned man, investigators needed to know whether the victim had been set alight at the scene or elsewhere. Mitch and Jay were tasked and indicated the use of an accelerant. Investigators subsequently found petrol about a metre deep in the soil below the man's body. This finding avoided the need for a massive sweep of the entire wood, which saved time and freed officers to work on the case. A man was subsequently sentenced to life imprisonment for murder.

In another incident, Trevor and the dogs were sent to an incident where a chip shop roof had been on fire. On initial inspection, it looked just like a normal chip shop fire but a closer look revealed the roof tiles had been

stripped off, a hole cut into the roof and accelerants poured in. The dogs searched the area and sniffed out a lighter and the abandoned gloves used by the culprit. What looked to be a pure accident turned out to be a serious case of arson. So, in some cases, the dogs are able to flag up a suspicious fire when their human counterparts are ready to declare it an accident.

In addition to their detective role, Trevor and the two dogs give displays at galas and fetes, and also visit schools with Community Safety Officers to help educate children on the dangers of fire and fire raising.

Outside of work the dogs are treated as pets — just regular pets until their harness is on. That's the trigger for them to work and they know they'll get their ball if they work hard. Says Trevor: 'They have a life of luxury until they are needed. Once they see me in my overalls they start to get quite excited. The dogs love their job or they wouldn't do it — that's the bottom line.'

assessors, carry out the tests. Once a dog has attained Novice they are put on the call-out list and regrading to a full grade is undertaken a year later. At this stage a dog is certified Fully Qualified for three years.

In the matter of fundraising, NSARDA Anglia might be able boast themselves a little more upmarket in the 'tin shake' stakes, thanks to a stand at London's prestigious Knightsbridge store Harrod's, but this is no less welcome than the cash from talks to local groups and supermarkets. Fundraising remains a struggle with members, in the main, forced to buy equipment for themselves. That said, Suffolk Constabulary has provided three Ford Focus estate cars, marked up with the NSARDA Anglia logo and Battenberg reflective markings. A Transit van, provided by a local company, also doubles as a command control vehicle and is marked up in the same way.

As a growing lowland resource, the Anglia dogs have been called to some high profile incidents over the last few years. The 'Ipswich murders' involved the deaths of five women, between 30 October and 10 December 2006. All the women were prostitutes working in the Ipswich area. All five bodies were found naked. Suffolk Police linked the killings and launched a murder investigation code-named Operation Sumac, drafting in police officers from several other police forces as well as a range of other resources — including search and rescue dogs. Two Anglia dog teams were deployed: Mark Green and his Golden Labrador Ollie, working with navigator Brian Gregory, and Kevin Waterson with his labrador/collie cross Bess, with Dave Bird (Buz) as his navigator. Mark and Ollie found clothing, and the next

TOP: MITCH AND JAY © TREVOR LYNCH.. ABOVE: MITCH INDICATING; JAY INDICATING © TREVOR LYNCH.

LOWLAND SEARCH DOG SOX AT WORK © PETE SHEPHERD.

day the first woman's body was found. Coincidentally, Mark is also a serving police officer and a team leader within the POLSA search teams who works with Anglia on his days off!

The third lowland organisation in England, the Lowland Search Dogs (LS Dogs), do not belong to NSARDA although there is a memorandum of understanding in place designed to engender a close working relationship. LS Dogs was formed in 2002 as the umbrella organisation for search and rescue dogs working in lowland areas. A number of regional units, the majority based in the south of England, comprise Kent, Essex, Sussex, Hampshire, Dorset, Berkshire, Buckinghamshire, Oxfordshire, Surrey, Cheshire and Norfolk. There is also a unit in South Wales. All the units are recognised by their local police force and, as with all the other dog teams across the country, handlers can only respond to formal requests from the police.

There are around four operational dogs and over 150 operational personnel across its member units. Dogs are trained to either air scent or trail depending on the particular interest of the handler. In operational terms, their use is confined to lowland areas such as farmland, forests and open downland. Handlers and dogs are not trained to search terrain that requires specialist mountain rescue skills or experience — their calls are invariably to search for vulnerable missing people.

In a key difference to their mountain search dog colleagues, who are usually required to be experienced members of their mountain rescue team and skilled in hill craft, lowland handlers must complete a recognised Search Technician Course before becoming operational, to demonstrate basic navigation skills and acquire a first aid certificate. Most are also members of their local ALSAR (Association of Lowland Search and Rescue) team. Each regional unit oversees the training of their own dogs before assessment by the association.

Their training and assessment procedures also differ. The organisation has developed its own standards and training procedures as well as its own internal assessment programme, with a number of national assessors spread throughout the country. Essentially, LS Dogs recognises three levels of search dog. Level 1 (Trainee) is a dog that is currently undergoing operational search training. The dog and handler do not attend call-outs but may be used for training exercises. Level 2 (Air Scent — Hasty) is a dog that has been assessed to work over a period of up to an hour, searching for multiple missing persons along a route, path or boundary. Satisfactory assessment requires the dog team to locate 100% of all persons. A Level 2 dog would only be used for searching hasty scenarios at day or night. Level 3 (Air Scent — Open Area) is a dog that has been assessed to work over a period of up to two hours, looking for multiple missing persons in an area of mixed terrain and difficulty. As with Level 2, satisfactory assessment requires the dog to locate all persons. The handler also is required to demonstrate key skills including sub-sectoring and search strategies as well as a knowledge of scent theory. Level 3 dogs are used to search any area deemed suitable by the handler and search manager on scene at the time of an incident. Levels 2 and 3 also apply to trailing dogs and successful dogs are identified as Trailing (Rural) and Trailing (Urban/Rural) respectively. Handlers can also train their dogs for one of a number of specialist areas such as Drowned Victim searching. In the case of Victim Recovery, dogs are trained and assessed to work over a ten acre area of woodland, and a building of approximately 200 square metres, to find body parts. Successful dogs may be deployed in urban or rural areas depending on the nature of the incident.

The length and nature of training differs from unit to unit but typically, training sessions are held once a week. Training to Level 2 normally takes around a year and then a further four to six months to move to Level 3. Dog teams are reassessed every two years to ensure the maintenance of standards and all formal assessments — which take place at a national assessment day — are preceded by a mock, pre-assessment check.

When Hamish MacInnes returned from his forays in the Alps back in the 1960s, he was highly motivated to investigate how dogs could be trained and used to search for people lost or avalanched in the Scottish mountains. He may have had a belief about how this might develop, but it is unlikely anybody could have foreseen how things would change and how the use of dogs for searching and helping mankind would expand and diversify to such a dramatic extent.

But clearly, the use of dogs goes far beyond their search and rescue capabilities. Besides this — and their obvious place as companion and friend in everyday life — we'd go so far as to say they're a cornerstone of modern society.

A year of searches

'I know it's important not to anthropomorphise or project human values onto dogs but I can't help feeling that they're just little hairy people with four legs and nice long noses going about their business.' Martin Clunes

Rescue teams across the country are on call 24 hours a day, every day of the year. And this is no less so for dog handlers, who are frequently called out in atrocious weather at unsociable times, any time of the day or night. This is a huge commitment for the handlers, although we suspect dogs probably see things differently. More an unexpected chance to play! Even so, it's likely that most days of the year, somewhere in the UK, a dog handler will be tasked by the police to search for a walker lost in the mountains, or a vulnerable person reported missing from home or hospital.

It wasn't always thus. When Hamish MacInnes returned from Switzerland, his focus was the training of dogs to search for walkers and climbers lost in the mountains or trapped in avalanches. He could hardly have anticipated the explosive increase in hillwalking, rock climbing and winter mountaineering which would occur over the next 25 years, or the associated increase in mountain incidents. Neither could he have predicted the reliance the police authorities would come to place on

dogs as a key resource in the search for people missing in urban and semi-rural environments. Nor the manner in which dogs are used for so many specialist purposes beyond the mountains — lowland searches, trailing and air-scenting, locating drowned victims, the search for casualties trapped under collapsed structures. The list grows ever longer.

SARDA has not only grown and diversified way beyond its original conception, its workload has increased significantly. Figure 1 (following page) shows the striking way things have changed in ten years, indicating the number of incidents each association was called out for, each year. (See Appendix 2 for a more detailed breakdown.) In fact, there has been a threefold increase in workload over the period — a rise which is only partly due to the formation of new associations, and their role in adding to the figures. It's been suggested, for example, that the police are much more knowledgeable now about using dogs as a search asset — which has led to a greater readiness on their part to request

dog teams to search for people reported missing in urban environments. It's also possible there is an overall increase in the number of mountain, lowland and urban incidents requiring deployment of the emergency services. It is widely recognised that the emergence of mobile phone technology has led people to become less reliant on their own navigation skills and more likely to call on support from mountain rescue. Only a few short years ago, if someone was mislaid or lost, they'd have used basic navigation skills to work out their position and determine the best way off the hillside or mountain. This, it seems, is a dying art!

So, we know the modern rescue team — and search dogs and their handlers — are involved in an increasing diversity of situations but how does that pan out across a year? What sort of incidents underpin the statistics? Many incidents have resulted in a positive dog find but this is not typical. In many cases, dog teams search areas where subsequent events show the missing person was somewhere completely different. At other times, members of the rescue team, or a helicopter searching overhead, find the missing person. And there are occasions when the person finds their own way off the mountain and returns home, whilst the various teams are still involved in the search. Whether or not they 'find', incidentally, is by no means a measure of a dog team's success. Often, their value to the police is in knowing a search area has been 'cleared' by a dog team and can therefore be eliminated from further searches.

Walk with us through a typical year of incidents — just a small cross-section of the hundreds of situations dog teams are involved in each year — and you'll quickly appreciate the myriad ways in which the different associations are tasked. And so to January...

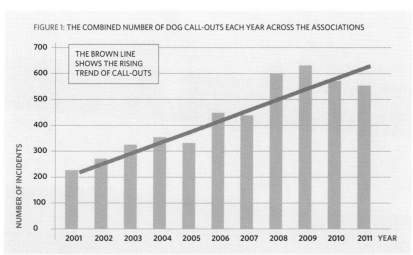

FIGURE 1: THE COMBINED NUMBER OF DOG CALL-OUTS EACH YEAR ACROSS THE ASSOCIATIONS

THE BROWN LINE SHOWS THE RISING TREND OF CALL-OUTS

January...

The start of our 'year' saw a man and a woman in their twenties, inexperienced in the skills required for winter mountaineering – much less the often extreme nature of a Scottish winter – climbing the east ridge of Ben Lui in the Central Scottish Highlands. It's a mountain described as 'the queen of all Scottish mountains' – a must for Munro-baggers.

When the man tripped and fell about 90 metres, conditions were so poor, rescue by helicopter was impossible. Team members, however, have no such constraints. Whatever the weather, where there's a need — provided it is safe for them to do so — out they go. Alongside members of Killin MRT, a dog handler from SARDA Southern Scotland and his dog set off on foot to find the walkers. The overnight search stretched well into the following day — with no improvement in the appalling weather conditions — until both were found. The woman was severely hypothermic, but otherwise okay, but her partner had suffered serious multiple injuries. Attempts were made to revive him as he was stretchered off the mountain to a waiting ambulance, but he was pronounced dead on arrival at hospital. It transpired this was the couple's very first experience of winter conditions and the first time the man had ever worn crampons.

At this time of year, the early-falling winter darkness often catches people out, especially if they've set off late or become lost and disoriented. In the Lake District, a 20-year-old woman walking alone lost her way and found herself benighted near Scoat Tarn, about two miles north east of Wasdale Head. She'd failed to pack in her rusksack any of the basic equipment — such as a torch and compass — that may have helped her find her way off the hillside, so Lakes search dog Pippa was called out, along with members of Wasdale MRT. Pippa found the woman, to the west of Scoat Tarn in Nether Beck, very cold and tired but able to walk off unaided with assistance from team members.

Over in the Isle of Man, the alarm was raised when a vulnerable person was reported missing in the Glen Maye area — about ten miles west of Douglas. Two Isle of Man dog teams were deployed, along with members of the Coastguard, Fire Service, Police and Civil Defence. The dogs were first tasked to clear fields, and the grounds of several large houses in the Glen Maye area. Once this was done, they were redeployed to search the area adjacent to the missing person's house as well as coastline to the south. Four hours into the search, the missing person was found alive and well by police officers, inland from the initial search areas.

In Ireland, handler Mick and Bono from SARDA Ireland responded to a call from the Gardai to search for a youth missing in Curracloe, about 40 miles from Waterford in County Wexford. This large-scale search involved members of the Civil Defence, the Irish Coast Guard, members of the Dublin & Wicklow and Glen of Imaal MRTs, the South Eastern MRA, and up to a thousand members of the public. It lasted three days with Mick and Bono clearing a variety of woodland, marshland and coastal areas. Sadly, the youth's body was found on the shore near Wexford town, some days later.

Back in England, in the lowlands of Kent, Steve Ball and seven-year-old Morgan, a Parson Russell Terrier from LS Dogs, located a seventeen-year-old youth who had overdosed near a river. Later in the month, handler Vanessa Courtney and Sam, her German Shorthaired Pointer, found an unconscious woman deep in woodland. Police indicated that, had she not been found, she would certainly not have survived the night in the extreme cold weather.

TOP: RICHARD BEECH (SARDA WALES) AND CELYN © RICHARD BEECH.
ABOVE: JOY GRINDROD LDMRSD) AND EINICH ON AVALANCHE TRAINING IN SCOTLAND © DARYL GARFIELD.

February...

You'd be forgiven for thinking – in the winter, at least – that mountain rescue in Scotland is always about climbers and ropes, crampons and ice axes, and snow. Plenty of snow. But sometimes the incidents involve those simply going about their day-to-day life in the mountains.

Early in February, near Oban on the west coast of Scotland, a 60-year-old farmer was reported missing having failed to return after gathering sheep from his local hills. He was known to suffer from mild dementia. Rescue teams from Oban, Arrochar and Strathclyde Police were deployed in the area where the man was last seen and, for the next eight hours, some 50 personnel — along with a Sea King helicopter from Royal Navy Gannet (Rescue 137) with thermal imaging equipment — were deployed to find the man. There were various reports of footprints in the snow — both dog and human — which helped lead the searchers to him. Then, just as a Southern Scotland dog handler was about to be deployed, in came news that contact had been made with the man after his dog was heard barking. He was found just inside a forest and fortunately was well, although a little disoriented. Stretchered to the road by team members, and then on by ambulance to Oban, he was later released after examination. Meanwhile, over 500 man-hours had been consumed by the search.

Back to the more adventurous side of the mountains — at this time of year, if it's not the snow, or the wind, or the dark that challenge you, it's the lack of preparation. Or the failure to carry all the kit you need to cover every eventuality. Often people have almost all the right equipment — except for one key item. Late in February, Durham Constabulary received a distress call from a 37-year-old man, lost in the Pennines in the dark. In fact, he was suitably equipped with a map and compass but couldn't actually use them — because he had no torch. Having spent a lot of time, crossing and recrossing small rivers in an attempt to identify his location, he eventually became disoriented and called for help.

Three dog teams from SARDA England set off to find him. Using the location of the man's car as a starting point, a hasty local search was carried out but, when this proved negative, a high level search of the hills to the east of Penrith, including Cross Fell (893 metres) and the Pennine Way, was initiated. The dog teams, along with members of Teesdale & Weardale MRT, were driven up onto the fells in the rescue team's vehicles to begin their searching. After about 30 minutes work, in very poor visibility, search dog Nut indicated to handler John and continued to indicate several times, each time extending further than the last, crossing and recrossing Trout Beck to the east of Cross Fell. Finally, the missing walker heard Nut approaching and — most untypically — made himself known by running towards the dog shouting 'Help!' Clearly relieved to be found, albeit very confused and frightened, he was otherwise in good health.

On the Isle of Man, dog teams Matt and Lola, Jim and Star, were called out mid-evening to search for a man missing in the Groudle area of Douglas. One pair, along with a police dog team, searched the cliffs to the north, where the man's car had been located, while the other searched cliffs to the south, towards Onchan. The area was searched extensively for several hours. Even when the Douglas lifeboat crew reported a body located below cliffs between the two search areas, both dog teams continued to search the Groudle railway and Groudle Glen until a positive identification was confirmed.

Meanwhile, SARDA Wales was called to help Llanberis MRT search for a group of missing hill walkers. It was lunchtime when the team received a call to say two hill walkers were lost in the mist and snow-covered ground on the south side of Snowdon. Two dogs were deployed. Following an initial drive in the team's Land Rovers, both dog teams struck up the hill on foot — Gaynor and Pero up the south ridge of Snowdon, Richard and Celyn by the Rhud Ddu path. About 90 minutes into the search, Richard found two sets of tracks leaving the path to the south east. He followed the tracks, with Celyn searching in front. Another twenty minutes on, they began to hear shouts for help then, suddenly, Celyn emerged from the mist and indicated to Richard before shooting back into the mist to the missing walkers. Glad to be found, they were unhurt but needed warming up before being walked to a waiting Land Rover for transport off the mountain.

The following day, just before lunch, Llanberis team members were called out again to locate a lone hill walker. He'd climbed to the summit of Snowdon but, on his descent, had slipped and fallen some 300 metres towards the cliffs of Clogwyn Coch, before coming to a halt on the edge of a large cliff. The man was badly injured but able to speak to the police on his mobile phone but, because his exact location was uncertain — and knowing he was in thick cloud — a small group of three team members, along with Richard and Celyn, were dispatched up the Snowdon Ranger path to search. An RAF Sea King was also deployed to explore the snow-covered slopes. At one point, word came through that the walker could hear the helicopter, but he thought it was on the other side of the mountain. By this stage, the mountain rescue group had reached

the top of the ridge and turned towards Clogwyn Coch. Conditions were extremely challenging: the snow was knee deep and visibility was down to twenty metres. Shortly after turning into the 'cwm', team members heard shouts for help but couldn't make out where they were coming from due to the echo in valley and the noise from the circling helicopter. Richard and Celyn, accompanied by a navigator, headed off to the north side of the valley, in the direction of the railway tracks. Just as they reached the tracks, Celyn shot off down the mountain and out of sight. Richard quickly followed and it wasn't long before he too could hear the man shouting for help. As he scrambled down increasingly steep ground, Celyn returned and indicated. On they went together, quickly finding the man who was holding on for dear life to a large spike of rock. The other team members were alerted and arrived on scene to make everyone safe and treat the man's injuries before securing him on a stretcher. Then, using a system of back ropes for safety, stretcher and casualty were lowered to the top of a crag, winched into the hovering helicopter and away to hospital.

Early in March, in Scotland, a 55-year-old man from England was spending a week camping and walking in a very remote area known as the Fisherfield Forest. Sometimes tagged 'The Great Wilderness', it's an area entirely devoid of permanent settlements. Towards the end of his expedition, he texted his wife from the summit of An Teallach, one of the Munros in the area, suggesting he would contact her again a couple of days later, once off the hill. Unfortunately, his message didn't get through. Concerned for his safety, the man's wife contacted Northern Constabulary and members of the Kinloss and Dundonnell MRTs, with handlers from SARDA Scotland, were duly tasked to search the area. The 'missing' walker's route plans were studied and it wasn't long before he was found, somewhat surprised to be 'discovered' relaxing in his tent by worried rescuers and a very excited dog!

Later in March, a school party was walking near Wolfscote Dale near Ashbourne in the Peak District. One of the students — a fifteen-year-old girl — slipped and injured her back, unable to continue. With very poor weather and unreliable mobile communications, it was extremely difficult to pinpoint the location of the party. Members of both Buxton and Derby MRTs, and dog team Dave and Megan from SARDA England, set about a search of the footpaths and surrounding dales. Eventually the injured girl and her teacher were found by Megan in Biggin Dale, about a kilometre from the expected location. The girl was stretchered off to the head of Biggin Dale whilst the remaining members of the party were escorted off to Hartington in cold and extremely slippery conditions. Fortunately, the group had been well

March...

Thankfully, hoax calls are rare but occasionally the police are called for what turns out to be a 'false alarm with good intent' – or a 'FAGI' as it's known in mountain rescue circles!

ABOVE: NEIL POWELL'S DOG FERN SNIFFS OUT A SUSPECTED DROWNED PERSON ON LOUGH NEAGH © NEIL POWELL.
FACING PAGE: TOP: THE CRASHED CESSNA © STEVE DOMENEY (CAVE RESCUE ORGANISATION).   BOTTOM: RESCUE TEAM MEMBERS SET ABOUT PROBING AVALANCHE DEBRIS © BOB SHARP.

equipped with plenty of spare food and clothing so, in spite of a long wait, there were no cases of hypothermia for the teams to deal with.

Frequently, mountain rescue team members and dog handlers are stood down before they even reach an incident — often entailing a round trip of tens, even hundreds, of miles. It may have been a false alarm. The missing person may have turned up safe and well, or been located by other team members. Perhaps a body has been found. Whatever the circumstances, and however frustrating at the time — and never more so when the handler leaves a warm bed, and any prospect of a good night's sleep, to go search through the night — it goes with the territory: part of the commitment. On one such occasion in Ireland, towards the end of March, SARDA Ireland dog handler Catherine, with search dog Lily, set off to the agreed rendezvous point after two female walkers reported themselves lost somewhere in the Galty Mountains south of Tipperary. Whilst they were still en route, team members from the South Eastern MRA had located the pair safe and well. In Penrith, another search — for a walker reported overdue in the Haweswater area — roused Penrith members, including search dog Ginny, from their slumbers at 1.00am. The team and Ginny were stood down forty minutes later, whilst still en route, when it was discovered the missing person had left a note in his vehicle stating his overnight plans. In Wales, a young man was reported lost on Moel Famau, but was found by rescue team members whilst the dog team made their way to the scene.

Elsewhere, in a large sand dune area outside Newcastle, County Down, an

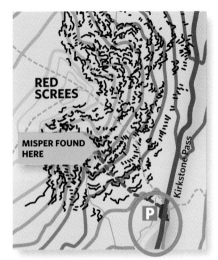

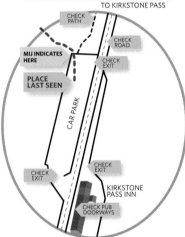

TOP: THE AREA ABOVE THE KIRKSTONE INN SHOWING THE VERY ROUGH, STEEP TERRAIN OF RED SCREES.

ABOVE: DIAGRAM SHOWS HOW IAIN SET ABOUT ELIMINATING POSSIBLE EXITS THE MISSING PERSON MAY HAVE TAKEN — THE RED DASHED LINE SHOWS THE ACTUAL ROUTE DETECTED.
THE GREEN ARROW MARKS THE EXIT POINT AT WHICH MIJ INDICATED, DIRECTING TEAM MEMBERS AND AIR SCENTING SEARCH DOGS UP RED SCREES TO CONTINUE THE SEARCH.

elderly man suffering from dementia became separated from his carer. Mountain rescue teams, the police, coastguard, fire and rescue service, Community Rescue, a coastguard helicopter and three dogs from SARDA Ireland North, were deployed to look for him. After a day and most of the next night without success, handler John and search dog Jodie found the man at 5.00am, still alive but suffering from hypothermia. This gentleman made a full recovery but not so fortunate was the man who was seen to throw himself into the river Boyne in County Meath in the Republic of Ireland. Gardai divers, and a number of civilian dive teams, searched the river for three long days without success. At this point, Neil Powell was asked to assist with his drowned victim search dog Fern. Having searched the river for thirty minutes, she indicated a spot in the middle of the river, about a half mile downstream from where the man had jumped in. His body was recovered from that location, where it had been trapped beneath a large boulder, held there by water pressure.

If mountain rescue has one distinguishing characteristic it's that no two incidents are ever the same. Each brings its own challenges and outcomes. It's not often that dogs are called to locate a crashed aircraft but, when they are, you might expect the location to be fairly obvious! But this wasn't the case when a small two-seater Cessna crashed on North Yorkshire moorland. The plane came down on Ingleborough Moor near Settle, late one evening, on its flight north from Blackpool to Kirkby Lonsdale. It was dark and visibility was very poor. Fortunately, both men survived the accident and the pilot was able

to report the crash, although there was some confusion over its exact whereabouts. Members of Kendal MRT and the Cave Rescue Organisation were tasked by North Yorkshire Police to search the area for the two men. Two dog teams from SARDA England were also tasked. Following an extensive search of the area, the aircraft wreck and the two men were located by search dog Glen and handler Bill, shortly after midnight. Both men had suffered minor injuries. They were treated on scene by cave rescue doctors then evacuated a couple of miles by stretcher to road ambulances waiting in Clapham.

Around 8.00pm, one evening late in March, Langdale Ambleside MRT received a call from Cumbria Police to help look for a 67-year-old retired professor reported missing from his home in Ambleside. He was known to be fit and in good health, and very familiar with the local hills but the alarm was raised when he failed to return from one of his regular trips on the fells. His vehicle was traced to the summit car park on Kirkstone Pass — the traditional starting point for the steep climb up Red Screes — where it had apparently been for about ten hours. The weather was cold and the ground covered in melting snow. Team leader Nick Owen decided to call in Iain Nicholson of SARDA Wales and his trailing dog Mij to see if they could help, before mobilising a full team call-out. His view was that because there was no lead as to where the man had gone (he could have taken to the high fells either west or east of the main road), and realising he was probably looking at a multi-team call-out for a night search of both sides of the car park, Iain and Mij could help reduce the search area by giving a clue to the man's direction of travel. With a number of personal items from the man's house to give Mij a scent to follow, she was tasked to check all exits from the car park, as well as the nearby roads and pub entrance. She gave one indication: at the gate that led to Red Screes. Mij followed the trail, picking up bits across the lower ground before it steepened up to Red Screes. The problem was that melting snow was tending to wash away the man's trail and, after a few hundred metres, they came to a blank with no further evidence of the trail. But, at least Mij had given the rescue team a head start and a good indication of the man's route up the fellside. At this point, Owen deployed his team members, along with Lakes handler Roger Pickup and his dog Beinn. They followed the line of the path uphill, sweeping the steep, broken ground either side and, after about an hour's searching, found the man's body just down from the path near the top section. Tragically, despite being properly equipped for winter conditions, it seemed he had stopped for a moment and put down his ice axe, perhaps to enjoy the view or take a break, then lost his balance and fallen down the steep ground.

The Grampian Mountains in Scotland comprise a number of quite distinctive mountain masses. Perhaps the best known is the Cairngorms but, to the south east is Lochnagar, famously the setting for *The Old Man of Lochnagar*, a children's story originally told by Prince Charles to his younger brothers. The range is cut into by a number of very clear glens such as Glen Clova, Glen Esk and Glen Muick. Surrounding the glens are many mountains over 914 metres, which offer superb walking and climbing opportunities, especially in winter. Coire Fee at the head of Glen Clova boasts several classic winter climbing routes. The family of a lone climber raised the alarm when he failed to return at the expected time from a foray into the area. Tayside Police and Tayside MRT, supported by a helicopter from RAF Lossiemouth, began searching late on Friday night. It was decided that 'B Gully' in Corrie Fee was the most likely area the man would have been exploring that day. The going was particularly difficult. A soft crust sat atop a deep layer of sugary snow. Team members split, dividing their time between the various climbing routes in the coire. A dog team from SARDA Scotland headed up 'B Gully' and searched as far as the dog could go. Searchers at the top of the crag reported footprints at the top of 'A Gully' but were unable to tell which way the person had been walking. It was decided to check the lower part of this gully so members in the coire headed over that way and began their search. They soon came across avalanche debris and, after only a short period of searching, the dog began to dig and located the man's body.

Whilst avalanches are very common in Scotland during the winter period, there are very few where walkers or climbers are injured or lose their lives. Indeed, the number of incidents involving people has been steadily decreasing for the past 25 years. But, unfortunately, when someone is caught in an avalanche, the chances of injury are extremely high and survival rates very low.

April...

Many incidents attended by dog teams are what might be termed 'non-mountaineering' in nature: unconnected to the traditional pursuits of walking or rock climbing. As far as the rescue service is concerned this doesn't really matter. If the police feel a dog team is the correct asset to use then, whatever the location or activity in question, the request goes out.

By April, following a long period of prolonged rain, Scottish rivers were unusually high. Many that could usually be forded were impossible to cross. Nevertheless, for those who work in the mountains, life — and work — must go on. When a shepherdess in the Borders attempted to cross a small, swollen burn on her quad bike, she was swept away by the force of water. Later in the day, a family member reported her missing when her overturned bike was found in the river. Members of the Moffat and Galloway teams, and dog teams from SARDA

Southern Scotland were tasked by Dumfries & Galloway Constabulary to find the woman. An extensive search of the river and banks downstream proved unsuccessful. Further searches in treacherous weather conditions were carried out over subsequent days by mountain rescue personnel and dogs, to no avail. Sadly, there comes a point, when lines must be drawn by the police and, all avenues seemingly covered, a fruitless search must be terminated. And often, despite the best efforts by the professional and voluntary agencies, missing people are found by unsuspecting members of the public out for a walk. Two weeks after searchers stopped their searching, a fisherman spotted the woman's body in the River Nith.

In the Lake District, a 77-year-old woman suffering from Alzheimer's was reported missing from a care home in Keswick. Six search dogs, along with police officers and members of Keswick MRT, commenced a search of the area. As the incident unfolded, Cumbria Police were given additional information, which suggested the lady was possibly wandering a short distance away in Portinscale. Search teams were mobilised in this direction and the woman was quickly found safe and well by a police helicopter using infrared heat-seeking equipment.

Another woman in her late seventies was reported missing in Dulverton, Somerset. She had been staying with family members in the area and wandered off alone without anyone knowing. Fortunately, a member of the public had seen someone meeting her description heading in the direction of local woodland. Members of Exmoor SRT were mobilised, along with SARDA England

handler Nicki with Cavos. They searched for several hours and, at one point, Cavos showed a great deal of interest in a particular area. However, due to the lack of wind, he was unable to give a clear indication. Shortly afterwards, Nicki located footprints that matched the footwear the missing woman was wearing. The area was immediately flooded with team members and a concentrated search ensued. Within a short space of time, Cavos found the lady — only 500 metres from the point where he had first shown interest — perfectly demonstrating that dogs can work on the slightest human scent, but really do need air movement to detect direction.

Meanwhile, in Kent, a seventeen-year-old female was reported missing in the village of Hawkinge. There was a suspicion she had been violently assaulted. Kent Police asked handler Jo and search dog Bryn, from NSARDA CanTech, to assist Kent SAR in a search of a large graveyard, surrounding fields and woodland. Evidence suggested the girl might have made her way towards a pond and it was known the graveyard had a pond within its grounds. The initial search took five hours, at which point Bryn was rested while Jo continued searching the local urban area with the foot teams. It was a further three hours before police reported that the missing person had been found alive and well.

May...

The nights may be getting lighter in May but allow insufficient time for an expedition – particularly one which ventures far beyond the nearest road head – and you might still find yourself benighted in the mountains.

Beinn Molurgainn is a very remote 690 metre peak in the South West Highlands north of Oban, hidden in the rough jumble of hills between Loch Etive and Loch Creran. A lone male walker found himself disoriented as darkness fell and contacted Strathclyde Police for help. Mobile phone communications were poor, making it impossible to gain a clear fix on his position. However, the message got through for him to climb a little higher until

he could see the flashing lights of the police vehicle. Communications improved once he gained height, and he was asked to flash his camera. Which gave the police an opportunity to take a compass bearing on his position. By doing this from two locations along the road they were able to judge his approximate position on the hill, a procedure called triangulation. A dog handler from SARDA Southern Scotland joined members from Oban and

Strathclyde Police mountain rescue teams and made their way to the man, none the worse for wear and able to walk off accompanied by the team members.

Occasionally, both air-scenting and trailing dogs are used on a search, each bringing their own distinctive, and very different, skills to bear on the situation. Whereas air scenting dogs are trained to pick up the scent of a person — any person — carried in the wind, trailing dogs start with an article from the missing person, such as a hat or pullover, and then attempt to locate that person by following their trail from a known start point. One such incident took place in Bolton when Greater Manchester Police called for assistance from Bolton MRT, along with Alison and Floss from SARDA England, and trailing dog team Iain and Mij. An elderly man, suffering with dementia, had been reported missing from his care home. Particular concern was expressed because of the home's proximity to a large reservoir. Team members searched all afternoon and evening but were stood down just after midnight with nothing found. Everyone expected to resume the search at first light but, thankfully, the man was located safe and well by police, outside the areas searched by mountain rescue.

Still early in the month, a despondent male was reported missing in Tonbridge. It transpired that a group of fisherman had seen a man fitting his description standing on a bridge, naked and clutching a bible. He wasn't seen to enter the water but clothes were found neatly piled by the bridge and, soon after, a bible was spotted floating nearby in the River Medway. Kent Police tasked two dog teams from NSARDA Cantech to search the banks and adjacent areas of the river along with numerous foot teams. One dog team, with a support team, searched one side of the river heading downstream, with foot teams deployed on the opposite bank. The other dog team set about working many miles downriver, tasked to search in the upstream direction using the path on one side of the river, the other side being inaccessible. Eight hours later, as all the dog and foot teams converged, the search was suspended with nothing found. A large and complex search of both rural and urban areas had been undertaken — all the relevant areas had been covered and there was no further information available. Unfortunately, some days later, the body of the missing man was found by divers underwater, adjacent to a lock.

June...

Very occasionally an incident occurs that takes on enormous proportions of scale and severity: the Lockerbie disaster, for example, or the 'Cairngorm Tragedy' of 1971, when five young children lost their lives on the Cairngorm plateau. At times like these, mountain rescue comes into its own, with immediacy and unquestioning commitment. Out come the stops, as every available resource is mobilised.

Occasionally also, dog teams are involved in incidents where there is a real or suspected element of criminality. In June 2010, a lone gunman went on the rampage in West Cumbria and Whitehaven, shooting at numerous people, killing twelve and injuring many others. Cumbria Police used every armed police patrol in Cumbria to apprehend the armed man suspected of the shootings. An immediate, large-scale search was launched, its Gold Command set up at Police HQ in Penrith to manage the incident. The response included armed vehicle and foot patrols, officers from Cumbria Roads Policing Unit, police dog units and air support from Lancashire. Handlers from SARDA Southern Scotland and Scotland travelled south to assist their colleagues from England and the Lakes, and mountain rescue team members from across the Lake District dropped what they were doing to join the operation. Tasked to look for injured or fatally wounded people throughout the region, who may not have been accounted for, they searched on foot along lanes and verges for two long days. Thankfully, there were no further victims.

A few days later, in Scotland, a 29-year-

AN RAF SEA KING HOVERS DURING A RESCUE DEMONSTRATION CLOSE TO IDWAL SLABS, NORTH WALES — ILLUSTRATES THE DIFFICULT GROUND THAT DOG TEAMS COULD BE TASKED TO SEARCH © JUDY WHITESIDE

old walker contacted the police to say he was cold and very tired, and lost in the cloud somewhere on Ben Wyvis — at 1046 metres, one of the highest Munros in the eastern Cairngorms. Following a search involving Dundonnell team members and a dog handler from SARDA Scotland, he was located by the dog at the summit, extremely cold but able to walk down accompanied by team members to the waiting vehicles. It transpired he was ill-prepared for his trip yet, carrying neither map nor compass, he had taken with him his laptop, loaded with mapping software to help him navigate down the mountain. He had clearly given no thought to using his computer in the driving rain, and was blissfully unaware it wouldn't have helped anyway!

Later in June, a dog team from SARDA Southern Scotland assisted Strathclyde Police and Arrochar MRT in the Loch Fyne area close to Inverary after the car of a suicidal missing person was located at the roadside. The dog team was stood down en route after the man's body was located by local team members near to a waterfall.

Sometimes, the absence of a find may be just as critical as actually finding somebody. In an unusual incident in Belfast, a gas explosion partially wrecked a house. Raph and his collapsed structure dog Jay, and Neil and Charco from SARDA Ireland North, were tasked by the Northern Ireland Fire and Rescue Service. Following an extensive search of the building, they were able to confirm that no one had been trapped in the rubble. Without this information, it would have taken much longer for the building to be considered empty and consequently demolished.

July...

It's a view commonly held by the general public that walkers shouldn't venture into the mountains alone, especially during the winter or when the weather is poor. However, this is a view not shared by the majority of hillgoers.

Those who hike the hills and mountains on a regular basis learn how to cope with difficult situations and invariably plan their days with due care and attention. The experience gained from travelling alone develops important skills — not least how to navigate in poor weather. It helps build confidence and generates a spirit of self-reliance — perhaps the most important quality of all, but sometimes things go wrong. In early July, two dog teams from SARDA Ireland, together with members of the Galway MRT, were called to search for a lone walker who failed to return home from a day's walking in Connemara, County Galway. Following a search of possible car parks, the Gardai located the man's car at the foot of Corcog, a popular area with walkers and climbers about 50 miles north east of Galway. Dogs and team members were tasked to search the mountain and, two hours later, one of the team, scanning the hillside with binoculars, spotted the man in a deep gully. Everyone made their way down the steep ground to the casualty who had sustained fatal injuries.

Every now and then, the rescue services are called to locate small groups of young people undertaking Duke of Edinburgh expeditions. The problem is less common these days, because the preparation and training is much more robust than it was many years ago but, even so, things don't always go as planned. In mid-July, members of Central Beacons MRT and two dog handlers from SARDA South Wales were alerted to a group of five teenagers overdue in the Brecon Beacons. When people are reported overdue, the emergency services may wait a short while before deploying personnel — the party may be perfectly safe and well, just making slow progress. Factors such as the composition of the group, details of their route and weather conditions will be considered. But on this occasion, as the weather was poor, and the group relatively inexperienced, team members were deployed as soon as word came through. Fortunately, search dog Jenna located the five girls very quickly — all in good spirits.

Fife in Central Scotland is not known for its mountain landscape but it has its fair share of missing persons. Two dog teams from SARDA Southern Scotland assisted Fife Constabulary in the search for a 75-year-old man missing from his home in the village of Auchtertool near Kirkcaldy. The man was last seen walking towards his home, so the search concentrated in fields and woodland near the village. The dog teams were accompanied by several police officers, one of whom found the man stranded at the bottom of a steep hill on the edge of a field — safe and well but suffering from exposure and minor injuries, resulting from a fall down the grassy slope.

In North Wales, it was a hot summer's day when a young man parked his car by a quarry in Llanberis, and was later reported as missing and suicidal. When the car was discovered, and concerns grew for the man's safety, the police called Llanberis MRT and SARDA Wales. Handler Helen Howe left her work and headed off with young collie Cluanie to begin a search of the roadside quarries and the immediate surrounding areas. Several other dog teams joined the search that evening, while members of the rescue team abseiled into the quarries to gain a closer inspection of the steep, complicated ground. The search continued all day to no avail with the man still missing. The following morning, Helen and Cluanie continued their search, with other Llanberis members and dog teams. Exploring the various quarries, they worked their way from top to bottom via numerous ledges and inaccessible areas. A short time into the search, Cluanie found the young man's body. The police underwater squad had to assist with evacuation as the only way out was either across a lake or along a narrow, very loose rocky ledge. By its close, the incident had involved over forty Llanberis team members and five dog teams from SARDA Wales.

Searchers on the Pilgrims' Way in South East England enjoyed a happier outcome when a despondent female went missing in the area of Vigo village, near a popular beauty spot. NSARDA CanTech deployed Jo, and newly qualified search dog Bryn, to search lengths of the route and a popular viewing point. Thirty minutes in, Bryn indicated to Jo that he'd made a find before leading the party to the missing woman.

August...

Early in August, a 65-year-old honeymoon couple reported themselves lost in the mist, somewhere on Matterdale Common in the Calfhow Pike area – about four miles east of Keswick and just north of Great Dodd (856 metres).

Members of Keswick MRT, including dog team Mick and Ginny, mounted an immediate search. Ginny located the couple, none the worse for wear apart from feeling somewhat embarrassed and they were duly escorted back down to the road where they were given a lift to their hotel!

An extensive search in mid-August involved members of two rescue teams, dog handlers from SARDA Scotland and a helicopter. Assynt is a wild and remote part of Scotland and the local rescue teams are responsible for many thousands of square kilometres of mountainous terrain. A female tourist on holiday contacted Northern Constabulary to say she was lost in the mountains near Kylesku, a tiny village only five miles from Cape Wrath, the most northerly tip of Scotland. Before any further information could be obtained, her mobile phone signal was lost. It was established she had no navigation equipment apart from an AA road map, but plenty of clothing in her pack. Members of the Kinloss and Assynt teams were deployed — along with two dog handlers and the Coastguard SAR helicopter from Stornaway on the Isle of Lewis — to focus a search on the high ground between Kylesku and Inchnadamph to the south. The operation was stood down at falling light. However, as teams reassembled the following morning, the missing woman was spotted by chance, by a team member on his way to the incident. She was quickly met by team members and walked to the rescue post at Inchnadamph. It seems she'd seen a helicopter the previous night on several occasions but hadn't believed it was looking for her!

Back on the Isle of Man, Matt and Lola,

The use of 'triangulation' to pinpoint someone's location

It's all about using basic geometry. Suppose the lost person is on the south side of the mountain in the dark and does not know their location, but they can indicate to others their location with a light, torch or mobile phone backlight. The rescuers can go to a known location (say A) and take a compass bearing on the light. In the example this is 320 degrees. They then move to another known location (say B) and take another bearing of 220 degrees.

With this information they plot two lines on the map, from the two locations where the bearing was taken. Where they intersect gives a good indication of the person's location. Searchers can now move to that location, or the person can be safely guided down with instructions from below.

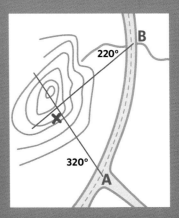

were called to search, alongside a police dog handler, for a man deemed to be at 'high risk' who had been missing overnight. Surprisingly, both dogs — one air scenting and the other tracking — detected the man after a short time of searching. He had fallen into a deep gorge and was severely hypothermic and in need of urgent medical attention.

September...

The majority of people rescued in the mountains are generally well dressed, properly shod and kitted out with good equipment. This is no guarantee they know how to use it however!

Take the man walking in the Scottish Highlands, in September a couple of years ago, who requested help when he became lost in bad weather. Asked if he knew his approximate location he replied he had a GPS receiver and would give the rescuers his grid reference. This he duly did but the set of numbers turned out to be a measure of latitude to longitude — a maritime measure. When questioned further, he admitted he'd purchased the unit the day before and only just taken in out of its box. He'd failed to realise it needed to be properly calibrated for terrestrial use.

Equally worrying was the pair who set off for a stroll one evening from their hotel in Glen Clova in the Eastern Cairngorms, dressed only in their everyday clothes. Weather conditions in the high mountains of Scotland can be as appalling in spring, summer and autumn as you might expect in winter. So, besides setting off in the appropriate kit, and allowing yourself sufficient time to achieve a particular route, it is generally advised to carry extra clothing, just in case — advice this couple might have heeded. Their footwear was appropriate only for street use and they had no waterproof clothing or navigation equipment. As they climbed up into the increasingly heavy cloud, weather conditions deteriorated and they quickly found themselves lost. They managed to alert Tayside Police using their mobile phone but were unable to describe their surroundings. Members of Tayside MRT and a dog handler from SARDA Southern Scotland searched through the night in what, by now, were appalling conditions and the couple were eventually located at daybreak next to a loch, about two miles from the hotel. Both were suffering from exposure and hypothermia and the woman was so serious she had to be stretchered off the mountain.

A missing English walker triggered an extensive search in County Kerry in the south-west corner of Ireland, when he failed to return to his car. It seemed he had been climbing Carrauntoohill which, at 1046 metres, is the highest mountain in the McGillycuddy Reeks. When an initial sweep of the most likely areas — by members of the Kerry MRT — proved fruitless, the search was extended to involve the Civil Defence, Air Corps, Gardai and dog teams from SARDA England, Wales and Northern Ireland. The extended search covered an area of high ground from Lough Acoose to the Gap of Dunloe to the west of Killarney and continued for ten days. At this point it was officially called off, although many team members continued searching at weekends and it was the following year before a body was found, by members of the Kerry MRT, during a search dog training session.

October...

When a large group of people go walking together there is always the possibility they will split because of varying levels of fitness or different objectives. When this happens, the chances of someone becoming lost is greatly increased.

Three men in their thirties were descending Ben Challum in Central Scotland when two noticed their friend was no longer with them. The mist was very thick but it didn't stop the pair retracing their steps back up the mountain to locate their friend. When he couldn't be found, they assumed he had descended another way and would be at the hotel on their return. When they discovered he wasn't, they raised the alarm. Four dog teams from SARDA Southern Scotland — along with Kevin Stead from England, and Lakes handler Dave Watt, with their dogs — joined members of Killin MRT in the search. Kevin and Dave were on hand, coincidentally, because they were working that weekend as external assessors for SARDA Southern Scotland. For one of the handlers putting himself to the test, this presented a particular challenge. Rupert Bonham, of SARDA Scotland, had already successfully completed three search areas for his upgrade assessment. Following a very stressful day, he then worked through the night on the incident before completing the final two assessment runs the next day with only an hour's sleep in between! Thankfully, he successfully gained the upgrade to full search dog. Despite a comprehensive search of the mountain and all possible descent routes, the man couldn't be traced and the search was eventually terminated early in the morning. The following day, members of the Lomond and Ochils teams were also called but, before they arrived, the man was spotted by helicopter, walking back to the road. It turned out that, after losing sight of his friends, he had become disoriented and began walking in the opposite direction to the planned descent route. As a result, he spent a wet and very

TOP: MACGILLYCUDDY'S REEKS IN COUNTY KERRY, THE REPUBLIC OF IRELAND © DON MURPHY.
ABOVE: RUPERT BONHAM AND LIZ OUTRAM WITH FAELAN © PETER SANDGROUND.

Doggie Tales

SEARCH DOG SAM AND THE ELDERLY LADIES

Suffering from dementia, she was — as is often the case — quite able to walk without difficulty. Having lived in the area for many years, she could easily have wandered some distance from her home. A search control was established and dog handlers deployed to specific areas. By this time it was nine o'clock in the evening, the temperature was falling and the situation urgent. The local mountain rescue team had also been called. The dog teams were given small areas to search and slowly moved further and further out from the lady's last known location. Just after midnight, Harold was given an area close to her friend's home to search, about two miles from the lady's own house.

'As my navigator and I looked through the windows of the house Sam, my search dog, went around the garden and garage. He came running back and barked his indication to me that he'd found something. I followed him to the garage, whereupon he started to sniff frantically around the garage door. I tried to open the door but it was firmly locked from the inside. I walked around to the side of the garage and looked in through the side window, where I was met by an old lady looking back at me! It did make me jump as I had been calling out her name for some time. Eventually, I opened the side door and made my way in to see her. She was unsure about my presence but was quite happy to have Sam alongside her.

'A quick radio call to search control brought the police and ambulance and Sam, courteous to the last, walked the lady to the door of the ambulance. Only when she was safely inside did he bound back to his proud owner!

'A few years later, Sam had occasion to find another elderly lady. I'd made plans to take my wife and daughter out for a surprise meal. The arrangements were in place and I was looking forward to a pleasant family evening. We were just about to leave the house when the telephone rang. Call-out! A lady had been missing for seven days. Police and police dogs had already been out searching along with the police helicopter, to no avail. The area for the search was semi-rural leading onto a hillside with a number of small wooded copse and farmland. I was asked to arrive at first light to begin the search with the mountain rescue teams and other SARDA Wales dog handlers. At least we could enjoy our family meal!

'At the briefing point we were given our search areas and a description of the missing lady. I told the search managers I'd have to leave at mid-day to pick up my daughter from the railway station, so I'd work quickly to finish the search off. The police inspector thanked me for the time I could spare and I left the briefing saying I'd find the lady for him as soon as possible. There was a look of doubt in his eyes as I walked away — how could anyone be so confident?

'I was to take trainee handler Dermot with me as my navigator, and to show him how to work a dog on a search. Within a couple of minutes of arriving, we were off searching for the lady. I cleared the

The use of search and rescue dogs is far from confined to the mountain environment. Harold Burrows of SARDA Wales tells the story of one old lady who went missing in the afternoon from a North Wales coastal town.

first wooded area and the fields around it and had to check a small depression covered with brambles. As we walked into the second area, Sam picked up a scent. He ran off towards the stream running through the search area, moments later running back to me barking to indicate a find. Off he shot again as I followed him back to the stream and what appeared to be a bundle of clothing lying next to the stream. Was this our lady and was she alive or dead? As I drew nearer, it quickly became apparent this was indeed our missing pensioner, fast asleep. She woke with my gentle nudge to her shoulder, very confused and dehydrated.

'We sat together for some time. I gave her a drink of juice and we talked about what she'd been doing for the last seven days and what she'd been eating. Dermot was on Cloud Nine and hardly able to speak for excitement of the find! He reported to control that we'd found the lady safe and well and would need an ambulance to take her to hospital for a medical check out.

'Back at search control, the police inspector came over to thank me, his wonderment at the speed of our find still playing on his face: was I just lucky or had Sam and I had just demonstrated super powers? Either way, great job done!'

cold night in an abandoned shepherd's cottage before finding a way to walk back around the mountain on rough tracks.

Late in October, six dog teams from SARDA England were called to assist Cornwall SRT in a search for a 24-year-old despondent man missing from hospital in Bodmin. Despite a comprehensive search, it was a member of the ambulance crew who eventually found the man.

November...

In early November, a false alarm with good intent occurred in Central Scotland, at the spectacular Falls of Dochart, a popular tourist attraction. As you enter the village of Killin, a narrow stone bridge across the river affords visitors a stunning view of the falls as they cascade magnificently in all directions, over the rocks and around the island of Inchbuie, the traditional burial place of the MacNab clan. A photo opportunity if ever there was one – but lethal, should you fall.

LEFT: HAROLD BURROWS AND SAM © SARDA WALLES.

ROGER PICKUP AND BEINN (OUT OF PICTURE!) ON A SEARCH OF MICKLEDON WITH LANGDALE AMBLESIDE MRT © PAUL BURKE.

A report came in that a man had climbed over the parapet of the bridge and disappeared from view. The river was in heavy spate following days of constant rain. Two dog teams from SARDA Southern Scotland assisted several other services, including the Central Scotland Police Underwater Search Team, the fire and rescue service, members of Killin MRT and a Royal Navy Sea King. The banks of the river were searched for several miles downstream of the bridge, but nothing was found and nothing has been reported since.

In Ireland, dog team Mick and Bono travelled to Wicklow late at night to help the Glen of Imaal and Dublin and Wicklow teams search for three female walkers overdue from a walk in the area of Mullaghcleevaun and Tonelagee, the second and third highest of the Wicklow Mountains. At five o'clock in the morning, as Mick and Bono began a search on Tonelagee, the walkers were found elsewhere — safe and well — by a rescue team search party.

despondent man was reported missing. Search dog Molly indicated at the foot of a bridge on the edge of a reservoir and, some time later, Skye also indicated in the same location. Nothing was found at this point but, when a police underwater team began to search the reservoir, they quickly found the body of the man in the water. He had probably entered the water at the spot where the two dogs had indicated.

This is just a snapshot of the many incidents dogs and their handlers are called to every year. Whilst there are some common features, every one is different in terms of the people involved, the weather, time of day, location and the emergency services called to assist. Some are done and dusted very quickly — sometimes within an hour or so. Others continue over many days. Sometimes a life is saved, sometimes an incident is fatal. In a very few cases, the missing person is never found. Whatever the circumstances, each and every incident requires care in planning, as well as detailed and thorough execution.

But do the dogs know about all this? And do they care? Clearly not. For them, it's a joy to be outside and a pleasure to be playing fun games once more, but to describe their behaviour in such simple terms is to miss three key talents: their amazing drive, their ability to work with their handler, and their keen sense of smell. Dogs are, in fact, incredibly bright creatures. So it's hardly surprising their place in society excels any other domesticated animal. Far beyond the world of search and rescue, dogs have continued to carve their own special niche in society in a multitude of ways.

December...

In the Lake District, in December, Cumbria Police received a call from a woman near the summit of Cat Bells who had been blown over by extreme winds. Repeated attempts to contact her by mobile phone failed, so Keswick team members mounted a search of the ridge whilst Lakes dogs Dottie, Flash and Ginny were requested to standby in case the search escalated. In the event, the woman had managed to make her way to the road (by crawling the first part!) and phoned in to say she was safe.

Leicestershire Police asked for assistance from Derby MRT with a search near Melton Mowbray in the Peak District. An 80-year-old man, known to be suffering from depression, had left his car on a country lane at around 3.00pm the previous day. SARDA England handler John Coombs and his dog Biscuit worked with a police dog team which had picked up the man's scent from his car. After some time the scent went cold and the search was discontinued, to resume at 5.00am the following morning with John and rescue team members involved in a more extensive search of the area. The man was eventually found by Biscuit on the edge of a wood only one kilometre from his car.

A large-scale search — involving members of both Swaledale and Teesdale & Weardale MRTs and five dog teams from SARDA England — launched in the north east of England, when a 24-year-old

BLACK BOB

THE DANDY WONDER DOG

Multi-talented

'A man whom neither of us had recognised strode by, whereupon my father (James Herriot) said to me, 'That's a suspicious looking character! I wonder what he's up to?' 'Why do you say that?' I asked. The man looked fairly normal to me. He gave the retreating figure another glance and smiled. 'He hasn't got a dog!' Jim Wight

Why is it that dogs permeate our society so? They appear in films, cartoons and on television. They feature in TV commercials, magazines and books. They help the farming community, police and rescue services and contribute to the safety and wellbeing of people with various disabilities. They've served in wars, helped the cause of science and made their mark in Greek mythology. Dogs have travelled into outer space, stood as parliamentary candidates and been the focus in popular music. And, as if this wasn't enough, they are one of the most popular pets on the planet and feature in many of our favourite sayings and idioms: 'Let sleeping dog's lie'... 'Raining cats and dogs'... and, as we said at the start: 'Man's best friend'. But it's not just their loyalty and companionship we love: their capacity to work and perform in such a wide variety of ways — attributes that have been exploited for many centuries — makes them the most versatile of all domesticated animals. Indeed, it's been suggested that, next to humans, dogs are the most successful animals on the planet! With proper training, they can be taught skills that show creative, caring, athletic and functional facets of their personalities.

Those involved in the structured training of dogs obviously have expectations about how their dog's behaviour will change. The ability to realise these expectations is always helped (both with canine and human learning) if you know something about the history of the dog or person you're working with — their present abilities and what they've done in the past. It's said that you're in a better position to know where you're going if you know where you've come from. Which is why handlers are always keen to determine as much about their dog's background and history as possible, before they embark on a training programme. Training can then be tempered to the dog's particular needs, abilities and potential weaknesses. In turn, it helps the handler to know something about how dogs learn, and especially how they've evolved across time, in order to fully understand the process of training.

Domestic dogs belong to the biological family of carnivorous and omnivorous mammals termed Canidae, which also includes wolves, coyotes, jackals, dingoes and foxes. All canids evolved from a primitive wolf-like animal similar to the Asian grey wolf (Canis lupus), although the nature of that evolution is different for each subspecies, as demonstrated in the diagram. The origins of the word 'dog' are unclear but it's been suggested it comes from the Old English word 'docga', meaning a 'powerful breed of canine'. The word docga, in turn, derives from the Germanic term dukkon, which translates as 'finger muscle' — perhaps an indication of the dog's early role as a worker. A 'domesticated animal', incidentally, is defined as one that 'has had its behaviour, life cycle, or physiology systemically altered as a result of being under human control for many generations.' In the case of the dogs we know today, this has happened primarily through the intervention of man and selective breeding.

It's estimated there are over 400 breeds of dog in the world, each categorised into seven groups based on their function or use, but why so many different kinds and how did they all come about? And, if every breed of dog (Canis lupus familiaris) descends from the ancient wolf, how did the change from wolf to domestic dog take place?

It is widely regarded — with supporting DNA evidence — that the dogs of today evolved from a small pack of wolves tamed by people living in China around 15,000 years ago. It's even been reported that all modern dogs descend from just three female wolves! Which means that, genetically speaking, every dog that shares our home, sleeps on our sofas and helps search for missing walkers is 99.9% wolf!

Indeed, comparative studies show that a dog's physiology and behaviour have much in common with their lupine cousins. Wolf cubs are similar to dog pups in that they frolic, and they greet adults of the pack in the same way a dog greets its owner when they come home. Wolves are also submissive to dominant wolves in the way that dogs are submissive to humans. And they have a predisposition towards domesticity in that, whilst born into a pack with a rigid hierarchy, they move on and live alone, find a mate and create their own pack. Dogs, therefore, are essentially wolves modified behaviourally to get on with humans. So, next time you look into your dog's eyes, reflect on the fact that you're actually looking into the eyes of a wolf! Finally, if you want a clear-cut difference between a dog and a wolf, how about this? Wolves will not give a human eye contact, but dogs will actively seek out eye contact — and wolves would never eat in the vicinity of humans, whereas dogs are very happy to be hand-fed.

But, if all dogs descended from wolves, how and when did this happen? Archaeological evidence suggests that the first domesticated dog/wolf appeared around 10,000-14,000 years ago. At this stage they appeared in rubbish dumps as well as burial sites, suggesting they were already used as food or as property or pets. However, genetic evidence suggests a much earlier diversification, about 145,000 years ago, between those animals destined to become pure wolves and those destined to become domesticated dogs. The exact process of change is subject to conjecture, but it's commonly thought that people living many thousands of years ago noted how skilled wolves were at hunting, and used these skills to their advantage. Specifically, they picked up on the wolf's ability to separate a chosen animal from a herd and bring it to ground. It is suggested that people learned to harness this characteristic to help their own hunting ability to track, kill and hold wounded game. Hungry wolf-cubs, scavenging around human settlements, may have been captured and reared as pets, or for food or work. As these animals proved their use on hunting expeditions or as guards — when their sense of smell and acute hearing could be used to protect humans from attack — they were bred for their useful traits.

In time, the relationship between people and wolves grew, so the overall process then was one of selection by humans. People decided to bring dogs into their community and select those animals with useful traits, actively removing those without. Some of these selected traits may not have been very useful for survival in the wild and would have included changes in both physical and behavioural features.

This constant seeking to refine and domesticate wolves to human advantage sparked an inexorable process of change, from single species to the large number of canine breeds we see today. People may not have known about the concept of genetics, but will have understood that 'like begets like' and, very gradually over many centuries, bred dogs for specific qualities — speed for hunting, strength for hauling, scenting ability for tracking, keen hearing for guarding, companionship and loyalty, and so on — and breeding out 'bad' elements in the process. With the passage of time, dogs with desirable characteristics were interbred to produce new breeds. So, people chose the best male and female dogs to breed and produce puppies with the desired traits of both parents. The domesticated dog began to evolve from its wolf ancestor, different breeds were created and, eventually, dogs came to be adopted as pets.

During the 1950s, Russian geneticist Dmitry Belyaev and his team devoted several years of research into how dogs become domesticated and the speed with which evolution takes place. He was intrigued how, given the same genetic make-up as wolves, dogs had evolved to have different coats. He didn't study wolves or domestic dogs but chose instead the Silver Fox because of their availability (bred in captivity for the fur trade). He selected only those foxes with the desired characteristics of a domesticated animal. For example, those that showed a lack of fear or aggression, or wagged their tails and whimpered when given food. The selected animals were bred, and those of their offspring which showed the most desirable characteristics were allowed to breed again. He discovered that after only ten generations of controlled breeding —

around 40 years — 70% of the fox population showed characteristics that identified them as being domesticated, each exhibiting many of the characteristics of the modern dog. They revealed no fear of people and often wagged their tails and licked people with affection. But their appearance also changed: they started to develop spotted coats, floppy ears and curled tails. Belyaev showed that, whilst it may have taken thousands of years for the Silver Fox to evolve from the grey wolf, it took only a few decades to become domesticated. It's no surprise therefore that the evolution of dog from wolf, and its differentiation into so many breeds, has been so rapid.

From wild wolf to versatile friend and workmate

Dogs were the first animals to be domesticated by humans and, in the first instance, they were employed for their guard dog skills. Today of course, they're well known for their working capacity and their ability to labour over long periods, often in poor weather. The annual Iditarod Train Sled Dog Race, which runs from Anchorage in south central Alaska to Nome on the western coast of the Bering Strait — a distance of eleven hundred and fifty miles — is completed by dog teams in ten to seventeen days. This corresponds to hauling a sled the length of Great Britain in just seven days! Many breeds of dog have a strong work ethic and this, coupled with their resistance to extreme cold weather, has made them invaluable for the Inuit people of Canada, Greenland and Russia. Inuit dogs are capable of pulling sledges over enormous distances, in temperatures well below zero and they frequently do this on a simple diet of dried meat and fish.

Dogs have traditionally been used to haul objects. Many of the Arctic and Antarctic expeditions undertaken in the past 100 years were only possible through their involvement. Roald Amundson used dogs on his expedition to the South Pole in 1912 and it is now recognised that a key to his success was the use of Greenland huskies to haul the sledges. Amundson actually used half of the dogs as food for the remaining dogs and his team, in order to reduce the weight of dog food to be carried. Bernese Mountain dogs were used at one time to haul loads of dairy produce and baskets to market and similar dogs delivered milk in Belgium and flowers in Holland.

Dogs are used extensively in many parts of the world to help the police and security agencies combat crime. German Shepherds tend to be the breed of choice because they possess a number of characteristics — intelligence, courage, toughness, tenacity, agility and obedience — which make them the ideal for this kind of work. Their record for devotion to duty is second to none and there are instances of dogs being injured or even killed in action. Police dogs are used wherever there are crowds to be controlled, criminals to be tracked down and arrested, frontiers to be patrolled, or property and people to be guarded. Similarly, police sniffer dogs are used with great effect to detect drugs and explosives. Dogs such as Springer Spaniels are capable of doing this however cunningly the items are concealed, and can even detect the smell of an object (such as a firearm) a long time after it has been removed from the scene.

It's well known that dogs play a universal role in guarding and herding farm stock — sheep, cattle and other animals, including deer. Many countries have developed their own pastoral breeds for this particular purpose. In Australia, for example, dogs

CLOCKWISE FROM TOP LEFT: P.A.T. DOG KATIE ON A VISIT © PERMISSION GIVEN BY P.A.T. DOGS; POLICE DOG IN TRAINING © SGT NIALL MACLEAN; ROBERT BLACKWOOD WITH GUIDE DOG KIRK ON PLANE; BRITAIN'S FIRST GUIDE DOG OWNERS IN 1931 — FROM THE LEFT, ALLEN CALDWELL WITH FLASH, GW LAMB WITH META, MUSGRAVE FRANKLAND WITH JUDY AND THOMAS RHYS WITH FOLLY; SIMON GROOM AND DEREK FREEMAN IN THE 'BLUE PETER' STUDIO WITH GOLDIE AFTER HER FIRST LITTER OF PUPS, IN 1981 © GUIDE DOGS.

are used to work huge flocks of sheep across vast ranges, often in extreme heat. For this purpose, farmers have developed breeds such as the Kelpie and Australian Cattle dog — the latter a mixture of many breeds, including the native Wild Dingo. Other countries have developed other breeds to serve as working dogs For example, France has four sheepdogs — the Beauceron, the Briard, the Picardy and the Pyrenean; Holland has two — the Dutch Sheepdog and the Schapendoes. The Samoyed people living near the Arctic Circle developed the breed which bears their name to tend herds of reindeer and, in Lapland, the Lapphund serves the same purpose. In the UK there's a long tradition of sheep and cattle dogs. Bearded Collies, Old English Sheepdogs, Rough and Smooth Collies have all been used for these purposes, but unequalled for working with sheep, the Border Collie is in a class of its own, universally employed as a farm dog and popular for showing and obedience displays.

Whilst dogs have been used in a working capacity for many years, their ability to help people in other ways has also been developed considerably in the past 50 years or so. A number of organisations now train dogs specifically to support people with disabilities of one kind or another. The use of guide dogs (typically labradors or Golden Retriever/labrador crosses) to help those who are blind or partially sighted is well known. More recently, dogs have been trained as 'hearing ears' for the deaf, a scheme which originated in the USA. Adopted in Britain less than 30 years ago, it has proved a great success. Hearing dogs are trained to alert their deaf owners to any sound such as a knock at the door,

whistling kettle, alarm clock, fire alarm or a crying baby. Dogs are also trained to help physically challenged people by, for instance, switching lights on and off, opening and closing doors, picking things up from the floor and helping their owners to rise from chairs or wheelchairs, or climb stairs.

One area where dogs have played a very distinctive role has also sealed their place in the world of entertainment. Dogs are great performers and, whilst they may not know it, they've amused generations of children and adults alike through the media of TV and film, magazines, comics and books. Dogs truly are gifted and capable animals. Their versatility and susceptibility to training knows few boundaries.

Being greeted by his or her dog at the end of hard day invariably brings a smile to its owner's face and owning a dog can actually provide long-term health protection.

It is well established that dogs (as well as some other animals) can help in the therapy and recuperation of those who are disabled or ill. James Herriot often drew attention to this in his stories about life as a country vet. In one particular case, he tells the story of a retired farmer who was bedridden through injury, and his pet dachshund. On one of his visits the farmer commented in a strong Yorkshire accent, 'Aye, it's a funny thing, but 'e allus sits there. T'missus is the one who has to take 'im walks and feeds 'im but he's very faithful to me. He has a basket over there but this is 'is place. I only have to reach down and he's there.' James Herriot commented many times in his stories about the therapeutic effect dogs and cats had on their owners, noting that they often stayed

close to their owner as if conscious of their role of comforter and friend. It's now well known that pet ownership can help people cope with pain and depression, speed up recovery from operations and even — as recent research suggests — reduce the risk of some cancers and heart disease. Indeed, it's been scientifically proven that the mere action of stroking a dog, or cat, slows down the heartbeat, reduces blood pressure, and can make someone who has suffered a heart attack much less likely to have another. An American study has shown recently that people who have regular contact with pets (be they dogs, rabbits, cats, whatever) are one third less likely to suffer certain kinds of cancer. A study of British GPs showed that almost half believe pet ownership can help owners recover after a stroke or nervous breakdown and speed up recovery from an operation. With people who are hospitalised for a long time, it is now accepted that a visit by a pet can be a very significant therapy.

This is the underlying principle behind the organisation known as Pets As Therapy, a national home and hospital visiting scheme. Established in 1983, it helps those who are confined to their home or hospital, or resident in a care home, by providing visits by qualified owners and their dogs. The scheme was the brainchild of Lesley Scott-Ordish who, until her death in 1997, was a highly respected authority on canine behaviour. She was inspired by the story of a dance instructor who gave classes in movement and community singing at several old peoples' homes in the London area. Scott-Ordish took her own dog to classes and the nursing staff noticed how eagerly the residents looked forward to his visits, especially those that had previously owned a dog and were not permitted to keep them in their new home. The nurses realised the beneficial effect the dog had on everyone; it seemed the residents gained as much, if not more, of a therapeutic benefit from the dog's company than from the formal class led by the instructor. This observation was the starting point for Pets As Therapy. Today, the organisation is a national charity and unique in providing good-natured dogs and cats with registered volunteers, to a wide variety of institutions — hospitals, hospices, residential care homes, day centres, special needs schools and many other establishments. Over the years its service has developed in a number of ways so that today, for example, P.A.T. dogs are used by occupational therapists to encourage stroke patients to use their limbs and talk, and by clinical psychologists to help those with clinical depression. There are approximately 5000 P.A.T. dogs and cats registered into the scheme throughout the UK and it's estimated that more than 140,000 people are visited every week.

It's well known that dogs have a highly tuned sense of smell but their sense of hearing is also very acute. Surprising then, that this ability wasn't fully exploited to help people with hearing disabilities until the early 1980s. The key role of the charity Hearing Dogs for Deaf People is to train dogs to alert deaf people to specific sounds they might otherwise miss — in the home, workplace or public building. It has its own breeding scheme but dogs are also selected from rescue centres and donated by breeders and members of the public. A variety of different dogs are used, but the mainstay are spaniels and poodles (and

crosses of), Golden Retrievers and labradors (and crosses of) and a few other smaller breeds. In order to qualify as a hearing dog, each dog is required to pass through different stages of training: socialisation, advanced sound work and home placement. Socialisation training takes place in a volunteer's home under the supervision of one of the charity's trainers. This ensures the dog becomes familiar with a whole range of situations including traffic, crowds of people and loud noises. The dog also attends obedience training classes at one of the charity's training centres. All dogs that pass through socialisation training commence an intense four months of advanced sound work where they are taught to respond to specific sounds, and to alert their handler by touching with a paw and then leading back to the source of the sound.

Training follows typical operant conditioning principles (more about this in chapter 7) where tasks are broken down into small, achievable steps and the dog rewarded when they get it right. In this way, positive associations are created between common sounds such as an alarm clock, cooker timer, doorbell or telephone, and rewards such as food, praise or toys. So, for example, the sound of a telephone may lead to the dog touching the person with their paw and then, when the person asks, 'What is it?' the dog leads them to the telephone (thanks to technological advances, many phones are hearing aid compatible). Dogs can also be trained to respond to danger sounds such as a smoke or burglar alarm. In these cases, the dog responds differently, perhaps by touching their owner with a paw then immediately lying down. In this way, the

owner knows there is danger and can take appropriate action. Before qualification, the hearing dog and their new deaf owner train together at one of the charity's two training centres — in Buckinghamshire and Yorkshire — before a period working together in the recipient home before final qualification as a partnership.

Hearing dogs help to identify the nature of their handler's invisible disability, because they wear a distinctive burgundy-coloured coat. To date, the organisation has trained and placed more than 1,500 hearing dogs throughout the UK.

Since 1931, guide dogs have helped over 21,000 blind and partially sighted people through the provision of carefully matched and trained assistance dogs. The Guide Dogs charity (originally titled The Guide Dogs for the Blind Association) was founded in 1934, and currently employs more than a thousand professional staff — supported by nearly 10,000 volunteers, including puppy walkers, brood-stock holders, dog boarders and local fundraisers. The organisation has four dog training schools, a breeding centre and 28 district teams located across the country where all the technical staff are employed. It has been breeding dogs for more than 75 years and is internationally renowned for its expertise in breeding and training guide dogs. Indeed, it is the world's largest breeder and trainer of working dogs and, every year, around 1,200 would-be guide dogs are born to brooding bitches especially chosen for their intelligence and temperament.

The key aim of Guide Dogs is to enhance the mobility and freedom of those who would otherwise find it very difficult, if not impossible, to lead a normal, everyday life.

Most people who own a guide dog do have some vision; they don't have to be formally registered as blind or partially sighted. Further, there's no age limit and no previous experience of keeping or caring for a dog is necessary. Guide Dogs provide all essential equipment and training and also cover the cost of vet bills and dog food. The only cost to the owner is a nominal 50 pence!

The organisation has a well established procedure for ensuring puppies become good guide dogs. It does this through selective breeding and thorough training. Around six to eight weeks of age, puppies are given their first experience of guide dog training. Volunteer puppy walkers (who, in effect, own the dog for the first year) introduce the young pups to the sights, sounds and smells of the world in which they will play an important part. This means taking them on buses and trains, into shops and along busy streets. Puppy walkers are responsible for basic obedience training and, most important, teaching puppies to walk ahead on the leash, not to heel. When the dog is about a year old, it returns to Guide Dogs for the next part of its training. Here, the young dogs learn the skills needed to guide a blind or partially-sighted person. Specifically, they are trained to walk in a straight line in the centre of the pavement unless there is an obstacle; not to turn corners unless told to do so; to stop at kerbs and wait for the command to cross the road, or to turn left or right; to judge height and width so that their owner does not bump their head or shoulder; and how to deal with traffic. Training is rigorous and not all young dogs make the grade but, for the majority that do, the introduction to their

new owner marks the start of a partnership that lasts around seven years. Most guide dogs retire when they are about nine or ten years old. Matching the correct dog with the correct owner takes skill and experience — the owner's length of stride, height and lifestyle all contribute to the type of guide dog they will be matched with. The couple spend up to four weeks of intensive training together until they qualify and the guide dog acquires its white harness, and Guide Dogs continue to help with regular aftercare if required.

Like Hearing Dogs for the Deaf and Guide Dogs, Support Dogs is dedicated to helping people with various kinds of disabilities through the use of specially trained dogs. It was set up in 1992 by an established dog trainer, John Rogerson, when he recognised the potential to train dogs specifically to help physically disabled people with a variety of everyday tasks. Early efforts proved very successful and this led to work training dogs to predict seizures in people with epilepsy. Dogs are trained to help their owner with a wide variety of everyday tasks such as opening and closing doors, picking up objects, assisting with dressing and undressing, switching lights on and off and carrying items. A number of breeds including labradors, Cocker Spaniels and various cross breeds are used and, whilst many start as family pets, some are rescue dogs. All are screened before training and undergo full behavioural and veterinary examinations. As with the guide dogs, training starts with general socialisation in a variety of situations and environments before specialised work at the charity's national training centre.

From its early beginnings, the charity now

trains dogs to assist people with numerous physical disabilities, including children with autism. To date, only a few dogs have been trained — mainly Golden Retrievers and labrador crosses — but the evidence shows clearly that autism-assistance dogs can help children increase their independence and safety and also bring about positive behavioural changes such as enhanced social interaction.

It is known that dogs can be trained to respond to seizure activity in their owners by, for example, bringing the telephone or pulling an alarm cord if they see their owner fall to the ground. These dogs are referred to as 'seizure response' dogs. The organisation is also involved in training dogs to predict the onset of a seizure — 'seizure alert' dogs — which are able to recognise the early signs of a seizure in their owners and are trained to respond in a manner (such as barking or pawing), which permits their owner to anticipate the seizure. Quite how dogs are able to anticipate seizures in humans is largely unclear. It has been suggested that seizure alerting is based primarily on visual cues such as facial expressions, postures and general movements, but physiological cues such as muscle tension, respiratory signs and perspiration might also be monitored by dogs. Dogs are able to warn their owners up to 45 minutes before a seizure begins — a substantial period of time to prepare for the seizure. Several breeds of dog have been shown capable of predicting seizures — collies and Golden Retrievers have both been used. In practice, seizure alert dogs have to be with their owner 24 hours a day and follow them wherever they go. The key advantage is that the means to alert someone to an imminent seizure provides the person with a greater freedom of movement and ability to control their lives when a fit takes place.

The police, of course, use dogs for many general and highly specialist kinds of tasks. The term 'sniffer dog', often used when referring to police dogs, strictly speaking only applies to those dogs trained in the detection of items such as drugs, currency, explosives and firearms. Springer Spaniels are excellent at this kind of work and labradors too are seen on duty in public places sniffing for drugs. Border Collies are also used for operational work in confined spaces.

In the nineteenth century, pet dogs sometimes accompanied police on their rounds — dogs such as Topper, a Fox Terrier who accompanied patrols from the Hyde Park police station in London in the late 1800s. Around the same time, bloodhounds were brought in to assist in the Jack the Ripper case, although these were only token attempts to use dogs. Their potential for deterring criminals wasn't fully recognised and exploited until much later. In fact, there was real concern at the time that dogs might prove dangerous and harm police-public relations. The story elsewhere in Europe was different. Police dogs were first used to good effect over a hundred years ago by the Belgian police force. The achievements of their trained police dogs spread to several continental countries and, by the First World War, dogs were being effectively trained to perform specific military duties as messengers, guards and sentries. Continued success with dogs by continental police forces in the 1920s and 30s eventually sparked an interest by the British Home Office. An experimental training school was established to examine training methods, and to identify which breeds had the greatest aptitude for police work. Two specially trained labradors were officially introduced to the Metropolitan Police Force in 1938, the idea that they would accompany police officers on their beats in the suburbs. However, it was not until after the Second World War — when dogs proved highly successful in recovering people from the London air raids — that their use was eventually extended throughout the different police forces in the UK. Police dogs are now an accepted, specialist arm in the fight against crime such that today, every force in the UK has a dog section.

The number of ways in which the police use dogs is very wide reaching — crowd management such as at football matches, protests and VIP visits, the searching of buildings and open grounds for missing or wanted people, or the recovery of evidence, tracking of suspects, maintaining public order and so on. Indeed, on an average day in a busy area, a 'general purpose' (GP) dog will almost continuously attend burglaries, abandoned stolen cars and all manner of suspects making off. Handlers track suspects with their dog at close range in harness and a ten-metre line. When this is not possible, or the person is contained in a building or an enclosed outside area, the handler will allow their dog to search free, using air scent. Unlike SARDA dogs, however, the dog is trained to remain with and detain the person, and not return to the handler.

We readily conjure up pictures of the big, tenacious German Shepherd apprehending its criminal 'catch' firmly by the sleeve. In situations like this handlers, have to be mindful of the Human Rights Act. Whenever a dog is deployed as a 'use of force' the handler has to justify compliance in that the individual's human rights were considered. Handlers of trained dogs, in the course of duty, have to account for injuries to anyone they apprehend and the risk of litigation is ever present. Injuries through a dog hold could be interpreted as grievous bodily harm and handlers run the risk of being investigated for a criminal offence for carrying out their duty. But police dogs and dogs in the service of the Crown are exempt from prosecution under the Dangerous Dogs Act for this very purpose — otherwise every police dog bite would result in the handler being convicted. It should be pointed out that dogs do not always have to be commanded to do something by the handler: police officers now have a variety of other tools at their disposal — including CS spray, batons, shields, plastic bullets and taser guns — all of which can subdue a person without risking the safety of a police dog. Typically, these would not be used in practice until the arrival of an armed response vehicle, making the dog the first back-up to police officers.

With the exception of specific searching tasks, the first choice of breed is the German Shepherd although Belgian Shepherd (Malinois), Dobermanns, Rottweilers, Weimeraners and German Pointers are also used, depending on their particular function. There is an abundant supply and, like collies, German Shepherds have highly developed senses, which are complimented by a high standard of intelligence. They have a characteristic stance and expression, which gives the impression of vigilance, loyalty and watchfulness and, once on task, stay alert to every sight and sound. Little escapes their attention. As one police officer said, 'A good police dog is like a good boxer — he works with a high level of controlled aggression within the rules of the game.' They are also very strong. It's been estimated that a German Shepherd's bite exerts 320lb of pressure compared to a human bite, which is only 120lbs! Their ability to track is excellent and it helps that they tend to be fearless, and display an automatic suspicion of strangers. Which is why it has been suggested they're a very effective tool against crime. Indeed, they are so good at what they do, that one officer commented, quite seriously, that 'if the dog could speak and drive then I'd be out of a job!'

Most police dogs are trained in special police training schools and every force spends a huge amount of time and resources training dogs. Some have experimented with gift dogs and puppy walking schemes where dogs are procured from reliable sources and then live with a volunteer during their formative months. Many forces, such as the Metropolitan Police Force, have their own breeding programme. The exact training programme varies across police forces but there are many common threads.

All dogs undergo extensive training, which begins when the puppy is around twelve weeks old. Puppies live with their handlers and this helps to generate a level of trust that is the essence of a good working relationship. Dogs and handlers then complete a twelve-week course with their handler at a training school. Training involves basic skills, obedience and agility exercises, principles of tracking, searching

for people and property and criminal work. Exercises start short and simple and build up in increments. Once the course is successfully completed, the dog and handler begin patrol work.

The key purpose of training is for the dog to react in the same way each time it hears a certain command or sees a visual sign from the handler. Handlers have to know their dog will react correctly and do so every time. So, for example, if sent to chase a suspect, a dog should know what is required to stop the person until called off by its handler. Having said this, there is also a degree of flexibility. Handlers work with their dog to find out what works best and apply it in a manner that suits their dog. Typically they use triggers, such as a hand signal or voice command, to let the dog know it is time to work. Once the dog becomes operational, similar techniques are employed on the job.

At the end of the training course, dogs are ready to go on the streets as operational police dogs, although they receive a certain amount of 'refresher training' carried out under the supervision of a Home Office Instructor. The amount depends on the age and experience of the dog/handler team. They also receive 'continuation training' carried out on a daily basis. This is not generally assessed and forms part of the day-to-day activity the handler does to boost the dog's performance and maintain its motivation. In addition, all dogs are required to be relicensed through a Home Office inspection once a year to ensure they are safe and effective and can carry out the tasks expected of them. All of this ensures standards are maintained at local and national level. Police dogs tend to have an average working life of about eight years

and live with their handler both throughout their working life and into retirement. Some police authorities, recognising a dog's long service, even provide retired dogs (who may only have two years of retirement) with taxpayer-funded pensions to cover expenses such as food and vet's fees.

It's not unusual for police officers to work both GP dogs and sniffer dogs. In a way, the distinction between the two is a little confusing because working both types relies on the dog's sense of smell. It's just that this is more pronounced with sniffer dogs. Drug and narcotic misuse is a problem that permeates all levels of society and sniffer dogs trained to detect drugs are used in a wide variety of settings to counter drug activity — airports, licensed premises, leisure events, business premises, schools and universities, or anyone who is suspected of carrying various kinds of drugs. Drug detection dogs are capable of locating all major illicit substances including, for example, heroin, cocaine, ecstasy, amphetamines and marijuana. Training is highly specialised and, as with GP dogs, takes place in special training centres. Training courses last around eight weeks and, during this time, dogs are trained to detect specific smells and respond accordingly. Dogs typically indicate by pausing momentarily — 'freezing' — in the direction of, and very close to the drug, or location where the drug is concealed. They are not trained to actually touch the source of the smell, as it could prove dangerous if ingested or absorbed through the skin. Training a dog to do this involves a crafty manoeuvre on the part of the handler/trainer where a ball magically appears over the top of the dog's head and lands on the source of the smell at the same time they indicate! In all cases, when a dog is onto a scent its demeanour changes as it becomes agitated, focused and insistent. Springer Spaniels are the choice of dog for this kind of work: they have a strong work ethic, exceptional sense of smell and are exceedingly persistent. Indeed, it's known that the nose of a trained sniffer dog is many times more sensitive than a human's. More than that, they can detect smells many years after the source has been removed. Training continues with reassessment every year in order to maintain the necessary license.

In action, sniffer dogs are used both proactively and passively. When searching a suspect area such as a person's bedroom, they are given relatively free rein to actively move in and around the area to locate any suspect objects. Typically, an initial routine inspection of the suspect area, be it a house, piece of airport baggage or container, is carried out. Where further investigation is deemed necessary, the dog

is released by its handler to carry out a more active search. Dogs methodically cover every section of the area they're sent to explore. The dog is rewarded and carries on working elsewhere once each job is finished. Dogs are also used in a more passive manner where they simply wait next to their handler and screen people as they walk past. This technique is used, for example, by police officers on patrol at train stations to identify travellers passing through ticket barriers, who may be carrying drugs and by other police forces to detect drugs at, for example, taxi ranks and nightclubs. Notably, whilst dogs are trained to detect specific smells above others they have the ability to identify related items. For example, a sniffer dog trained to find drugs will seek smells related to illegal drugs and respond if it picks up the scent of other known objects or substances. One advantage is that, even when illegal drugs have been deliberately masked by other strong smells in an effort

to disguise them, a dedicated working dog will not be distracted from its prime task. Quite apart from the technical work undertaken by dogs and their handlers, their visible presence at mainline stations and other public buildings goes a long way to creating a sense of public reassurance.

Other tasks that sniffer dogs undertake include explosives detection, searching for cash or bank notes, ammunition and fire arms. Cadaver dogs are trained to search for dead bodies in disaster areas and missing person investigations. There have been cases where dogs have identified blood spots that were so small, and had been covered by other substances, that only a microscope could confirm they were there. In recent times a number of dogs have been trained to locate accelerants, under the auspices of the UK Fire and Rescue Service. These dogs are trained to detect the presence or otherwise, at the fire scene, of flammable liquids such as petroleum.

Canine capers...

In many and varied ways, dogs are woven into the very fabric of our society, not least because of their tremendous capacity to entertain. The video clips of dogs, on TV programmes such as *You've Been Framed* are abundant proof of the lighter side to a dog's personality. Indeed, in the area of light entertainment dogs have excelled

themselves, often taking centre stage.

Dogs have appeared in hundreds of feature-length films across the years. One of the earliest examples was *Lassie Come Home*, first shown in 1940. The eponymous Lassie was a female Rough Collie and a courageous and highly intelligent dog, selflessly devoted to her owner. The film

spawned a long-running TV series in which many dogs were used to represent the heroine. Notably, all nine generations were bred from the same family but, whilst Lassie was depicted as a female, she was always played by male dogs, which tend to have longer coats and are considered more photogenic! Playing the lead was not without its perks — legend has it the canine actor who played Lassie earned more for his part in the film than the young Elizabeth Taylor, making her screen debut in the same film at the time.

There are many other notable examples. In *The Wizard of Oz*, Toto — a Cairn Terrier — appears throughout the film as Dorothy's pet dog. In police comedy Turner and Hooch, the French mastiff Hooch plays it for laughs alongside Tom Hanks, as Turner's slobbering, mischievous sidekick. Doc Brown, in *Back to the Future*, enjoyed a series of canine companions, all named after scientists: in 1955, his dog was named Copernicus and, by 1985, his dog was a Catalan Sheepdog named Einstein. In the animated series, Einstein became anthropomorphic and much smarter, helping Doc with his inventions for travelling to the past and the future. A Neapolitan mastiff played loveable giant Hagrid's pet in the *Harry Potter* films and a Border Collie called Fly befriended Babe in the film of the same name — and, of course, a number of black and white spotted dogs featured in the film *101 Dalmations*!

Dogs have long had a special relationship with television: Duke, Jed Clampett's bloodhound in *The Beverly Hillbillies*... K9, the canoid robot in *Doctor Who*... and, long before these programmes were aired, *Lassie* and *The Adventures of Rin Tin Tin* were essential viewing for those who could afford the new-fangled black and white TV sets. Shown in the late 1950s, *The Adventures of Rin-Tin-Tin* starred Rusty, a boy orphaned in an Indian raid, who was raised by the soldiers at a US Cavalry post. He and his German Shepherd, Rin Tin Tin, helped the soldiers establish order in the American West. Nearer home, in recent

years, the series *Doc Martin* featured a shaggy, grey dog called Gremlin. Martin Clunes, who played the lead character, discovered that Gremlin took a natural shine to him, following him everywhere given half the chance. The doctor, meanwhile, devoted a good deal of futile time and effort attempting to shake off his doggy friend — including throwing a stick over a cliff and telling him to 'Fetch!'

The long-running children's programme *Blue Peter*, first screened in the early 1960s, featured a wide variety of animals. The initial aim of including them in the show was to help teach children how to look after and care for their pets and, for those that didn't have a pet, it was hoped the animals would act as surrogates. Many of the show's animals were dogs including Goldie, a Golden Retriever, Mabel a Blue Merle Collie and Barney, an Irish Setter/dachshund cross. Petra was the first *Blue Peter* dog, appearing between 1962 and 1977. She was a mixed breed female with, apparently, a somewhat bad tempered disposition. Today, a bust of Petra stands in her memory in the *Blue Peter* garden at the BBC TV Centre but Border Collie Shep, born in 1971, was perhaps the most famous. Shep and presenter John Noakes became inseparable and the dog's excitable nature became a regular feature on the show, with Noakes's constant refrain of 'Get down, Shep!' a catchphrase. Shep left *Blue Peter* when Noakes departed in June 1978, and he died in 1987. Border Collie Meg featured alongside her owner, presenter Matt Baker, for six years from 2000. During that time, she delighted viewers when she gave birth to a litter of puppies. One of those puppies, named Corrie, is now a

search and rescue dog with SARDA Southern Scotland — more about her later.

Of course, dogs have always played it larger than life in the cartoon world, not least the world created by Walter Elias Disney. A dream to stylise, let alone humanise, dogs continue to inspire celluloid alter egos with such exciting and oddball personalities, and a level of charm and wit, far beyond your average pooch. Disney led the way in the attribution of human characteristics to just about any creature, but dogs have been a recurring theme: Pluto, Goofy, Lady and the Tramp, all those dalmations, Scooby-Doo... Each character spawning its own range of merchandise: soft toys, board and interactive games, rucksacks and clothing, dog treats and feeding bowls, breakfast cereals and snacks, action figures and ornaments, wallpaper and bedding — it's big business.

Pluto took form in 1930. Appearing most frequently as Mickey Mouse's pet dog, he also had an independent starring role in a number of short cartoons up to the '50s. He never spoke, communicating in a series of barks, facial expressions and body movements. In fact, Pluto was unusual for a Disney character — cartoon in nature, yet presented as a normal dog, with normal, canine characteristics — but he was one of the first to have thought processes and is now credited as one of the most popular cartoon characters of all time. He is seen in almost every type of merchandise and was listed as the fifth most popular Disney character after Mickey Mouse, Donald Duck, Minnie Mouse and Goofy. The good-natured, yet rather dim Goofy was clearly distinguishable from those around him, not so much by his appearance but his raucous laugh. Unlike Pluto, who was characterised as a pet, Goofy was created as a human character, so he walked upright and had a speaking voice. There were 48 *Goofy* cartoons — primarily in the 1940s and '50s — but he also appeared in many cartoons with Mickey Mouse and Donald Duck. In 1988, Goofy also appeared briefly in the fantasy comedy film *Who Framed Roger Rabbit?*

Walt Disney created many animated feature-length films which are now recognised as classics of animation. Lady and the Tramp, released in 1955, centres on a female American Cocker Spaniel named Lady who lives with a refined, upper middle-class family, and a male stray called Tramp, a footloose and collar-free character who takes every day as if it were his last. Ever one step ahead of the dog-catcher, he's too busy playing with danger to be scared of it. He lives by his wits and learned long ago that if you have a little charm and a lot of finesse, the world can be your dinner bowl. But Tramp has a major weakness — the ladies. As one of his friends in the dog pound comments: 'He has an eye for a well-turned paw, but if he ever falls under the spell of true love, the poor chump will grow careless.'

Well, needless to say, Tramp falls in love with Lady, overcoming a variety of scrapes in the process, and eventually becomes a hero. He joins Lady's family, and gets his own collar and license and, in classic fairy-tale style, the story ends with a smile as Lady and Tramp produce their own family, a litter of four puppies. Happy ever after!

If Tramp is skilful and confident, then Scooby-Doo is just the opposite. This long-running American cartoon began in 1969 and continues to the present day. The original series, *Scooby-Doo, Where Are You!* was created by Hanna-Barbera Productions and, although the format of the show has varied significantly over the years, the most familiar versions feature the talking dog, Scooby-Doo, and four teenagers. These five characters drive around in a van solving mysteries by exposing seemingly otherworldly ghosts and monsters as flesh and blood crooks. In the early design stages, Hanna-Barbera couldn't decide if Scooby-Doo should be a large, cowardly dog or a small, feisty one. Once they'd decided on the former, the options were large, goofy German Shepherd or big, shaggy sheepdog. But, after much consultation, they settled on a large, goofy Great Dane, complete with overly-bowed legs, double chin and a sloping back. The entire show was overhauled in 1980, at which point Scooby-Doo began to walk and run on two feet rather than four, just like his teenage sidekicks.

And then came Aardman with their ground-breaking technique of animating model characters to real-life conversations. Nick Park's *A Grand Day Out* launched in 1989, putting Wallace and his faithful dog Gromit firmly in the limelight, in which they continue to bask. The stop-motion animation employed is a very time-intensive process. Using plasticine models, the film is shot one frame at a time with the characters moved very slightly between frames — in a similar way to traditional cartoon animation where cell after cell, each depicting a tiny change in position, creates the fluidity of movement you see on screen. Gromit, of course, is much smarter than his owner. Indeed, he spends most of his time saving Wallace from various scrapes. And, unlike Scooby-Doo, he's clearly an intelligent dog, having graduated from 'Dogwarts University' with a double first in Engineering for Dogs. He's often seen reading books — *The Republic* by Pluto, *Crime and Punishment* by Fido Dogstoyevsky and a 'How-to' guide entitled *Electrical Surveillance for Dogs* — and he's very handy with electronic equipment. He can cook, tell the time, wash and dry the dishes, and even drive vehicles. He listens to Bach, knits and solves puzzles with ease and reads the daily newspaper, usually at the breakfast table. He even has a 'love interest' in Fluffles, a pet poodle. Gromit doesn't express himself with spoken words, but he hardly needs to. One twitch of a brow or tiny blink of an eye and we know all we need to know about how he feels!

Dogs have featured in ads and TV commercials for many years. The Andrex puppy (a labrador/retriever cross) has been the company's mascot for almost 40 years. Insurance company Churchill too make masterful use of canine charm with their Churchill dog — an ironic take on the much derided nodding dogs gazing benignly from rear view windows. Blessed with a captivating smile, and a limited vocabulary, his 'Oh yes!' catchphrase always trumps the cynics. Those who doubt his celebrity friend-list, or ability to accomplish great deeds, to rescue people from the midst of crisis, are soon put straight. Needless to say, soft toy versions of Churchill very soon became available for that rear view window.

Optical retailer Specsavers also employ a string of hapless characters in their long-running Should've gone to Specsavers message, not least the myopic farmer whose Border Collie suffers the indignity of a shearing, alongside the flock he is guarding. We suspect the average collie would be far too clever to fall for this, but they're clearly not as bright as multi-talented mongrel Harvey. Harvey features in a marketing campaign for Thinkbox, a company that helps advertisers get the best from the televisual medium. When a young couple visit the dog's home, looking to choose a pet from the countless lost souls housed there, they're stopped in their tracks by Harvey, as he deftly turns on the TV behind him. Cue his very own TV commercial, a blistering showcase of his amazing skills: playing chess, doing the school run, cooking, ironing, mowing the lawn and cleaning windows. The perfect pet!

Dulux Paints also struck gold when they hit upon the idea of using a dog to front their product. Their Old English Sheepdog was first introduced in the early-1960s and has been a constant and highly popular feature of the company's advertising ever since. In fact, the association is so strong that Old English Sheepdogs are often referred to as 'Dulux dogs'. Most of the dogs used over the years have been selected from a closely related line of pedigree dogs, and many are Cruft's qualified.

Aside from TV and films, dogs have played key characters in many well-known books and magazines. Bill Sykes has Bulls-eye in *Oliver Twist*, and Kep the collie features in Beatrix Potter's *The Tale of Jemima Puddle-Duck*. A huge hound plays a prominent role in *The Hound of the Baskervilles* and two dogs featured in the stories of young wizard Harry Potter — Fang is Hagrid's faithful, but somewhat wimpish, companion throughout the tale, whereas

Black Bob picked up the little toddler by his vest and carried him from the advancing flames.

Fluffy is the giant vicious, three-headed dog once cared for by the hairy giant, and guardian of the Philosopher's Stone. Timmy the mongrel made up the fifth member of the Famous Five in Enid Blyton's classic books. The list is almost endless, as is the list of canine characters that have appeared in comic strip form:

Charlie Brown's pet beagle, Snoopy... Dennis the Menace's Gnasher and Gnipper in *The Beano*... and, of course, Black Bob — hero of *The Dandy* comic and *Black Dog* books, perhaps the closest of all animated dogs to the modern search and rescue dog.

'BLACK BOB TO THE RESCUE!' FROM 'THE VERY BEST OF BLACK BOB' PUBLISHED BY DC THOMPSON 2010
© DC THOMPSON.

Beside the crook lay Andrew Glenn's pipe, jacket and cap. Bob sniffed the pipe. It was still warm, so Black Bob knew his master could not be far away. The collie climbed on top of the rock and scanned the hillside, but nowhere could he see any sign of the shepherd.

So Bob jumped down and started to circle the rock with his nose to the ground. If only he could pick up his master's scent he would soon find out which way he had gone.

A fictional Border Collie from Selkirk in the Scottish Borders, Black Bob started life as a text story in The Dandy in November 1944. He later progressed to a cartoon strip in The Weekly News, which continued through to 1967. Drawn by Jack Prout for publishers DC Thomson, the popular black and white sheepdog appeared regularly in The Dandy from his debut until 1982 — even after Prout's retirement in June 1968. The series even spawned eight Black Bob annuals. True to life, Black Bob was depicted as a highly intelligent dog, described by DC Thomson as 'handsome in his black and white coat, and so wise in the ways of sheep and men that he handles the great flocks, which are in the charge of his bearded master, with seldom a word to direct him. Bob has many adventures, not all in the sheep pasture or even in the Selkirk, Scotland area, where he lives. He is often a hero and always saves the day.' Shortly before his retirement, Prout acquired a black and white Border Collie and, to mark the occasion, staff at DC Thomson presented him with a spoof dog licence, allowing the animal to keep Jack Prout as a pet. The document was 'signed' with Black Bob's paw print.

It isn't just the worlds of film and television, or publishing in its many forms, where dogs have provided creative inspiration. Music too has felt the force. Readers of a certain generation may recall the sad old Elvis Presley song, *Old Shep*. Written by Red Foley in 1933, it was first sung live by Elvis in 1945 — when he was just ten years old — and tells the story of a faithful dog who had to be put down by its owner. Nine years later, Presley went on to record *Hound Dog*, which topped the charts, forerunner to sixty-odd years of pop songs featuring dogs, from *Lonely Pup in a Christmas Shop* (Adam Faith) and *How Much is that Doggie in the Window?* (Patti Page), through *Me and You and a Dog Named Boo* (Lobo), *I Love My Dog* (Cat Stevens), and *Puppy Love* (Donny Osmond). We could go on...

They've even made it onto the stage. In 2010, the nation stood by its remotes for the final in the BBC's hunt for a dog to play Dorothy's faithful sidekick Toto in Andrew Lloyd Webber's reworking of *The Wizard of Oz* in London's West End. The search for Toto was almost as gruelling as the search for a leading lady, with dogs from across the country vying for the role. In a live final of *Over the Rainbow* Miniature Schnauzer, Dangerous Dave, from Rossendale in Lancashire, with his trademark red scarf and a noted ability to leap right into his owner's arms from a standing start, beat off the competition. He made his West End debut on 21 April 2010 in a special performance of the musical, in aid of Comic Relief.

Way find!

So. Multi-talented. In so many ways, on so many levels. But despite their undisputed flair on stage and screen, it's probably their extraordinary power of smell which has truly changed the lives of mankind. If a dog can save a person's life by finding them when all other methods have been exhausted, then this is certainly true. The vast majority of search and rescue dogs are trained and assessed to search off-road terrain, from flattest farm to serious mountain, day and night, whatever the weather, for many hours at a time. That said, a dog's effectiveness depends on ground and weather conditions as well as the speed with which they are deployed. If other people have passed across the search area before a handler is tasked to search, and report back on how confident they feel the area has been covered (eg. 75% probability of detection), this too can impact on a dog team's success.

Most dog teams, particularly in Scotland, are trained to search for walkers or climbers trapped in avalanche debris. Whilst the risk is very low, people are avalanched every year in Scotland and

Doggie
Tales
TEALLACH
A TRUE SCOTTISH
MOUNTAINEER

Dave Whalley's dog Teallach was the softest, long-haired Alsatian you could ever meet. He was also a keen Munroist, 'compleating' his first round in 1985. He'd just twelve left for his second round when he passed away, in 1992.

I feel sure Hamish Brown's dog Keltie completed his round before Teallach, but he was certainly one of the early dog Munroists.

'He completed many outstanding walks in his life including two complete traverses of Scotland, a north to south and an east to west and 145 Munros in seven weeks — very hard on the paws!

'Many of his early expeditions were the Welsh classics and winter routes in Scotland and the Lakes. During my posting in North Wales, the lesser hills proved good training for Scotland and, every six weeks or so, we'd take a trip to the big mountains in the north where he excelled and, during my time with the RAF MRTs at Kinloss and Leuchars, there were many big mountain days. His mountain logbook describes the Skye Ridge in two days, eleven traverses of the South Clunnie ridge, six of the North Clunnie Ridge, nine of the Mamores and seven of the Fannichs, three ascents of the Shenavall Six and three of the Affric Munros. And he completed The Tranter Traverse in Kintail. He was a regular user of the CIC hut at Lochaber — until the members banned him! Something to do with excessive snoring and pungent odours!

'The most difficult Munros were on Skye, where we experienced a wonderful two-day traverse of the Cuillin Ridge. My rock climbing ability is limited, so getting to the very summit of the Inaccessible Pinnacle with him was a major operation but, with help from my climbing friends, we succeeded. The remaining sections of the ridge showed that Teallach had exceptional route finding ability. Typically, he'd run ahead, vanish around a ledge, and arrive before us, completely unfazed by the technical challenge and exposure. In fact, he really was an accomplished climber on rock and ice, often soloing steep ground with ease. Once, on the Cioch Nose in Applecross, we left him attached to the rucksacks at the bottom of the route. On our return, we found him in the loch over a mile away, rucksacks still tied to his collar!

'A regular at Glenmore Lodge, he was eventually banned for annoying the instructors assessing students in the Northern Corries. The trouble began as he waited at the bottom of a climb. If he heard my climbing calls, he'd think I was calling to him for help then interrupt the instructors by trying to find his way up steep Grade II gullies! But on rescues he was always well behaved. He knew

when we had a fatality to deal with, or when the situation was serious. Then, he kept out of the way. He was also a very willing and warm bivouac partner for any casualty.

'Though not a trained search dog, Teallach was superb on the hill and could sniff out all manner of hazards in any weather. His area knowledge was exceptional and, whilst he never used a map or compass, he always found his way to the summit where he invariably left his mark! He had two big falls, the first on Creag Meaghaidh, where he slid 300 metres in a whiteout. He was out in front as usual and at the overconfident stage in his mountaineering career. I descended into the coire expecting to find him in a bad way but, apart from being a little shaken, he was fine — although now very 'cornice aware'! The second incident was on Lochnagar. An epic on Spout Buttress left us descending in poor weather late on a wild winter's night. The only way off was over the cornice and down Black Spout Gully. Our descent was fine until two following climbers dislodged the cornice, which took us six hundred feet down the gully. Teallach arrived on scene and began digging us out, even though the avalanche had also hit him. We

eventually returned in the wee small hours, battered and bruised, but still alive.

'Back in the 1970s, snowholing was fashionable. One night on the Cairngorm plateau, after the usual few drams, we all drifted back to our own holes. Just as we were falling asleep, I heard a noise outside and, thinking it was a raid on our whisky store, sent Teallach out to chase them off. Even though he was a big softy, in the dark and around the snowhole, he must have looked fearsome. Imagine my consternation the following morning, when I went out and found two climbers curled up and shivering. It seemed they'd left their sacks below a climb and couldn't find them. Having seen our light they thought they were safe, only to be met by a huge dog, who barred their entrance to the snow hole! Feeling somewhat guilty, I brought them in and made a brew. As we later descended to the car park, we met members of the Cairngorm team coming to search for our 'lost' friends.

'Teallach always had an eye for a comfortable position. Back at the bothy, after a day on the hill, he'd search out a soft spot — usually a comfy sleeping bag, make himself comfortable, then fall asleep. Few owners were brave enough to move the huge Alsatian and many a novice team member had a cold night curled up on the floor. If there was a fire in the bothy, he'd invariably find a position very close. Once, following a very long hill day, he crawled next to the stove, lay down for a while, and immediately burst into flames. Needless to say, he moved away very quickly!

'In his later years he enjoyed walking up to the crags with us and watch our epics on the classic routes, occasionally pinching any food left in open rucksacks. Even after a long climbing day he would still be there twelve hours later. He'd even work out our descent routes and wait for us there. He acquired a love for sea stacks and would happily swim around the stack as we climbed — and his love of water extended to a dip in every loch he could find, whatever the weather or season.

'I rarely saw Teallach tired. But once, whilst completing the Big Three in Torridon, (Beinn Eighe, Liathach and Ben Alligin), the heat got to him and he refused to add Beinn Dearg to the day. Instead, he headed off down the glen on his own to the vehicle. With advancing years, ageing began to take its toll. Problems with his hips and back became chronic, but he still loved every minute on the hill. Teallach was an exceptional dog, well behaved at all times and no problem with sheep or wild life. But, most of all he was a great companion; the ultimate party leader, always looking out for everyone and rounding up any stragglers. He wasn't just a Munro Bagger but an all round Scottish Mountaineer. He was even able to jump and climb deer fences in his prime, although on one occasion he nearly hung himself when his karabiner caught in the top wire! He always wore a screw gate karabiner round his collar and this was one of his hallmarks. In the middle of the night when he was thirsty, he'd head for the toilet for a drink. The noise of the karabiner on the toilet bowl woke everyone!

'I miss him to this day. He had a wonderful life and was a true friend.'

ABOVE: TEALLACH WITH THE SCREW GATE KARABINER ROUND HIS COLLAR © DAVE WHALLEY.
IMAGE ON PAGE 80: TEALLACH ON HIS WAY UP THE INACCESSIBLE PINNACLE ON THE CUILLIN RIDGE IN SKYE © DAVE WHALLEY.

occasionally lives are lost. In the ten-year period to 2009, eleven people died in avalanches. Those who are buried have a short life expectancy. Many are injured by the weight of snow and ice, there's a high risk of asphyxiation and those who are buried certainly suffer from hypothermia. Their best chance of survival rests with those in the immediate vicinity who escaped or witnessed the avalanche. If search dog teams can be deployed quickly, a likely area can be covered in minutes where it might take line searchers an hour or more. Dogs can carry out a 'hasty' search before rescuers begin work with avalanche probes. Records show that dogs are capable of indicating where the scent of a victim buried in snow emerges at the surface, even when the person is buried metres below the surface.

A fairly recent project looked into training dogs to detect and indicate human scent from people who have drowned making it possible to determine the approximate location of a body. Then, by taking into account water currents, depth and temperature, divers have a considerably better chance of locating the missing person. Dog teams have been used to search extensive areas of water such as lakes, ponds, quarries, reservoirs, rivers and streams. Handlers who search fast flowing water and expansive areas of open water are knowledgeable about water hazards and the necessary safety precautions and always work in conjunction with members of other emergency services.

Some dogs are trained to identify the unique smell of cadaver items such as bodily fluids and decaying corpses that are hidden or buried. So-called cadaver dogs, or human-remains dogs, are trained to search a specific area of land or part of a building and indicate when they pick up a smell. As you might expect, they are used extensively by police forces to help locate victims of crime. By using mainly ground scent, dogs can locate remains which have been buried for many years. They can even locate minute materials such as hair or fingernails, which are virtually impossible for a person to locate by eyesight alone. Cadaver dogs were used to great effect to search for remains of victims of the 9/11 attacks in 2003.

A number of organisations across the world train dogs to search for survivors or bodies buried under the debris from collapsed structures. Here in the UK, the fire and rescue service has a statutory responsibility to respond to emergencies involving the collapse of buildings and other structures. A number of UK urban search and rescue dog teams were established in 2001 to give the service a search and rescue dog team capability. These teams are on standby 24/7, made up of fire fighters from individual stations across the country. Whilst they may be called to help overseas their primary role is urban search and rescue in the UK. There are a number of other, non-government organisations that specialise in searching for people trapped in collapsed structures and buildings, such as RAPID UK and the International Rescue Corps. At times of international disaster, many different organisations from across the world are called to assist. In the Haiti earthquake of January 2010, over 50 international search and rescue teams, comprising more than 1700 people and about 170 dogs, were mobilised. Disaster or collapsed building search dogs may be called to a wide variety of situations — fires, hurricanes, explosions or earthquakes, plane crashes, rock falls, floods and mudslides. Collies, labradors, German Shepherds and spaniels undertake work that is often hazardous and usually occurs when weather conditions are at their most extreme. Usually, they work off-lead but close to their handler and focus on debris piles and voids, or access paths too small or dangerous for the handler to enter. Dogs are trained to alert in a similar method to other air-scenting search dogs in that they give a scratch and bark alert where the scent emanates from the rubble pile at its strongest point.

Trailing dogs work in a different manner to their air-scenting cousins, trailing the scent of a specific person through an item of their clothing. They work on or off-lead and are oriented to scent which has drifted to the ground downwind of a person's route of travel, then follow on or close to the route walked by the missing person, although they may work some distance from the actual footsteps. They are particularly useful for locating missing people when their last position is known.

So, as we said: multi-talented and amazingly versatile — and, on top of this they're extremely faithful and rarely, if ever, complain. By and large, they are very low maintenance, costing relatively little for the pleasure they provide their owners and the work they undertake — but sometimes things do go wrong.

5 The very best of health

'I quickly found a grass chute splitting the steep rock face and followed it down to the bottom of the crag. Looking around I spotted Coco standing on top of a boulder. Rushing over to him he started to wag his tail, but he wasn't moving. There was a trail of blood below him on the boulder.'
Mark Hogarth

Most dogs are pretty hardy creatures. Indeed, they have a much higher tolerance for pain than many other animals — some a lot bigger, such as horses. But even so, working dogs need care and attention. They suffer injury and illness, they experience stress and discomfort and they need a considered diet and exercise regime and, like their human counterparts, their physical capabilities deteriorate with age and may be prone to debilitating disorders symptomatic of their particular breed. So, just like their handlers, dogs need looking after. Their health, safety and wellbeing are vital. Of course, for the vast majority of owners this is not an issue. Many, if not all search and rescue dogs are also family pets and no owner would think twice about doing whatever it takes or costs to help their dog through a difficult illness and to ensure their comfort and welfare. In fact, some might argue many handlers take better care of their dogs than they do themselves! We couldn't possibly comment!

But how does the aspirant handler decide which dog to train in the first instance? How do you recognise — if indeed this is possible

at all — which breed has the potential, temperament, intelligence and physique to become an effective search dog?

The best breed and type of dog for use as a search and rescue dog has been a subject of intense and sometimes heated debate, probably for as long as SARDA has been in existence. Dog owners and trainers are often fiercely loyal to a breed and it may be impossible to change their point of view by argument... only experience can do that. Border Collies, German Shepherds and labradors are by far the most common breeds for search dogs, but there have been many successful individuals from other breeds. Spaniels, pointers, retrievers and their crosses are all represented and have their champions among handlers — even counting a lurcher, a large Munsterlander and a Huntaway amongst their ranks. There are, however, certain aspects of anatomy and health that are generally agreed by everyone. A dachshund, for example, because of its very short legs, would not make a mountain search dog.

A mountain rescue search dog must be

big enough and sufficiently agile to negotiate difficult terrain, and continue working in such terrain for hours at a time. Practically speaking, this means it is likely to weigh somewhere in the range 15-40kg (small collie to German Shepherd). Smaller dogs have the advantage of being light to lift and carry over fences, or off the hill in case of an accident, whereas a big dog might require a stretcher for evacuation but may have a speed advantage.

Ideally the dog's coat should be adequate to allow it to work without an insulated jacket in any weather conditions. Search dogs are usually worked wearing a very light jacket but the purpose of this is to act as a signal it is working rather than protection from the elements. It may also carry a lightstick so the handler can see the dog in the dark, and sometimes a small GPS receiver so the dog's movement pattern can be identified and subsequently downloaded onto a map to help inform overall search management. A thin skinned dog with a very short coat, such as a greyhound, will find it difficult to keep warm in winter when it is not actually working, although insulated jackets of many types are available and frequently used when dogs are not actually deployed. Much of a search dog's life is spent waiting — for deployment, for transport, for someone else to finish training in the area about to be entered, for someone to come and collect the casualty it has just found — and it can get very cold. Equally, the dog with a very long, thick coat may suffer in summer when it has to work in the heat. Heat exhaustion (hyperthermia) may be very serious if not recognised early. In fact, the very first rescue for Bob Sharp, one of the authors, was to recover a German Shepherd suffering from hyperthermia on the top of one of Scotland's mountains. The dog seemed to enjoy the ride down on the stretcher, although the rescuers carrying it were greeted with strange looks from walkers when they realised the occupant wasn't human!

In days gone by long coated working collies such as the Bearded Collie and the Old English Sheepdog were often shorn at the same time as the sheep to prevent this problem. At the other extreme, long coats may also be a handicap in snow. Snow adheres to some types of hair — balling up — and this creates all kinds of problems for the dog. We have seen working spaniels and collies almost unable to move, weighed down by snow on their ears, legs and belly after some enthusiastic exercise in fresh snow.

Dog boots, designed to protect a dog's paws and possibly enhance traction, have been used in arctic conditions to protect from ice cuts — for example, with sled dogs running in the Iditarod race — but they are rarely used in the UK and only then in a veterinary context as a short-term measure

to retain a dressing for a dog with a paw wound. The only other circumstance where dog boots have a use is when a neurological disorder in the dog causes their paw to knuckle over at the metacarpophalangeal joints. This tends to wear out the dorsal surface of the paw and boots can help alleviate the problem. However, dogs are past masters at trying to remove unnatural attachments, whatever their nature! Plaster casts, stitches, wound dressings and even the mirth-inducing lampshade-like, protective medical device worn by dogs to prevent them from biting or licking at their body, or scratching at their head or neck, while wounds or injuries heal — the Elizabethan collar. So, even if they were given a shiny new set of boots to wear, it's likely they'd do their best to remove them, cut paw or not!

Dogs also sweat between their toes so putting on a boot would cause their feet to become moist, which in turn, would encourage interdigital infections. In truth, there is no other, valid need for dogs to wear boots of any kind. Indeed, contrary to aiding traction, their use may be positively dangerous for a dog on snow and ice. Dogs tend to manage fine with their natural claw 'crampons'. Boots remove this natural asset, making them more likely to slip, as well as reducing their confidence. The main thing here is for handlers to recognise the dangers of sheet ice and take adequate precautions by avoiding such terrain, or else tethering their dog for the duration of travel when on sheet ice.

It is difficult to generalise about temperament in dogs as there are always exceptions to any rule but it's safe to say that good search dogs are generally friendly, motivated and eager to earn a

reward. A strong play drive is a valuable trait as play is the reward most commonly and easily used in training. Much of an adult dog's temperament is decided by its breeding, early socialisation and handling. A pup that is handled a lot and introduced to many different sights and sounds in the first sixteen weeks of its life will usually be more able to deal with stressful and varied events later in life. A major factor in determining a dog's temperament is what it inherits from its parents in terms of confidence, and also what it learns from its mother and other dogs during the first few weeks of life. Occasionally, a dog's temperament can cause serious problems for its owner — so much so that drastic action has to be taken. The dog may have to go to a new owner or even be put down. Fortunately, there are many experts in canine behaviour who can help with such challenges. One such is Jacquie Hall, a training and behaviour adviser at the Northumberland Canine Centre in Alnwick. Here's what she said about the challenge of one particularly wilful dog.

'One of my roles as training adviser to SARDA England is to make an assessment of every puppy's temperament. On this basis I can advise handlers (whose temperaments I also note!) on how to bring on their puppy accordingly so its full potential can be realised. The word 'dominant' is often used to describe a dog's disposition, but I tend to look at temperament issues quite differently and describe them in terms that are easier to understand. Most puppies are fairly well balanced but there are problems at either end of a behavioural continuum ranging from those that lack confidence to those who have too much. Confidence levels tend to be genetic in that shy, anxious dogs are generally born from parents of a similar disposition. Dogs like this tend to be nurtured as shy and anxious dogs and treated with kid gloves by owners who don't know how to change these traits. Similarly, confident dogs are also born that way, and they can become over-confident if behaviour boundaries aren't set down early and clearly enough. Whilst I'm not involved in the puppy selection process, I do get to see puppies as early as ten weeks old, which gives me time to influence change if required.

'Many of the puppies are Border Collies, bought from farmers who breed their own working dogs. Some farm-bred dogs tend to be highly driven with an over-riding herding instinct, which can be difficult for inexperienced handlers to manage without expert advice. The majority of puppies prove to be straightforward to handle but, occasionally, I see puppies which, when put into a strange environment, can fall apart emotionally. This is more evident in those bought at a later age who've only lived with littermates and parents, although I have seen puppies as young as twelve weeks cowering behind an owner's legs, trembling with fear. That same puppy may well have appeared quite confident in the litter where it was comfortable and relaxed.

'This may not look encouraging for a search and rescue dog, as an anxious emotional state is not conducive to learning, and training will prove difficult if a dog cannot be brought through it. But all is not lost! Success can be achieved but it requires a full understanding of how a dog thinks and behaves. For both shy and outgoing puppies the treatment is actually quite similar. Basically, all dogs need (and

indeed like) a strong and confident leader. How this relationship is achieved with dogs of different temperaments is the same... but with subtle twists. The key to raising (or lowering) a dog's confidence and gaining respect and control is primarily through the use of games. Possession (of toys, articles etc) is very important to all dogs; it reflects status, strength and tenacity. So, in playing games with puppies, I advise handlers how play can be used appropriately with dogs of different temperaments.

'The key with shy puppies is to allow them to win games of possession in subtle, believable and non-condescending ways. This helps raise their self-esteem and confidence. The opposite is true with over-confident or excited dogs. These dogs must earn possession of what are now the handler's toys... through compliance! So, I encourage all handlers to play possession games, particularly tug of war, but with subtle twists appropriate to each individual dog and handler. All games must be motivational as that is what will eventually keep a dog searching for many hours in the most horrendous conditions... a game with their toy!

'Let me give an example of how this approach has worked. Through an interesting twist of fate, and through observation and understanding of temperaments both human and canine, I was able to match a dog with a handler, which eventually saved the dog's life and provided SARDA with a very successful dog team.

'Alex Lyons from Dartmoor graded two search dogs prior to training his lab/collie cross Glen. The two previous dogs he'd trained successfully had been very confident and suited Alex's style of handling

well. However, Glen was not a confident dog and it was obvious to me in the early stages of training he was suffering emotionally under the pressure. It wasn't that Alex was being too harsh but he wasn't rewarding Glen enough to raise his self-esteem. As a result, Glen was losing confidence. When dogs get to this stage they can often display what we call 'learned helplessness'. In this state, even though they desperately want to please, they just stand and do nothing because they lack the confidence to try something and risk making a mistake. I witnessed this with Glen and alerted Alex to the problem but it was going to be hard to overcome the problem at Glen's late stage in training.

'At the same time, in my professional capacity as a behaviourist, my local vet asked me to work with an over-aggressive twelve week old Border Collie. On first meeting Max, he appeared very confident and strutted into my training arena as if he owned the place. His owner described him as 'attention-seeking' and resistant to any control. He was also very possessive and had bitten on a couple of occasions whilst guarding his toys. I smiled to myself, thinking here was yet another owner exaggerating the problems about how difficult it is to control a twelve-week-old puppy.

'How wrong I was! When I put a lead on Max to start taking some control he simply made his point by sinking his sharp, baby teeth into my calf! He was already supremely confident at playing tug-of-war, and displayed this not by targeting the toy but the hand that was holding it! Max had obviously already developed a highly self-indulgent approach to life — in only twelve weeks! Fortunately, I had a littermate of

TOP: BALLING UP, ABLY DEMONSTRATED BY ABIE.
ABOVE: IN-BUILT 'DOGGIE CRAMPONS' ALLOW ABIE TO GET A FIX IN THE SNOW. IMAGES © BOB SHARP.

Max in for training around the same time. Whilst he wasn't quite as bad as Max, he too was posing a problem to his owners with his attention-seeking naughtiness and lack of respect for control. I worked with Max, his brother and their respective owners for a few weeks until both owners admitted they could cope no longer. Max's owner admitted he actually disliked Max, whose behaviour was getting worse by the day. Indeed, he said he didn't want to keep him and was now put off owning dogs for life after having had a lovely companion dog for many years prior to Max. Similarly, Max's brother was swiftly returned to the breeder.

'At this point, I had one of those light bulb moments! Max was never going to make it in a pet home and if returned to the breeder would probably be put down — as I fear may have happened to his brother. Meanwhile, I felt Alex was never going to make it through final assessment with Glen, whose temperament just wasn't strong enough to cope with the pressure... but who would make a perfect family pet! So, the notion of a switch occurred to me. After a short telephone call, Alex agreed. I transported Max to a SARDA training session in the Peak District the following week, and made arrangements for Glen to be brought up to Northumberland to be placed with Max's brother's former owner a few weeks later. Glen settled into his new home immediately and, with instructions from Alex on which commands to use and games to play, Glen was officially retired from SARDA and became a family pet! However, all was not too well in the Lyon household. Max was causing mayhem! But, as I had hoped, Alex handled it superbly and, in spite of many bites, chewed furniture and attention-seeking barks, Max went on to qualify as a search dog. Furthermore, he played a starring role in the BBC's *Real Rescues* and received a 'Shining World Hero Award' for his efforts in locating and saving the life of a missing elderly woman in November 2008.

'I like to think I saw the potential in Max and the belief that Alex was the right person to handle and train him. Max clearly needed specialist handling. He had a temperament problem which needed to be addressed in a highly specific manner by someone who, equally, had the patience and required skills. Today, Max is not only a well-balanced family companion, but also a competent search and rescue dog.'

With over 200 breeds recognised by the Kennel Club, through highly selective breeding, breeders try to achieve predictable results in their litters. This may be colour, shape and size, length of leg or ear or, probably more important, but unfortunately not always prioritised, temperament. It is less possible to be certain that a certain dog and bitch of the same breed will give offspring of a particular temperament than it is to predict, for example, their coat colour or the length of their legs. However, it's more likely that if they are both of good temperament, their pups will be too. Parents of different breeds may produce a range of different characteristics in their offspring. Some of the nicest dogs we've ever known have been collie/German Shepherd crosses but equally we've come across some very difficult animals of this cross, which have inherited all the worst traits of both parents. It's hard to know what you're getting, which is why so many working dogs are pure bred. The advice to would-be owners to

see both parents of their pup is always sensible, but never more important than with a pup of a mixed breed.

In thinking about search dog breeds the question of soundness must be considered. A healthy dog will probably be qualified or graded by the time it is three years old and, depending on its breed, health and level of fitness, may then have up to ten years of working life before being retired. Some breeds have a number of inherited conditions that would render the dog unfit to work and much time and effort can be wasted training a dog that goes lame or blind quite early in life. Unfortunately, some of these occur in breeds that are otherwise ideal for the job. Some can be detected before the dog is selected for training, by genetic or other tests. Border Collies can suffer from a disorder of the retina called retinal atrophy, which is a progressive and incurable disease causing blindness. The heritability of this condition is fairly well understood and much commendable effort has been made by breeders in the last 30 years to eradicate this.

Some other conditions can be detected by expert ophthalmological examination of the eyes. The working collie show and trials organisers have been cooperative in facilitating these examinations at their events to detect the condition as early as possible and enable breeders to avoid mating affected individuals. It is wise to purchase collies from parents that have been certified free from eye diseases. Some of these — for example collie eye anomaly — can be seen in pups as young as seven weeks old so an eye examination on the pup is also advisable.

German Shepherds and labradors, and

some other large breeds are prone to hip and, more recently, elbow dysplasia — a sometimes crippling abnormality of the joints in which the normal well-fitting joint surfaces do not develop as they should. This causes instability and sometimes partial dislocation of the joint resulting in arthritis and pain. Breeders are attempting to eradicate the condition by X-raying animals prior to breeding. While a good hip or elbow score is no guarantee a dog will have sound offspring (inheritance of these problems is more complicated than retinal atrophy) it is a sensible place to start in trying to improve the soundness of the breed and does seem to be having some effect in reducing the number of dogs suffering from these painful conditions. These dysplasias cannot reliably be diagnosed in very young pups in a clinical examination though they may be suspected. There are other conditions more common in some breeds than others, such as idiopathic epilepsy that sometimes affects Border Collies, but they are not common enough, or the mode of inheritance is not sufficiently well understood, for eradication programmes to have been developed.

Generally, it is advisable to purchase pups for search work from parents that are at least two years old when bred for the first time, as many conditions will have shown up in the adult by that time. The common and sensible practice of trying to find a pup one of whose parents is a proven working dog, if not a search dog, has much to recommend it. Choosing a dog for search work can involve making difficult decisions. The prospective handler would be wise to take advice from an experienced trainer and also not be afraid to discuss health issues with their vet.

TOP: NERO MAKES IT DOWN THE HILL, THANKS TO MEMBERS OF OGWEN VALLEY MOUNTAIN RESCUE TEAM © OGWEN VALLEY MRO. ABOVE: MILLY TAKES TIME OUT TO RECOVER AFTER HER DRAMATIC ACCIDENT © HEATHER MORNING.

There is no doubt that dogs suffer injuries from time to time. A dog travelling at full speed across a steep and broken mountainside is at risk of colliding with sharp rocks or falling significant distances. At night time when visibility is poor and in bad weather when the ground may be slippery, the risks are even greater. An injured dog must be given first aid in the same way as an injured person and, in many cases, the treatment administered is the same. The whole point of first aid is to help prevent any condition worsening, alleviate pain and help save life. Injuries to dogs can vary from minor soft tissue damage to limb fractures and serious internal trauma. Dogs are hardy creatures and generally know what is good for them, so they tend not to tackle anything too dangerous but, occasionally, they break legs, rip claws and tear pads. Injuries such as torn pads and minor lacerations can be dealt with by the handler on the hill. For example, a crepe bandage, found in the first aid kits of most rescuers, can be used for a variety of purposes. They're simple to use and can be adapted for a wide variety of purposes. And, hopefully, a crepe bandage applied to the injured part of the dog will suffice until it is off the hill and can be taken to the vet.

More serious problems such as internal trauma caused by a long fall, or a compound fracture may require a carry-off on a mountain rescue or improvised stretcher. A dog with a suspected or obvious leg fracture, or a dislocated joint, may require the injured site to be stabilised and protected to avoid further injury. However, animals are better able than humans to tolerate an unstable fracture due to their inherently higher pain threshold, greater number of weight-bearing limbs and lighter body weight. As a consequence, fracture stabilisation prior to transport is much less crucial for canine than for human casualties. Serious bleeding is a different matter and would be managed by local pressure and some kind of semi-tight binding. Veterinary experts suggest the majority of injuries are best left alone if the animal is conscious. An injured dog, even if well trained, is likely to behave in the same way as an injured wild animal if in pain. Its fight or flight reaction could easily result in a bite wound to the handler or would-be first-aider, or anyone else trying to restrain and help. Most medical interventions to traumatised animals should be performed after appropriate sedation and/or anaesthesia and these are clearly best left to trained professionals. In summary, unless it is clear that immediate action is required — to stem heavy blood loss, for example — it's better to leave the dog's injuries alone and arrange for prompt evacuation of the animal under its own steam, if possible to a vet for professional assessment, advice and management.

A dog that does suffer a serious injury will most certainly need a protracted rest before it recommences work. As was the case with search dog Milly. Collie Milly and her owner Heather Morning are members of SARDA Scotland. Heather, who was a Ranger on Cairngorm mountain at the time, was helping skiers and boarders onto the tow at the bottom of the Coire Cas. Milly was standing close to Heather simply watching the world go by. As the tow tugged a boarder away from the start, his board sliced through Milly's left rear leg severing a major artery. Like most accidents, things happen unexpectedly.

Heather was suddenly faced with a life-threatening situation and had to respond very quickly. Milly was in distress and rapidly losing blood. Heather reacted immediately by stopping the tow and reaching for her first aid kit. With help from a couple of skiers, she pressed a triangular bandage onto Milly's leg and bound it with additional slings to help compress the wound. Unfortunately, dogs don't seem to understand the RICE principle: rest, ice, compression, elevation! Unable to elevate Milly's leg, Heather had to get to a vet, and quickly. Members of the ski patrol had already been alerted and were on hand to whisk Milly by sled further down the mountain to the car park. From here Heather drove her to the vet in nearby Grantown-on-Spey where she was operated on immediately. Milly lost half her blood volume and was on a drip for three days. She remained with the vet for three weeks and was a sorry sight on her return having lost much weight. But she recovered quickly and now continues her role as a qualified SARDA dog as if nothing had ever happened.

A very different but still serious plight overtook Nero, the Black Labrador, when out walking with his owner in North Wales. Ten-year-old Nero was on a long walk with owner Alex when he began to suffer from what appeared to be heat exhaustion. The two of them had walked up to the Devil's Kitchen, then on to Glyder Fawr and Glyder Fach. Alex planned to continue on to Tryfan but at this point Nero started to appear tired, so she abandoned the traverse and made tracks to return. This involved descending a steep, rocky path towards the plateau from where Nero was ultimately rescued. It was on the descent that Nero

began to limp and then his back legs gave way and he laid down and started to whimper. Two passing walkers helped Alex carry Nero a short way down the steep section of the path, but it wasn't easy. One of the men tried to carry Nero in his arms but lost his footing and fell on his back with Nero on top! At this point, Alex decided she needed outside help so she dialled 999 and asked for the police. Half expecting the mountain rescue team not to bother, she was overjoyed when they told her to 'stay put and wait for us.' Members of the Ogwyn Valley MRO responded and climbed up to Alex and Nero, carrying with them a pack frame and large zipped bag. Initially, Nero was placed in the bag and strapped to the pack frame and carried down as if on a small stretcher. There was concern he might be overheating in the bag, so it was decided faster progress would be made by carrying Nero over team members' shoulders. Three team members took it in turns carrying the dog, while the fourth escorted Alex off the mountain and down to the team base at Bryn Poeth.

Alex took Nero to the vet the following day for a thorough check up. It turned out he was in good health except for several blistered paws. It was probably the pain of walking on rough ground that halted his progress down the steep, broken track. Dogs, as we've said, do have a relatively high threshold for pain and it is probable that Nero's pads had begun to blister earlier in the walk, but he gave no indication. Happily, he suffered no long term effect, which is perhaps more than can be said for the backs of his rescuers!

David Warden and Ben are members of SARDA Southern Scotland. They were out training one summer's day when they experienced something David will never forget. Ben was running across an open field when he suddenly yelped and jumped into the air. He had been bitten by an adder. At the time, it didn't occur to David and his wife Lynne, who is also a dog handler, that anything was amiss — Ben simply carried on searching for the body. However, once they were home, he began to show signs he wasn't quite right. A close inspection showed he had developed a huge abscess on his hip, which burst on the way to the vet. Ben was forced to undergo an emergency operation which involved removing a large expanse of skin down one side of his leg. It turned out the adder bite had caused an infection which had eaten away an area of soft tissue around his hip joint. Another operation was required and this was followed by months of regular physiotherapy. It took eighteen months of additional training and fitness work before Ben was back to call-out status. He was left with a slight limp although this didn't affect his work as a search dog. In fact, within a short period of being back on call, he had three successful finds, one of which involved locating a badly injured glider pilot in thick woodland.

Search and rescue dogs are no more susceptible than other dogs to any of the common or more obscure canine infections. There are a number of these and, whilst some are easily treated, others can be extremely dangerous and often fatal. Ear infections, which are common, skin infections and upper respiratory infections such as Bordetella (kennel cough) are not dangerous but do require veterinary attention. Other infections are more dangerous. Parvovirus, which is spread through infected faeces, is an extremely contagious, painful disease. Puppies are especially vulnerable because of their underdeveloped immune systems and the majority die if they catch it. Canine distemper is another dangerous infection, which can progress to seizures and, in fifty percent of all cases, results in death. The most deadly infection is rabies for which there is no known cure and is always fatal. Fortunately, the likelihood of a dog (or human, for that matter) catching rabies is extremely remote in the UK. In fact, the rabies virus was eradicated from the UK over 100 years ago.

The key thing is that all canine infections, including hepatitis, distemper, rabies, Weil's disease, kennel cough and parvovirus, are preventable by vaccine. The majority of responsible dog owners — and certainly all dog handlers — ensure their dogs are vaccinated regularly and given boosters every twelve months to keep them safe. The routine visit to their vet also provides an opportunity for a thorough physical health examination including checks on the dog's weight, body condition, heart, lungs, airways, limbs, paws, eyes, ears, nose, mouth, skin and coat, back and abdomen. Regular trips to the vet also give handlers a chance to ask about and discuss any medical, behavioural or physical concerns they have about their dog. And when the dog is given a clean bill of health, it gives the handler (and their association) confidence that the dog is fit for purpose for another year.

If there is a particular problem for search and rescue dogs it's that they're prone to picking up ticks, the blood-feeding parasites often found in tall grass and bracken, where they wait to attach to a passing host. That host might be a grazing sheep, horse, cow, deer, dog or human being. They are found in most wooded or forested regions throughout the country, on moorland, heathland and livestock pasture, and are particularly abundant in areas where there are large numbers of deer. Most prevalent in the spring and summer months of the year (normally March through to October), they can still be active on milder winter days. They fix themselves to a host by inserting their mouthparts into the skin then gorge on the host's blood, eventually dropping off when full.

In dogs, ticks are most frequently found in crevices, in and around the ears, the areas where the insides of the legs meet the body, between the toes, and within skin folds. The majority of tick bites on dogs and humans are harmless but there is a small but significant risk of contracting Borreliosis (Lyme disease) from these parasites. The causative bacterium, Borrelia burgdorferi, may take several hours to transmit to a host, so the sooner a tick is located and removed, the lower the risk of disease. All dog handlers know about ticks and check their dog regularly for likely tick infestation.

Ticks can be prevented and there are several products and medications available over the counter, from online veterinary pharmacies or from a vet. Some vets suggest putting a tick collar on the dog, although no method provides 100% protection. It's advisable to discuss tick control with your vet and use veterinary prescribed products. The pyrethrum-based active ingredients of over-the-counter products have been implicated in cases of direct poisoning to dogs, or contamination poisonings of other pets which have close contact with the dog. Typically, vets take into account the age and health of a dog, plus its animal companions at home, and prescribe a product taking into account all these factors. It is also worth noting that many tick-control preparations don't actually repel ticks, as commonly thought, but act as a systemic acaricide (tick killer), which kills the tick once it starts feeding.

When ticks (alive or dead) are found on dogs, removal is a delicate operation because a piece of the tick's mouthpiece could break off and remain in the dog's skin, increasing the risk of localised infection resulting from the foreign body. Many methods have been proposed but a popular device called the O'Tom Tick Twister is a proven way to both remove the whole tick and minimise the risk of disease transmission. This is a small plastic device with a 'V' cut into the lower part. The 'V' is introduced under the body of the tick and twisted a few times, releasing the barbed mouth parts of the tick and allowing it to be lifted out. Many long-used methods of tick removal, such as smothering it with butter, petroleum jelly, spirits or other substances, or burning it with a cigarette or hot match head, are now considered likely to cause the tick to regurgitate saliva and its stomach contents, increasing the risk of disease transmission.

Snake bites are not infections but, as we heard with David Warden and Ben, they are a problem and can lead to infections. Although extremely unlikely, search dogs that work on moors, heath land and warm mountain tracks and slopes run the risk of being bitten by an adder. Most snakebites tend to occur between March and October when snakes are more active due to the warm weather. Adders are more likely to bite a dog than any other animal because

of their general inquisitiveness and predisposition to explore undergrowth and perhaps disturb a snake when it is basking. Adder bites result in pain and inflammation, but are not usually fatal. First aid measures such as sucking out the venom or applying a tourniquet are not recommended — they are ineffective and may even cause further harm. If an adder bites a dog, it is always considered to be an emergency and prompt veterinary attention should be sought. The most effective treatment is anti-venom but supportive treatment such as anti-inflammatory drugs, intravenous fluids and antibiotics may also be given as and when affected dogs need them.

Dogs, in their turn, can be carriers of infections which they inadvertently spread to others. Hookworms are a common intestinal parasite and dogs that are not wormed can carry hookworm. Not only do they drain their host of blood, to the tune of up to 10% per day, they can cause death. It's thought that around half a billion people worldwide are affected by the hookworm parasite. Hookworm eggs pass with a dog's faeces and then become free-living organisms in the environment where they can then be picked up, not just by other dogs, but also by humans (especially children), resulting in a nasty inflammatory reaction. In a farming context, unwormed dogs can pass worms to cattle and sheep. Responsible dog owners always have their dog wormed at least twice a year.

Another problem is fleas. Dogs that aren't washed regularly or treated with professional medication may carry fleas, which can then be passed to other animals and household items. And whilst they do not use humans as a host, they can bite. A major problem is the potential for dogs to

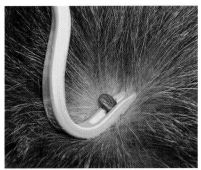

FROM TOP: A TICK ON HUMAN SKIN; A BLOOD FILLED TICK; THE TICK TWISTER REMOVES THE TICK FROM ITS PREY. ALL IMAGES SUPPLIED © BADA UK (BORRELIOSIS AND ASSOCIATED DISEASES AWARENESS UK).

spread foot and mouth disease. Dogs are not susceptible to the virus that causes foot and mouth disease, but the virus can be transmitted on their fur and paws. Dogs can also carry tuberculosis, although transfer to humans is highly unlikely.

The environment too, can take its toll on a dog. Whilst they are tolerant to a wide variety of conditions, there comes a point when the environment begins to have a negative effect. Dogs are able to adapt relatively well to drops in temperature (they generate heat through exercise and maintain heat via their fur coat) but they are less able to cope with rises in temperature. On hot summer days they have difficulty regulating body temperature and will show early signs of discomfort such as extreme panting and lethargy. Any dog handler will spot these signs early on and take avoiding action by stopping their dog working or by moving them to a cool location, into the shade or a pool of water.

High wind also has the potential to affect a dog's balance and progress, particularly as it works into the wind. However, because the wind slows down close to the ground it will, in general, affect dogs less than their handlers. We suspect handlers are more likely to take avoiding action in extreme wind conditions, before their dog begins to suffer adversely. The same applies to bad weather in the form of heavy rain, blizzard and hail. In these cases, handlers probably get out of the weather by sheltering behind a crag, trees or hollow, before their dog begins to suffer. An exception is blizzard conditions where handlers can don goggles but their dog cannot. In these circumstances, a dog will not only suffer extreme discomfort but also lose its ability to move safely and surely.

But, as we've said before, handlers are highly responsive to situations where they can take some kind of evasive action, which is denied to their dog.

Ground conditions can make life difficult for dogs. Deep heather and tussocky grass, ice-covered rocks and sharp rocky terrain can slow progress for both dogs and their handlers, and also consume unnecessary energy. Ground covered in ice or loose rocks above a steep crag can easily compromise a dog's balance and leave them exposed to a serious fall. Unlike their handlers, who can compensate by using crampons, dogs only have their claws to gain a purchase on slippery surfaces. These can be effective but they're certainly not bullet-proof. In these instances, handlers either back away from such terrain or attach their dog to a safety lead. Deep snow can also have a serious effect on both dogs and their handlers in terms of slowing their progress and increasing energy expenditure. Depending on the type of snow, dogs can suffer a serious balling-up of snow on their bellies. This adds to the weight they have to carry, makes it very difficult to move and is extremely difficult to remove — more often than not, the snow/ice has to be thawed in a warm room before it can be removed.

In all instances of inclement weather, handlers are extremely sensitive to the negative effects on their dog, and more than capable of dealing with potential problems. We're confident that the vast majority of handlers always put the health, comfort and safety of their dog first and only consider their own plight once they have their dog sorted. Indeed, it's worth noting here again a point we've made before about the relationship between handlers and their dogs and in particular the handlers ability to 'read' their dog's behaviour when in search mode. We believe this extends to the skill of handlers to perceive much more about their dog than their searching capability. Handlers are highly competent in detecting when their dog is unwell, unfit, distressed, anxious, fatigued, hungry, disinterested, injured and so on. This is all part of the 'skill package' that makes for a good dog team.

Search and rescue dogs are typically more active than their non-working counterparts. Not only do they get their daily walks, they're also active during training and operational work. This additional workload — which is regular and sometimes intense — means that they're probably much fitter than the average domestic pet. This raises questions about whether they should receive additional or special physical training/exercise or special diets. There appears to have been very little research on this subject, but informed opinion suggests it is unnecessary to provide additional training — in the way you might for a competitive sportsman. Dogs improve their fitness as they exercise on a gradual basis and acquire a level, which is commensurate with the demands placed on them. Over time they become used to working long and hard without showing any adverse signs. This is certainly the case with working farm dogs. All they require following a hard exercise is a well-deserved rest and a decent-sized meal. For a dog that is fit and well fed, working for a long time shouldn't cause any problems, although we did hear of one case where a dog was working very hard for several hours and suddenly collapsed. The handler thought it had broken a leg as it was impossible to encourage the dog to stand up. However, it turned out the dog was not injured but suffering from a very low blood-sugar level. It had simply run out of energy and couldn't move. The handler gave it a sachet of food and the dog very quickly recovered, although its work for the rest of the day was terminated! Various dog food companies, of course, sponsor several of the associations so handlers are assured their dog receives food that is nutritious and well balanced.

Mark Hogarth was the training coordinator for SARDA Southern Scotland. He is also a qualified handler with a black and white English Spaniel. In October 2009, Mark and his trainee dog Coco, a chocolate-coloured cocker spaniel, were undergoing their bi-annual assessment in the Trossachs in Central Scotland. The area used for assessment is typically rough, boulder-strewn and sprinkled with numerous small crags and buttresses that rise to a height of around 30 metres. Mark and Coco were having a good day until Coco decided to have a tussle with gravity.

'After having been given my search area by the two assessors, I went away, looked at the area and planned a search strategy. This involved judging the strength and direction of the wind, any difficult parts and also identifying useful landmarks in the area. After a few minutes' consideration I returned to the assessors and described my plan of action. This is very important as it's part of the overall assessment.

'I walked a few yards into the area and tried to put on Coco's working jacket. As usual this was a struggle, as he knew he was about to work and he becomes really excited. Anyone who knows spaniels will recognise this built-in work factor that dominates their lives. On the command 'Find him!' I sent him off and away he shot at breakneck speed, barking madly. After a quick radio check we settled into our mode of working. It was a beautiful, warm sunny day, Coco was working well and I found myself relaxing about the assessment — I was actually beginning to enjoy myself.

'My plan had been to work the left hand side of the area first, taking out a strip of land between two gullies. This involved an ascent of about 500 metres to get me to the top of the area. This is normal practice and it gets the hard work of gaining height out of the way first.

'In the glen that day, another five assessment areas were being used at the same time. As I made my way up to the top, my radio crackled to life with news that other handlers had found their first body. This always creates a sensation of unease and you find yourself asking the question 'Why haven't I found yet, have I missed someone?' But I quickly resumed my own task and made my way along the upper boundary of my area. Scent always rises up and over a ridge so having reached the top left hand edge I started to move to the right hand side of the area. This would take out a strip of land about 100 metres-wide below the top boundary.

'As I crossed the top of a large crag, Coco's body language changed and I knew he had picked up the scent of a body. I encouraged him and he began criss-crossing the top of the crag. I was expecting him to make his way down the side of the crag to where, hopefully, the body was. I turned away from the crag to shield my radio microphone from the wind to tell the assessors that Coco was showing interest and I would work him down the crag. This was critical as it meant a change to my search strategy. Immediately one of the assessors came on the radio to say that Coco had fallen. I turned around and Coco had vanished. The assessor then came back on the radio and said that Coco was on his feet and running. When I asked for confirmation about the fall I received a definite: 'That's an affirm.'

'By now the radio was full of chatter and it was clear there was some confusion as to whether it was a dog or handler that had fallen. I quickly found a grass chute splitting the steep rock face and followed it down to the bottom of the crag. Looking around I spotted Coco standing on top of a boulder. Rushing over to him he started to wag his tail, but he wasn't moving. There was a trail of blood below him on the boulder.

'After what seemed an eternity, I managed to collect myself and shift into first aid mode. It wasn't easy trying to examine him — all Coco wanted to do was cuddle into me. But I needed to be firm and methodical with him. Both his eyes were bloodshot and there were two puncture wounds, still bleeding, on his top lip. Fur was missing from his chest and there was some superficial grazing. So far, so good! I checked his legs for any deformities and they all appeared okay.

'The assessors were now asking about Coco and I told them he looked alright but I was worried about internal injuries. I tried to get him to walk but he wouldn't. So I picked him up and started to descend the difficult ground below the crag. People were asking if I wanted any help as I was stumbling and falling over. I agreed and sat down to wait. I turned and looked back up the crag. I couldn't believe that he had fallen so far and yet looked to be alright. I

CLOCKWISE FROM ABOVE: COCO RELAXING WITH HANDLER MARK HOGARTH © SARDA SOUTHERN SCOTLAND; THE SCENE OF COCO'S FALL © BOB SHARP; COCO AND KYLE © PETER SANDGROUND.

picked him up again and set off but within a few metres, I fell over and nearly landed on top of him. I think we both decided that carrying Coco was not a good idea and we set off again, this time with Coco walking very slowly and stiffly behind me — but at least he was walking.

'Fortunately, Kenny, who is a trainee handler acting as a body on the day, is a qualified vet and he started to make his way quickly to join us. Coco and I continued to move down very slowly before being met by another dog handler. Calum described the extent of Coco's fall. He had fallen head first, some ten to fifteen metres onto a ledge, then somersaulted another 30 to 40 metres to the bottom of the crag. He then got up and ran to the boulder where I had found him. Calum then proclaimed that both assessors were in agreement Coco had scored ten out of ten for artistic merit! Typical mountain rescue black humour but, as always, it eased the situation! We tried to carry Coco using a jacket as a makeshift stretcher but he wasn't happy about this and preferred to walk.

'We were met by Kenny who gave Coco a thorough examination. He confirmed my early diagnosis and suggested medication and then observation for the next couple of hours to see if there were any internal injuries. We made our way back to the car. My other search dog Kyle was in the car so I let him out and the two dogs wandered away together as if for a quiet chat.

'A short while later I put them both together in the car. As I was driving away from the search area to find a quiet spot, it suddenly hit me that Coco could have died. The worst thing about it all was that it would have been me that had caused it. It was me who was training him to do what I

enjoyed. At that point all I could think of was that I was going to pack it all in and resign from SARDA. I took both dogs to a sunny spot where we could watch another dog and handler working. Whilst chatting to my friends it was pointed out to me that lots of accidents could have happened to Coco during his time as a search dog. Also, I should recall the enjoyment he got out of it. I had been working Kyle, as a qualified search dog, for six years and he had only ever suffered from a cut pad, but had acquired sprained legs from chasing tennis balls in the park and cut his tongue from fetching sticks. I looked over towards Coco, lying on his back in the sun being fussed over by everybody and enjoying the attention. I began to reason that if he hadn't suffered any injury then maybe we should continue our work training to become a qualified dog team.

'I now felt much better about the situation and, after an hour or so, we started to make our way back to the car and home. As we approached the cars we met up with another handler and his dog carrying his favourite toy. Without any thought about his recent ordeal, Coco, in his usual friendly manner, went up to the dog who immediately turned on Coco. He let out a yelp and ran back to me. Almost immediately, a mountain biker came speeding by and nearly ran him over. As I looked down into his two bloodshot eyes, I couldn't help but think that it just wasn't Coco's day!'

Mark monitored Coco for several days and weeks following his adventure with the crag but, happily, Coco suffered no long-term injury. Mark rested him for a week before giving him the all clear. In contrast, Mark himself is still a bag of nerves and

anxious whenever Coco is given freedom at top speed above steep ground!

Just before Coco tumbled over the steep crag, he had picked up the scent of the person he and Mark were trying to find. Mark had no idea where the person was, but Coco had used his extraordinary sense of smell to locate the person's scent. Of course, this is the reason we use dogs to locate missing persons. Their incredible ability to detect the faintest of wind-borne smells puts them in a league of their own, and certainly more capable than any man-made robot designed to smell. But, what makes a dog's sense of smell so much more sensitive and efficient than our own and how do smells travel in the wind? A number of well-held myths persist about the movement of smells over the terrain. Perhaps we can help dispel a few.

Doggie Tales

BANNED FROM THE CORNER SHOP...
DIDN'T LIKE SHOPPING THERE ANYWAY...

Yesterday, I was at my local corner shop buying a large bag of chews for my loyal pet. I'm in the checkout queue when a woman behind me asks if I have a dog. What a stupid question. Did she think I had an elephant? So, since I'm retired and have little to do, on impulse I told her that no, I don't have a dog, but was starting the 'Dog Chew Diet' again. I quickly added that I probably shouldn't, because I ended up in hospital last time.

I lost two stone and I woke up in intensive care with tubes coming out of most of my every orifice and IVs in both arms.

I explained it was essentially a perfect diet — the way it works is, you load your pockets with chews, then simply eat one or two every time you feel hungry.

I have to mention here that practically everyone else in the queue was now enthralled with my story. Horrified, the woman asked whether I'd ended up in intensive care because the dog food poisoned me. I told her no (pause for comic effect) I'd just stepped off a curb to sniff an Irish Setter's bum and a car hit us both.

I thought the guy behind her was going to have a heart attack he was laughing so hard.

Perhaps not surprisingly, I'm now banned from the corner shop.

GIVE ME A BREAK...

An older, tired-looking collie wandered into my garden. I could tell from his collar and well-fed belly that he had a home and was well taken care of. He calmly came over to me. I gave him a few pats on his head then he followed me across the garden, onto the patio and curled up and fell asleep.

An hour later, he went to the garden gate, and I let him out. The next day he was back, greeted me in the garden, walked across to the patio and resumed his spot next to the chair and again slept for about an hour. This continued off and on for several weeks.

Curious, I pinned a note to his collar: 'I would like to find out who the owner of this wonderful sweet dog is and ask if you are aware that almost every afternoon your dog comes to my house for a nap.'

The next day he arrived for his nap, with a different note pinned to his collar: 'He lives in a home with six children, two under the age of three — he's trying to catch up on his sleep. Can I come with him tomorrow?'

SEARCH DOG MEG HAVING FUN © PETER SANDGROUND.

6 The nose knows

'Ask a person which sense they feel is the most important – the one they would least like to lose. They will invariably reply sight. Ask a dog which is their most important sense and they'll tell you it is smell!' Ralph Haber

The senses are our windows on the world. Without them we'd never know what was happening around us or, for that matter, within us. But what senses do we have and are some more important than others? Vision is obvious. So too is hearing, taste, smell and touch. These are the five classic senses. And, whilst each of these is physically very different, they can provide the same kind of information. How do we know this? Imagine a pig had walked into your living room. How would you know it was a pig? You'd undoubtedly look at it and surmise from its shape that it was a pig. You might listen to its snorts and grunts and these would indicate with confidence that it was a pig. Or you might decide to close your eyes, get close, and run your hands over the contours of its body. This might take some time but it would undoubtedly let you know it was a pig. Again, with your eyes closed and hands cupped over your ears, you might smell that it was a pig — they have a very strong odour, which is quite unmistakable. Which leaves one more sense: taste. Now, it's highly unlikely you would do this, but imagine taking a

bite. If you had the inclination and survived the onslaught from what would now be a very angry pig, then we're sure the taste in your mouth would tell you it was a pig! So, in a way, all your senses provide the same kind of information about the world, albeit in different ways and with differing levels of accuracy or precision. Integration of the senses like this helps give a full picture of the world in which we live and also provides compensation if one sense goes down.

But it's possible to add a few more to the list. These would certainly include pain as well as kinaesthesis and orientation. Kinaesthesis tells you about limb movement and how your limbs articulate in relation to one another. If you hold your arms out wide in an attempt to keep them horizontal, it is the sensory receptors in your joints that tell you where your arms are. The labyrinth of your inner ear tells you whether you are upright, lying down, rotating, accelerating and so on. And dogs have a highly specialised sense of movement and balance as reflected in their capacity to move quickly and effortlessly across broken ground.

Why is scent important? In a nutshell, dogs are a superb asset in the search for people missing in the outdoor environment because of the speed and efficiency with which they can operate. They do this by picking up the airborne scent arising from that person and then leading their handler to its source. All humans release groups or rafts of dead skin cells, which are carried away in the wind. Their concentration depends on a variety of factors including wind speed, any turbulence in the air and the distance the cells have been carried, and scent also diminishes with increasing distance or the wind speed.

The notion of a 'scent cone' has been used to describe the flow of rafts from a person. It suggests that scent disperses in a uniform manner. We're not sure it happens quite like this and suspect that dispersal is fragmented and dictated by even small aberrations in the terrain. Research has shown that the air turbulence at ground level can be quite pronounced with extreme variations in wind speed just a metre or so above the surface. The image on the following page is a clear illustration

FACING PAGE: **CLOSE UP OF A DOG'S NOSE** © PETER SANDGROUND.

of this, and suggests to us that a better description is the word 'plume' rather than 'cone'. Under these conditions, the challenge for the dog is to detect very low concentrations of scent, which may be moving in a rather complicated manner, often across complex terrain and in poor weather conditions.

Scent and smell

Now, we could embark upon a full scientific treatise of this subject and talk about the chemical composition of scent, the fine anatomy of a dog's nose, the histology of scent detection sensors and the physiology of scent detection. Aspirant handlers, and even well-seasoned dog handlers, might wish to agonise at length about the minutiae of scent characteristics but there are numerous other sources on the subject — some listed in the appendix. What we wish to do is demonstrate the key features relevant to a wilderness search dog handler, in the simplest manner possible.

For humans, the sense of smell or olfaction enables us to interpret odours, which exist in the surrounding air. Smell is often referred to as a 'distant receptor' because it allows us to make contact with the world without physically touching it. Vision is another example. The perception

TOP: SKIN RAFTS ARE LESS DENSELY POPULATED, FURTHER AWAY FROM THE PERSON © JUDY WHITESIDE.
ABOVE: A VERY COLD DAY WHERE THE GROUND WAS FROZEN AND THERE WAS NO DETECTABLE WIND — NOTE THE NON-UNIFORM NATURE OF THE SMOKE'S DISTRIBUTION AND THE PLUME (NOT CONE) SHAPE © BILL JENNISON.

of a scent is a two-stage process. First there is the physiological part, which is the detection of compounds by receptors in the nose. Second is the interpretation by the individual of the scent. Perception is an individual reaction, related to a wide variety of things including a person's gender, age, state of health and experience. It provides information about the ingredients of the substance or object emitting the scent — garden roses, roast beef cooking in the oven, ammonia — but that may not be the sole purpose. Products such as soaps and perfumes are designed simply to evoke an emotional response and don't require the individual to analyse their chemical origin! What, we wonder, does a dog think when it picks up the scent of a person? Does it say to itself, 'Missing human that has to be found' or simply 'My favourite toy is not far away'? — more likely the latter.

Smell is a powerful sense, capable of evoking very early memories, even from childhood — maybe even as distant as 50 years previously. It's relatively highly developed in newborns, enabling them to root for milk, although it is very quickly overtaken within a few months of life by the other senses, particularly vision. As adults, we're able to perceive many different kinds of smell, each of which can generate different feelings, sensations and behaviours. Some are strong and others weak. Some may be pleasant and others less so and a variety of words are used to define different categories. For example, the terms 'fragrance', 'scent' and 'aroma' are used to describe pleasant odours. Many people feel happiness when smelling roses or garden wallflowers. In contrast, words such as 'reek', 'stench' and 'putrid' are used to describe unpleasant odours.

Smells such as ammonia or hydrogen sulphide are noxious and potentially harmful and these are not only perceived as unpleasant, but often elicit defensive behaviours such as holding the nose or moving away from the source.

In the world of search dogs, the word 'scent' is typically used to describe the smell or odour given off by people — those rafts of dead skin cells. It's a combination of molecules/particles given off by an object that can be detected by the olfactory system of an animal or human. Scent has a number of key characteristics. It is made up of chemical compounds with low molecular weight. It can be detected by the olfactory system and therefore evokes a neural response. It is volatile and appears as a gas or vapour. And it is water and lipid soluble (dissolves in fat) both of which are essential to enable detection by the olfactory system.

Human scent is critical to the work of a search dog and our bodies (both internally and externally) are clearly at its source. Scent is specific to the individual — except in the case of identical twins — because the chemical composition for each of us has a unique profile. This is because the molecules that make up our scent are determined by a wide variety of factors. They include the bacteria that live on us, our diet, bodily secretions from sweat glands, dead cells or rafts shed from our skin, the soaps or cosmetics we use and our lifestyle, diet, clothing and exercise levels, as well as genetic and environmental factors. Considering that each of these can vary in a multitude of ways it's not surprising the overall profile for every person is different and unique. Of all these factors, the main ingredients of

human scent are the bacteria acting on the dead cells. Bacterial action causes cells to break down into amino acids which, in turn, are broken down into chemicals such as ammonia, methane and hydrogen sulphide. These clearly have characteristic odours which, in large quantities, are easily perceived by humans.

People shed bacteria-laden dead skin cells, as well as cells from the respiratory and the digestive tracts, all the time. It's been estimated we each shed 40,000 dead cells every minute and up to 70% of household dust is composed of dead skin cells. Some skin rafts are readily visible to the naked eye, especially on dark, rough fabrics rubbed against the skin. However, rafts are too big for the olfactory sense to identify. It's the molecules carried by these rafts of cells that dogs detect. Because a person's body temperature is typically higher than that of their environment, the skin rafts and molecules move from the body by convection and consequently leave the body by air currents.

One member of SARDA England has carried out an interesting study in the dog's ability to pick up a scent from human hair alone. A sample of hair (which might have been up to a year old) was taken from a hairdressing salon and used to replace the body. The hair was packed in a mesh bag and placed on the ground. Every dog that was tested picked up the scent and indicated to their handler, albeit not as enthusiastic as usual, confirming that — whatever the particular composition of human scent — dogs can detect it in very small quantities and low levels of concentration. This is the key to their remarkable ability to locate people using smell alone.

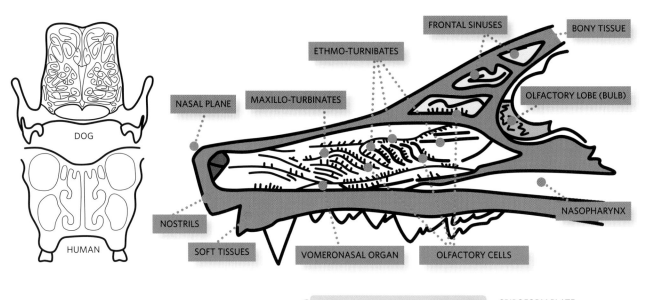

FRONTAL SINUSES

BONY TISSUE

ETHMO-TURNIBATES

OLFACTORY LOBE (BULB)

NASAL PLANE

MAXILLO-TURBINATES

DOG

HUMAN

NOSTRILS

NASOPHARYNX

SOFT TISSUES

VOMERONASAL ORGAN

OLFACTORY CELLS

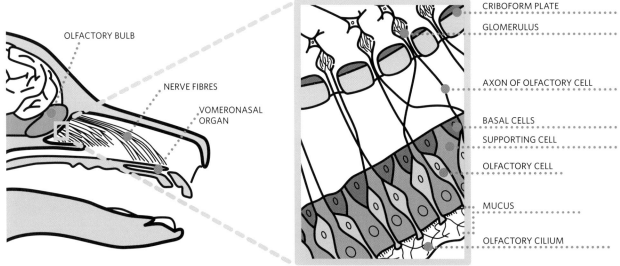

OLFACTORY BULB

NERVE FIBRES

VOMERONASAL ORGAN

CRIBOFORM PLATE

GLOMERULUS

AXON OF OLFACTORY CELL

BASAL CELLS

SUPPORTING CELL

OLFACTORY CELL

MUCUS

OLFACTORY CILIUM

TOP LEFT: CROSS SECTION OF THE POSTERIOR PART OF THE NOSE IN THE DOG AND THE HUMAN. THE LABRYNTHINE FOLDS OF THE ETHMOID TURBINATE BONES AND THE ADJACENT CARTILAGINOUS STRUCTURES IN DOGS PROVIDE THE SENSORY EPITHELIUM WITH A VERY LARGE SURFACE AREA.
TOP RIGHT: CROSS SECTION OF THE ANATOMY OF A DOG'S NOSE: THE OLFACTORY CELLS ARE PRIMARY SENSORY CELLS EQUIPPED WITH AXONS FORMING SYNAPSES WITH NEURONS (MITRAL CELLS) IN THE OLFACTORY LOBE.   ABOVE: A LARGE NUMBER OF OLFACTORY CELLS FORM SYNAPSES WITH A SINGLE MITRAL CELL IN A TUFT OF NERVE ENDINGS CALLED A GLOMERULUS. ILLUSTRATIONS © JUDY WHITESIDE

The olfactory system in dogs

When a person goes for a leisurely stroll in the countryside their prime sense is sight — they focus on their visual surroundings. In contrast, a dog is less interested in what it sees and much more focused on what it smells. Indeed, a person's brain is dominated by the visual cortex (part of the convoluted outer layer of the brain), whereas the olfactory cortex dominates a dog's brain. Olfaction is a dog's primary special sense and serves as a key source of information about the outside world. It enables them to find food, navigate the terrain, communicate with each other and find sexual partners. The olfactory bulb, which is a central part of the olfactory cortex, is physically 40 times larger in dogs compared to humans. It's been suggested that the proportion of a dog's brain that specifically deals with scent and scent detection varies from about twelve to 33 per cent. And about half of the dog's internal nose area contains cells dedicated to scent detection. So, given their underlying physiology, it's not surprising that dogs live in a world of scent. It's a world humans rarely come into contact with. A dog's sense of taste and smell are also closely related — so much so that they gain more information about food from its smell than from its taste.

The anatomy and physiology of a dog's olfactory system is very complex. Like a human's, it consists of soft tissue, bones and nervous tissue. The outer, hairless part of a dog's nose is called the nasal plane and it houses the nostrils (or nares) which are used for inhaling air and odours. Moisture on the surface of the dog's nose helps dissolve scent molecules in the air. When a dog inhales, the nostril openings widen and direct air into the nasal chamber where most of the olfactory receptor cells are located. Just inside the nasal chamber, a structure called the alar fold (not in the diagram) opens, to allow air into the upper nasal passages. When the dog exhales, the alar fold closes off the upper nasal passages and pushes air down and out of slits on the side of the nose. This prevents new scent being flushed from the nose, thus improving the dog's capacity to detect weak scents.

The nasal chamber houses a number of bony ridges called turbinates. The turbinates capture and delay the movement of air as it passes through the chamber. What this does is maximise the amount of time the receptor cells react with the scent molecules, increasing the dog's sensitivity to smell. The labyrinth-like structure of the turbinate bones is covered in mucous membranes that are home to the olfactory receptor cells or sensory epithelium. These are responsible for detecting the air containing the scent molecules. On first entering the nasal cavity, the air meets the maxillary turbinates which create turbulence and moisten the air. This allows the scent molecules to dissolve and come into contact with the receptor parts of the olfactory detection cells. The maximillary turbinates are less rich in receptor cells than the ethmoturbinates that are located further back in the cavity. These fill around half of the nasal chambers and have the greatest concentration of receptors. When a dog sniffs, air is forced back over the ethmoturbinates and along the sinus openings where mucous membranes enclosing receptor cells also play a part in scent detection.

In addition to the turbinates and associated receptor cells, a dog's nose also contains a further olfactory chamber called the vomeronasal organ that is rich in olfactory receptor cells. It starts near the front of the nose and runs along the floor of the nasal cavity. All of the olfactory receptor cells contained within the various nasal chambers are connected via the olfactory nerves to the olfactory lobe in the brain where information is decoded to give the dog its sense of smell. Many cells have a dedicated nerve fibre passing to the olfactory lobe in the dog's brain and this is one feature that makes a dog's sense of smell so acute. One thing a dog does to

CLOSE-UPS OF THE NASAL PLANE AND NOSTRILS, MODELLED BY ABIE © BOB SHARP.

enhance its scenting capability is to hold its breathing and sniff rapidly — at a rate of up to 200 sniffs per minute. Further, by exhaling through their mouth and turning their head towards the wind, they maintain a continuous flow of air through their nose for long periods of time. So, by disrupting the normal breathing pattern through a series of rapid, short inhalations and exhalations, it allows scent molecules that are unrecognised in a single sniff to accumulate (the alar fold coming into play), and these interact with the olfactory receptors to maximise scent recognition.

But how do dogs detect the direction of scent? Well, they use their nose again, but in a completely different manner to detecting scent itself. It's all down to their wet nose. It's often thought that a dog with a wet nose is a healthy dog and vice-versa, and there's some truth to this. It transpires a healthy dog spends more time licking its nose compared to one that is unhealthy, but a dog with a dry nose is not necessarily unhealthy. The outer skin of a dog's nose contains cold receptors, which are sensitive to cooling. As the air moves across a dog's nose, it cools the moisture at the point of contact (the so-called wind chill factor). This tells the dog the direction of flow. A good analogy is when a person wets their finger to detect airflow. The part of the finger that feels cold points into the wind.

Interestingly, breeds of dog with long muzzles have more scent receptors than those with short noses. For example, a German Shepherd has twice as many receptor cells compared to a dachshund. Dogs such as bloodhounds, specially bred for scent work, have the added advantage of long ears and facial features including numerous wrinkles, which help to gather

scent. It's been calculated that a dog's sense of smell is so sensitive, it can detect a single drop of blood in 55 gallons of water. It is estimated that dogs can discriminate odours at concentrations nearly 100 million times lower than humans can. This superior sense of smell is reflected in the relative number of receptor cells dedicated to smell (around 220 million receptor cells in a dog's nose but only five million in humans), as well as the size of the olfactory system dedicated to interacting with scent molecules (four times larger than in humans). If this isn't remarkable enough, a dog can also generalise scents.

Wilderness air-scenting search dogs are trained to detect and follow any human scent they come across rather than detecting the scent of one particular person (unless trailing). So, whilst their training involves searching for and locating only a relatively small number of different people, they're still capable of picking up the scent of someone they've never ever come across before. This is the whole point of using air-scenting dogs. Whether it's a real rescue, a training session or even an assessment, it doesn't matter that the dog has never encountered the casualty or body before. It is still able to extract, from the windborne scent, characteristics that indicate the source is human. It's also the reason why dogs are able to work well in recently contaminated areas. This is most noticeable during an assessment where the same areas will have been used for two or three consecutive days. Dogs can, after a short period of time, disregard the scent of the searchers which means that, when required, several dogs can be used simultaneously in a line search.

The effect of weather and terrain on scent

If you throw an object such as a ball or frisbee for a dog to retrieve, it will run in the direction it sees the object thrown and will probably anticipate direction from the person's arm or body movements. If the object is out of sight when it lands, the dog will use airborne scent from the object to home in. If there is no wind then the dog may move in the general direction but then move left or right, often very near to the object, in an attempt to find it. It may even display exaggerated sniffing behaviour to pick up any faint smells to help it locate the object. The presence or absence of wind is absolutely critical to the dog's ability to find the object or a person. It's not surprising, therefore, that dog handlers are obsessed with wind and talk about it with great authority! Indeed, the absence of wind is often cited as the main reason a dog fails to find the missing person.

The flow of air, and hence the movement of scent, is very important for handlers to understand if they wish to give their dog the best opportunity of finding a missing person. Unfortunately, predicting airflow (like meteorology as a whole) is not simple and numerous factors, including the prevailing weather and the terrain, affect the flow of air across the ground. Much is said about scent cones, dead areas, dumping and air movement, but there is little documented evidence to support

informed wisdom. On occasions, unexpected things take place, which question some of the key assumptions. For example, there are instances when dogs strike from what is believed to be an upwind location and other times when a dog is virtually next to the body, but shows no sign of indicating. There have even been instances of staged demonstrations when a handler knows the direction of scent, positions their dog for a find, but the dog fails.

To provide a more objective slant on this subject, we undertook a short investigation using visible smoke to assess the movement of air across different types of terrain, mindful that smoke may not necessarily have the same physical properties as human scent. This was borne out through consultation with 'smoke' suppliers who indicated that smoke with the same properties as airborne human scent is extremely difficult to manufacture. Our best option was to use out-of-date orange marker smokes used by mountain rescue teams for communicating with helicopters. Manufactured smoke is neither physically nor chemically the same as airborne human scent. It is heavier, coloured, produced in a high concentration and is forced out of a smoke generator with only a two to three minute production period. We were fortunate to gain access to a military training area that included large

areas of open moorland and forest. Testing took place on a number of clear days in September when the wind speed varied from calm to gentle breeze. We placed smoke canisters in a variety of different locations then, once these were ignited, retreated to observe and photograph what happened.

Many factors such as air pressure, precipitation, cloud cover, temperature and wind determine the weather and its effect on people, but wind is critical for search dogs and handlers. Handlers are not especially interested in how wind moves on a global basis, but understanding wind movement, speed and direction at a local level is more valuable in helping them deploy their dog effectively.

Wind is directly related to air pressure. If there is a difference in pressure between two locations then air flows between those locations. If there is no pressure differential then there is no wind. So synoptic charts, which focus on areas of low and high pressure and describe the changing patterns of air pressure across a given region, are a vital source of information in helping to understand wind direction.

With an area of low pressure — often called a depression — the air circulates around and inwards in an anticlockwise direction. The weather associated with a depression tends to be changeable with

TOP LEFT: ROUGH GROUND ON A WARM, DRY DAY WITH A GENTLE BREEZE — NOTE HOW QUICKLY THE SMOKE BEGINS TO RISE.   TOP RIGHT: TAKEN MID MORNING ON AN OTHERWISE STILL DAY, THE SMOKE RISES UP THE HILLSIDE.   ABOVE LEFT: A FREEZING COLD DAY WITH FROZEN GROUND WITH NO DETECTABLE AIR MOVEMENT IN THE WOOD YET THE SMOKE SHOW THE PRESENCE OF AN AIR FLOW.   ABOVE RIGHT: THE MOVEMENT OF SMOKE FROM A GULLY 3M DEEP ON A VERY COLD DAY SUGGESTS THAT THE DOG COULD RUN ALONG THE EDGE OF THE GULLY AND STILL PICK UP THE SCENT FROM THE BOTTOM © BILL JENNISON.

TOP LEFT: COMPARE THIS SMOKE FROM DENSE WOODLAND WITH SMOKE FROM THINNED WOODLAND.   TOP RIGHT: LATE AFTERNOON ON AN OTHERWISE STILL DAY WHICH SHOWS SMOKE EXITING FROM A WOOD, ACROSS A TRACK AND DOWN A SMALL VALLEY — SMOKE COULD BE SEEN FOLLOWING THE VALLEY FOR OVER 500 METRES.
ABOVE LEFT: A WARM DRY DAY, WITH A GENTLE BREEZE — SMOKE RISES FROM A GULLY THREE METRES DEEP. WATER IN THE BURN IS RUNNING FROM RIGHT TO LEFT YET THE SMOKE IS MOVING LEFT TO RIGHT!   ABOVE RIGHT: APPEARANCE OF SMOKE PLUME OVER A GREATER DISTANCE. © BILL JENNISON.

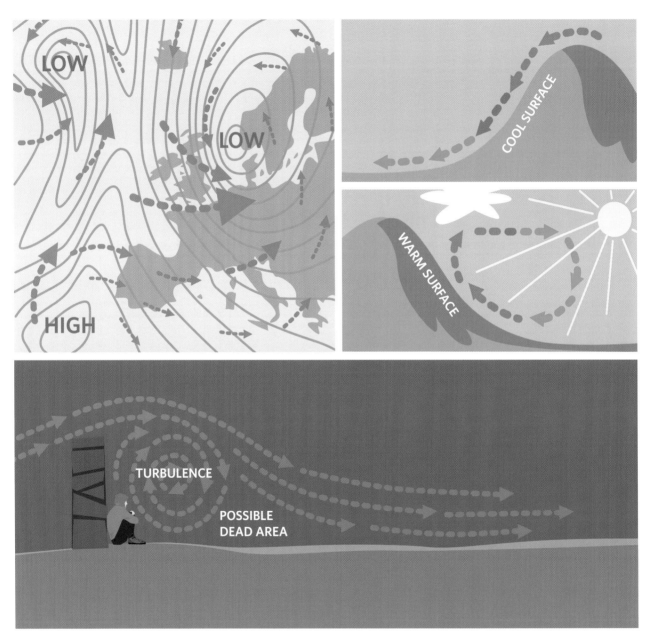

TOP LEFT: SCHEMATIC SHOWS HOW WIND DIRECTION RELATES TO PRESSURE. TOP RIGHT: THE DOWNWARD FLOW OF KATABATIC WINDS. MIDDLE RIGHT: THE UPWARD FLOW OF ANABATIC WINDS. ABOVE: GROUND OBSTACLES SUCH AS WALLS MAY GENERATE 'DEAD' AREAS OF MOVEMENT. ILLUSTRATIONS © JUDY WHITESIDE varying levels of precipitation, temperature, wind strength and direction. This causes problems, as handlers need to keep an eye on changes to make adjustments to how they deploy their dog. If a search is being conducted in an area of low pressure, the handler might expect changes in wind speed and direction over the course of a few hours. An area of low pressure with associated warm and cold fronts passing through the area would typically result in winds that change direction from the southwest to the west and then to the northwest. As the cold front passes the area, wind speed would pick up and air temperature would drop. Fronts can appear very quickly — often within minutes — resulting in rapidly changing conditions of which handlers need to be mindful. The opposite is true for an area of high pressure or anticyclone. Here the air circulates clockwise and the associated weather is generally stable for long periods. High pressure presents other problems. For example, if a search is taking place at the centre of an area of high pressure, handlers should expect little or no wind and perhaps little change over a period of hours. So whilst high pressure typically heralds favourable weather conditions, it is unhelpful for searching since dogs find it very difficult, if not impossible, to detect airborne scent in still conditions.

Most mountain rescue personnel are familiar with synoptic charts and their interpretation. Obviously handlers cannot alter the weather or the search location, or choose to carry out their search on another day, but the ability to forecast the weather from a synoptic chart — especially characteristics of the wind — puts them in a good position to fully exploit their dog's air scenting capabilities. At the very least it helps them recognise that, in some conditions, using their dog may require a slightly different strategy.

Terrain too plays a role in determining how a dog is worked, not just from a safety and workload point of view, but also how it affects air flow and scent behaviour. There are a number of general principles that help in the understanding of the terrain and how it affects airflow but two in particular are key. Firstly, as air passes over the tops of hills and mountains, it is effectively squeezed between the high ground and the upper layers of air. As a consequence, it accelerates through the narrower gap and wind speed increases. Similarly, when it is squeezed through valleys and across the saddles or cols it also accelerates and therefore moves faster. So, saddles and summits tend to be much windier than the surrounding countryside as the air is funnelled through a narrower space. The same applies as air passes through any kind of narrow gap such as the space between two large boulders. To give an idea of the magnitude of this effect, it has been calculated that — all other factors being equal — wind speed on the summit of a 900 metre mountain is about three times what it is at the mountain's base.

Secondly, the pattern of air movement changes over a 24-hour period. During the day, hills and mountain tops are warmed by the sun, which in turn heats the air just above it. Because the air over the mountain top is warmer than the air at a similar altitude around, a lower pressure region is created into which the air at the bottom of the slope is pulled upwards through convection which results in a general flow of air up the mountainside. Wind which blows up mountainsides is anabatic — very common on hot, cloudless summer days. So, even in the absence of a true wind, anabatic convection currents tend to produce a gentle uphill breeze. For this reason, theoretically, during the day, dogs are best used to search at the tops of hills or ridges, where they can pick up any scent rising from the valleys below.

By night, a temperature reversal sets in when cold, dense air sinks downhill as a shallow weak katabatic wind. So — also theoretically — at night time, dogs are best deployed lower down mountainsides or in valleys where they can take advantage of descending scent. Katabatic winds can become dammed up behind crags, large boulders and forest edges to create areas of cold, stale air so a missing person located in one of these positions might be difficult for a dog to detect, as the person's scent may stay trapped in the pool. Of course, whilst it is theoretically desirable to use dogs on ridges during the day and lower down at night, this isn't always practical. Searching for a missing person is more likely to be an emergency where the police want dog handlers to react immediately with little choice to work in ideal conditions. Dog teams may not have the luxury of searching with the wind to their advantage. In fact, they often have to search with the wind at their backs or in gusting and variable wind directions. Their only option may be to put their dog across the wind as best as possible and into situations where they have the greatest possibility of lifting a scent.

Knowledge of anabatic and katabatic airflow is a general aid to helping handlers place their dog in the best position but air movement is determined by many other

Doggie Tales
BONNIES FIRST FIND

German Shepherds were once the breed of choice in SARDA, much less today, but John Coombs, of Edale MRT in the Peak District, is undoubtedly a fan. With Bonnie and Biscuit – both German Shepherds – he can count a number of successful dog finds during his long career as a handler.

Bonnie passed away in 2006, aged thirteen, with fourteen finds to her credit but Biscuit continues the family tradition, with more than seven finds to her name as we write. The story of Bonnie's first find perfectly demonstrates the importance of her innate sense of smell during a search in poor conditions.

Derbyshire Police received a mobile phone call at around seven in the evening. Two walkers and their dog had been overtaken by darkness on Kinder Scout in the Peak District National Park. They had no torch and had alerted the police in an effort to prevent a major search being mounted. In the best of conditions, Kinder Scout is acknowledged as wild and exposed. Not the sort of place you would want to be lost in darkness with a storm brewing. Richard Gilbert, in his *200*

Challenge Walks in Britain and Ireland gives out a word of warning to those setting out in winter '...darkness falls quickly and the deep groughs and oozing bogs make progress imperceptible. The Kinder plateau, at over 630 metres, is not the place to be benighted. Accurate compass work is imperative and a wide margin of safety must be allowed.'

It was in this context that Edale MRT decided to mobilise a small party to escort the walkers to safety. Five members, including the team leader, one of the team's doctors and John with Bonnie, set out from Grindsbrook Booth. The walkers had described their location as the edge path of the main Kinder Scout plateau, at a point where a small stream falls over the crags into Grindsbrook, about four kilometres

from the start point and a climb of 300 metres. The group searched towards the location in three pairs, Bonnie and John following about 500 metres behind the doctor and his companion along the edge path, which runs right round the plateau at an altitude of 600 metres. By the time they reached the plateau, the forecasted storm had arrived with a vengeance.

The familiar path quickly transformed into a trench of liquid mud but, as the human search party struggled against gale force winds and visibility at just 30 metres, Bonnie appeared unconcerned by the conditions, using the wind to her advantage. She appeared and disappeared in the mist as she quartered the moor to the north of the path. By nine o'clock, all six members of the search team met near the reported position of the two walkers, having found nothing. By this time, radio conversation with Edale base revealed that the missing persons' mobile battery was now flat. The rest of the Edale team were called out, including another dog handler and his dog, Haggis. The situation was now developing into a serious incident.

Conditions were too severe for Bonnie and John to continue working alone, so another member joined the pair as they began a new search pattern westward across the moor towards Crowden Tower. They made good progress by keeping off the boggy path and out of the peat hags. Five hundred metres on, they heard shouts and a distress whistle. Bonnie pricked up her ears and disappeared, the lightstick around her neck bouncing away into the darkness. The shouts and whistles increased so John moved quickly after her. Within minutes, Bonnie came running back to indicate her find. The group were soon together and shaking hands. A flare was fired and a radio message sent to base to indicate all was well. One of the walkers had apparently twisted his knee earlier in the day. To carry him off by stretcher would have extended the rescue by another four or five hours. Instead, he bravely limped off with the aid of two walking poles. The party finally arrived at base an hour later where a welcome was waiting for the missing walkers and Bonnie — fresh from her first find.

factors, not least of which is the texture or nature of the ground. Planted fields, meadows and water, for example, tend to retain heat and generate a general downward flow of air. In contrast, sandy areas, ploughed fields and rough ground reflect heat, which causes air currents to ascend as thermals.

In an ideal world, all searches would take place on open ground, clear of any features such as crags and trees that might otherwise disturb the air flow. Indeed, many searches are conducted on open ground such as parkland and fields, to which people suffering from conditions such as Alzheimer's tend to be attracted. The flow of air across flat, open fields is reasonably uninterrupted which makes it relatively easy for a trained dog to pick up and follow an airborne scent, but this is not typical of most mountain searches where numerous large and small features complicate the terrain and make it extremely difficult to negotiate. Low vegetation such as small bushes, heather or bracken disperses the air making it challenging for a dog to pick up a scent.

Features such as walls, crags, forests, drumlins, water courses and uneven ground interrupt the regular flow of air even more. Woodland and forest present particular difficulties — not only do trees make progress physically difficult but also, depending on their density, there may be little or no wind at all. Open woodland may permit the passage of a gentle breeze but forested areas with dense undergrowth may prove extremely difficult to search because of the complete absence of airborne scent.

Although the prediction of air movement follows well established aerodynamic principles, the complicated nature of mountain terrain doesn't always make it simple. Occasionally, air moves in unusual ways that make it very challenging for a dog to pick up or follow a scent. Looping is sometimes found in still wind conditions. When this occurs the scent is carried above its source, transported aloft for a distance where it may be airborne for a considerable length of time and then dropped back down. This happens when a local thermal causes the scent to rise until it meets a layer of cooler air. The scent is then carried along until it has cooled to a temperature lower than the air below it. At this point it falls back to ground. Under these conditions, a dog may indicate but then lose the scent because there is none between the source and the point where the scent fell to ground. Continuation of a normal search pattern may resolve the problem. Sometimes, chimney effects take place where the upward airflow caused by warm air creates a thermal effect. Winds can also generate thermals to produce complicated spiralling air currents. Generally, it is the task of the handler to try to get downwind of an area to work but isolated convection cells or turbulent eddies can trap scent on the downwind side of buildings or sharp downhill slopes, making detection downwind difficult.

Another complication is eddying. Eddying occurs on the downwind side of linear features such as cliff faces, large rocks and tree lines and may trap scent or disperse it in several directions. In some cases, wind direction may be reversed. While scent in these conditions may cause some confusion for the dog, a skilled team should have little trouble working it through. Pooling is another problem. Low areas collect scent, just as they do water and pooling takes place in natural hollows, behind crags or along man-made features such as ditches. Scent pools may produce an alert but the dog may find it difficult to work to its source because of shifting winds. On these occasions, handlers assess the terrain to see what features may have funnelled the scent to that particular location. Pooling is frequently seen on a cool evening when katabatic winds carry airborne scent downhill.

Precipitation can also play a part in compromising airflow. Rain can depress airborne scent and, if severe enough, even wash the scent out completely. Similarly, falling snow can scavenge scent particles from the air making it impossible to detect. Together, the combination of weather and terrain may make it very difficult but experienced handlers learn to adapt their strategy to the existing conditions and experienced dogs learn to range persistently to find the source.

In practice, handlers adopt a pragmatic approach and use their own senses to judge wind direction. There are many telltale signs such as watching the direction in which clouds move or looking at the way tall grasses or tree branches lean in the wind. Feeling the wind on your face or even holding up a wet finger are practical indicators of wind direction and strength — although not always reliable. We know one handler who ties a length of pink silk ribbon around their wrist to check wind direction. (Although whether her chosen colour of ribbon is important, or not, is uncertain!) However, whilst handlers might agonise over all these things, they are ever mindful that their dog — the natural born hunter with thousands of years of evolution and experience — knows all of this. Of course, they don't think about it or have a meeting before they begin — they just get on with the job. Indeed, there is no better sight in search dog handling than seeing an experienced dog pick up a scent, lose it, circle back to find it again and continue to work — and this can go on for a very long time without any input from the handler.

The use of trailing dogs

There is a view that conventional tracking using air-scenting techniques may not always be appropriate in search and rescue. A number of handlers in England and Wales have been experimenting with trailing dogs since the early-1970s but it is far from a new phenomenon. Since pre-Roman times they've been used to track runaway members of the aristocracy, thieves, poachers and slaves so, clearly, dogs have a role in using their tremendous scenting capability in ways other than air scenting.

In contrast to their air-scenting cousins, trailing dogs rely on a different set of criteria. They're taught to follow a specific set of scents or smells on or close to the ground. Trailing involves the dog wearing a harness with the handler holding a long line and following behind. The dog follows the trail of the missing person using a combination of ground scent, and the air scents either side, by means of a scent article belonging to the person such as a hat or glove. This is so the dog can discriminate the lost person's scent from the scent of everyone else in the area. If the missing person's vehicle is available and the police can gain entry, the dog might be able to work from a swab of scent from the seat or elsewhere inside the car.

The key factor here is that the place the

which to begin. For example, if the PLS is a roadside car park, this can effectively halve the search area by concentrating resources to one side of the road/area. Where there may have been a sighting on a hilltop or path, a trailing dog can be deployed to that point to see if it can indicate the presence of that person's trail, and thus confirm or discount the sighting as correct or not. Where a missing person's PLS is known to be in a building — such as a nursing home — a trailing dog can simply ring the perimeter of that building, and see if it can acquire an exit trail. If none is evident, there's a possibility the person is still in the building.

So, how do trailing dogs follow a

follow a scent the correct way! Once the scent has been located, the dog follows it as best as possible — ideally to the missing person waiting for help to arrive. A great deal of effort is spent training dogs to discriminate between scents and much time is devoted to search games before a dog is given the opportunity to try a trail. Eventually, dogs are taught to find a specific scent they are given, and to indicate on that particular scent. In effect, it means they are trained to find where an individual person has been and to indicate where that person has gone.

In addition to their work with air-scenting dogs, some members of SARDA Wales have focused on training trailing dogs and

person was last seen, or was known to have been, must be available in order to give the dog a start. In most searches for people missing in the mountains, there is no 'point last seen' (PLS), so trailing may be an impractical search method. However, if the PLS is known, and a scent article available, a trailing dog can begin to track the person on a reasonably clear line. If nothing else, this helps to give other searchers a head start and a direction in

particular human scent? There are over 370 different scents identifiable on a human body. About fifteen of these are specific to any individual human and it's this group that a trailing dog learns to work with. Dogs instinctively move the correct way on a trail, and this is rooted in their natural desire to eat. Basically, if a dog follows the correct trail it is rewarded by food. If it's a wrong trail, it goes hungry! Consequently, it's seldom necessary to teach a dog to

their first dogs achieved qualified status in 2005. In practice, and when possible, handlers of trailing dogs work alongside those with air-scenting dogs. This has proved successful — in some cases actually reducing the time to find people lost in the mountains and other urban/rural environments.

The use of a trailing dog proved successful a few years ago when a child on holiday with her parents went missing

IMAGE SEQUENCE: **PREPARE TO GET WET FEET! TRAILING DOG MIJ LEADS HANDLER IAIN NICHOLSON ACROSS THE RIVER AND ONTO THE OTHER BANK** © DARYL GARFIELD.

on a crowded beach. Several thousands of people were enjoying a day out at the seaside when the young girl went missing, wearing a distinctive pink jersey. The police were unsure where to start and the air-scenting dogs already deployed couldn't operate effectively as the air was contaminated with the scent of so many people. As luck would have it, one of the police officers present — Tom Middlemas — had recently attended a seminar given by an expert in trailing techniques. It turned out that Tom lived only a short distance from the incident location. He was alerted and the mother of the missing child gave him a T-shirt worn by the girl to work with. Tom and his dog joined the many hundreds

with a friend and was now wearing a blue one. And who was the dog sitting next to? The missing girl, of course!

In another case, police had been searching for a vulnerable elderly person for 24 hours. Around a hundred police officers, including dogs and specialist search teams, had been involved in the search over that time, before mountain rescue and SARDA were called. A trailing dog and handler were deployed to the missing person's house, and a scent article collected. The dog trailed from the house, across a busy A-road and into some shrub land before entering what appeared to be a small rabbit run into a bramble bush three metres high and ten metres in

to good effect — vehicles abandoned by the driver, road traffic accidents, people who go missing from their home or hospital, children who disappear when on a family outing/picnic. In these situations, trailing dogs can provide direction for searchers and help close an area down for further searching when a trail goes cold. Trailing dogs are prone to mental tiredness but they can work in areas contaminated by the scent of other people as well as areas hazardous to humans.

The skill of a handler is in training their dog to use its remarkable sense of smell to good effect. It might seem fairly easy to train a dog to carry out a simple task such as to sit down or retrieve a thrown ball, but

of other people in the search and set off along the crowded beach. As they made their way, he repeatedly used the girl's T-shirt to remind his dog of the girl's scent. After a short time, Tom's dog suddenly turned and moved to a group of children playing with sandcastles. The dog sat quietly beside them. Initially, the police officers were indifferent as nobody was wearing a pink jersey. However, it transpired that the girl has swapped jerseys

diameter. When the handler shone a torch into the bush, along the small hole leading in, the missing person could be seen deep inside.

The use of trailing dogs is obviously limited when a walker is missing in a mountain or wilderness environment because trailing only works when there is a scent article and a PLS for the missing person, but there are numerous specific situations when trailing dogs can be used

a task which is simple in our eyes may take a dog many months of continuous practice to acquire. Even then, the dog may not always perform the task on demand. When it comes to search dogs, training a dog to follow a scent, return to the handler and indicate it's on to something, then take the handler to the source of the scent, is actually a complicated sequence of skills which takes years for a dog to acquire.

Doggie Tales

DAY 983 OF MY CAPTIVITY: THE CAT

My captors continue to taunt me with bizarre little dangling objects... They dine lavishly on fresh meat, while the other inmates and I are fed hash or some sort of dry nuggets....

Although I make my contempt for the rations perfectly clear, I nevertheless must eat something in order to keep up my strength. The only thing that keeps me going is my dream of escape. In an attempt to disgust them, I once again vomit on the carpet.

Today I decapitated a mouse and dropped its headless body at their feet. I had hoped this would strike fear into their hearts, since it clearly demonstrates what I am capable of. However, they merely made condescending comments about what a 'good little hunter' I am.

There was some sort of assembly of their accomplices tonight. I was placed in solitary confinement for the duration of the event. However, I could hear the noises and smell the food. I overheard that my confinement was due to the power of 'allergies.' I must learn what this means and how to use it to my advantage. Today I was almost successful in an attempt to assassinate one of my tormentors by weaving around his feet as he was walking. I must try this again tomorrow, but at the top of the stairs. I am convinced that the other prisoners here are flunkies and snitches. The dog receives special privileges. He is regularly released and seems to be more than willing to return.

He is obviously retarded.

DEAR CAT OWNER...

I thought you'd like to know how we dogs think a cat should be cleaned up. This is my advice:

Raise both lids of toilet and add small cup of pet shampoo to water in bowl...

Pick up and soothe cat while you carry him/her to bathroom.

In one smooth move, place cat in toilet and close lid. NB. You may need to stand on lid.

At this point, cat will self-agitate and make ample suds. Disregard any noises coming from the toilet – the cat is actually enjoying this!

Flush toilet three or four times – this provides a Power-Wash and Rinse.

Have someone open the front door of your home. Be sure there is no-one between bathroom and front door.

Stand well back and quickly lift the lid. Cat will rocket out of toilet, streak through bathroom, and run outside where he/she will dry him/herself off. Both toilet and cat will be sparkling clean.

Yours sincerely, The Dog x

ITS A DOGS LIFE: THE DOG

08.00: Food! My favourite thing! 09:30: Car ride! My favourite thing! 09:40: Walk in the park! My favourite thing! 10:30: Got rubbed and petted! My favourite thing! 12:00: Lunch! My favourite thing! 13:00: Played in the yard! My favourite thing! 15:00: Wagged my tail! My favourite thing! 17:00: Milk bones! My favourite thing! 19:00: Ball games! My favourite thing! 20.00: Wow! Watched TV! With the humans. My favourite thing! 23:00: Sleep! On the bed! My favourite thing!

7 Theory into practice

'Training their first search and rescue dog is the second hardest thing most handlers will do in their lives. Training their second search and rescue dog is the hardest.' Anon

We imagined, when we set out to write this, that everything there is to know about training dogs would be clear and unequivocal. But things are never quite so simple. It's probably safe to say that just about everyone in the dog world has his or her own way of working — there is no concensus. Not that this is a bad thing per se — indeed, there are often many ways to solve a problem whatever its nature, be it designing a car, curing a headache or training a dog to find missing walkers.

We don't confess to be experts in the training of dogs — or, specifically, the training of search and rescue dogs — but we've owned and trained dogs, and been involved in the training of many others over several years. We've also worked alongside dog teams on countless searches. So we know that, whatever the form of training or assessment, it is vital dog teams don't move onto the call-out list at any cost. Rather, it's imperative that only good dog teams find their way there. For this to happen, training must be thorough and systematic, with rigorous and objective assessment.

There are those who adopt a very pedantic approach to training, whilst others are prepared to watch and listen and modify their actions to suit changing circumstances. We have met with people — and organisations — who argue that their approach is the only way to do it. They seem firmly fixed on a single method and will not budge under any circumstances. That's okay if it works for them, and as long as they don't attempt to impose their approach on anyone else. Some argue that as long as a dog is not harmed during training (physically or psychologically), and that training achieves the desired results in a reasonable period of time, then it doesn't matter what method was used. The fact is, there's little new in training dogs. Every expert started somewhere by watching someone else, reading a book or watching a video. As they progressed, they altered things to suit their own circumstances and adapted along the way to produce a style that suited them.

In the world of search and rescue dogs, there are a number of different approaches and each association has its own accepted style. This is vital because any newcomer to an organisation needs a set of guiding principles and a set plan to work from. Search and rescue dog training isn't driven by time constraints or budgets in the way that, for example, the police authorities are when they train their dogs for general or specific police work. Because dogs and their handlers are all different (there will be fast and slow learners) and the work is voluntary in nature, there is a need for training to be time-flexible. For this reason, SARDA has produced excellent dog teams when other professional bodies might have rejected them — something of which each association is very proud.

When Hamish MacInnes started out in the 1960s, his key focus was training dogs to become 'air scenting wilderness search dogs'. Since then, this relatively narrow definition has expanded to include avalanche work, urban searches, and disaster work involving collapsed buildings and civil contingencies, as well as water-based rescues. In some cases, specialist dog teams have evolved for this type of work but the basic premise has not been lost and training today remains focused on developing dog teams to air scent in a wilderness setting.

FACING PAGE: **SEARCH DOG ANGUS** © PETER SANDGROUND.

Training fundamentals

With a few exceptions, all trainee dog handlers are full members of a mountain rescue team. Most associations insist that trainees are involved in mountain rescue and on the call-out list of their team, although in some cases probationary members may be accepted. A recommendation is usually required from the team leader as to the trainee's overall mountain rescue competence and commitment. It is also expected that potential trainees have worked as a body or worked alongside qualified handlers — perhaps as their navigator — to provide them with a good insight into the work of SARDA. The criteria may vary between associations, but whatever the exact details, every association has to be convinced about the commitment and potential of those who apply. Indeed, the early months of training are an opportunity for handlers to see for themselves how the association operates and to appreciate the demands placed on them, during training and afterwards when they become operational. This initial period allows both handler and association see whether or not they fit well together.

Many aspirant handlers own a dog before they embark on the road to training their dog for search work. They have rarely progressed beyond basic obedience training, although a few may have worked dogs in a semi-professional or professional capacity. A very small number start with a blank sheet, having never owned a dog. In this case, SARDA is more than able to provide advice on the type of dog they should obtain. Whatever their background and level of experience of working with dogs, everyone is incorporated into the training procedures of their association and works to the protocols and assessment criteria developed by that association. There are several key principles which form the basis of that training.

One of the very first things all handlers need to recognise is that, paradoxically, searching is not always about locating missing people: it's about clearing an area so the search controllers can deploy assets (human and canine) elsewhere. So, depending on the circumstances, dog teams have to be clear, from the beginning, that finding the casualty will not happen every time they are deployed. With this in mind, success at finding bodies has to be put into the context of the whole search, so a sense of balance prevails about what the job really entails. Of course, it's important for dogs (and handlers) to achieve early success in making finds. The maxim 'nothing succeeds like success' is as true in canine learning as it is in human learning, but it's vital this is balanced. At the end of the day, the success of a dog team is judged by its ability to clear a given area of land. If that area contains the missing person and the dog makes a find, then great but, if the person isn't in the area, the handler must be able to report they have cleared the area with a high degree of confidence.

Training is an extraordinary commitment. It takes not only time, but exceptional patience and discipline. For many handlers, it takes over their lives and dictates their work pattern, domestic harmony and financial resources. Dog handlers rarely have a hobby beyond caring for and training their dog. It's not just the time requirement — training involves working on a regular basis in all weathers and conditions. There are no holiday breaks or down periods — the pressure to work, exercise and train is a never-ending cycle. Yet it still has to fit in with work, family responsibilities, other mountain rescue commitments and life in general. Even those members who are retired cannot put aside a full working day, five days a week, to train their dog. So, it's up to the handler to find the right kind of balance — never a simple task. On top of all this, it is increasingly the norm for handlers to maintain a log of their training and assessment experience. This permits trainers to keep up with what trainees are actually doing during their own training sessions, and also serves as a permanent record of experience and training — useful if this has to be seen by others.

They say that patience is a virtue. Well, dog handlers in training need patience in abundance. When you consider that any single behaviour is only firmly embedded — truly learned — if it has been repeated several hundred times, over very many hours, days and weeks, progress is very slow. It's easy to see why prospective handlers want to get on and become qualified and expect things to happen reasonably quickly but, because their expectations are rarely met soon enough, some give up early or their training fails. This is one reason why experienced handlers have a responsibility to pace learners and convince them that the route to becoming an excellent dog handler is a slow and enduring one. That route has to be exact with no short cuts because it's quite possible a newly qualified handler can be called out within mere hours of passing the assessment, and a life may be at stake. Meeting strict assessment criteria is a must.

Training is not a simple process. There are twists and turns, regressions and plateaus, and progress doesn't always follow the rule book. It may be relatively simple to teach a dog fundamental obedience skills in the warm confines of a village hall but it is extremely difficult to train in the field where dog/handler dynamics, weather, terrain, background scents and stress all affect performance. Handlers can't expect their dog to behave in the same manner when not working as when it's working. Skills such as scent detection, communication and ranging, which are not everyday requirements in the dog's life have to become natural events in a work situation. Similarly, dogs that range naturally when on a regular walk may not do the same when the handler asks the dog to go away to find.

Without exception, training is a team affair — dog and handler together. Training a dog is as much about changing the behaviour of a dog as it is about helping the handler to understand their dog, how it learns and behaves in particular ways and how to maximise its potential. It's not always easy to convince trainee handlers about this. There's a tendency to think the dog should work for them and all they have to do is dictate or control its actions. It's a common misconception. For the dog — and to a slightly lesser degree the handler — the interaction between dog and handler has to be the most important thing in their lives. Ask any handler's wife, husband or significant other who is more important, them or the dog, and the chances are you'll get a very honest reply! Yes, dogs are fitter, faster and possess greater stamina than their handler. Their nose is more sensitive than that of the handler and, as a species, they've hunted for thousands of years. Knowing this, it might be easy to think that all the handler need do is translate what the search manager wants into dog language and communicate that to the dog, which will respond accordingly. But it's not quite like this — the training/learning process is two-way. Both dog and handler learn together in a shared manner. The dog learns to respond to the handler's commands and the handler learns to understand how to get their dog to act accordingly.

A good example of dog-handler teamwork is the way farmers communicate with their dogs. Many use the same basic herding dog commands:

'Come bye!' or 'Bye!' — the dog goes to the left of the stock, or clockwise around them.

'Away to me!' or 'Away!' — the dog goes to the right of the stock or anticlockwise around them.

'Lie down!' or 'Wait!' — the dog stops.

'Walk on!' — the dog walks forward closer to the stock.

'That'll do!' — the dog stops working and returns to the handler.

'Look back!' — the dog returns for a missing animal.

Just a few simple commands are all that's needed for both farmer and dog to work sheep successfully. Search dog handlers don't use the same set of commands to communicate with their dog, although they may use one or two. Basically, every handler has their own and, even though two handlers may differ, in time their dog gets to fully understand what each command means.

A key part of the handler's learning is gaining a thorough understanding of their dog. When dogs are working, they actually provide a lot of information to their handler. The handler's task is to understand and recognise what their dog is communicating. They have to be encouraged to get to know their dog, to watch out for subtle changes in behaviour — movement of their ears or tail — which give clues to what the dog is doing. Learning their dog's body language involves keeping a watchful eye on it at all times. It's no good the handler ploughing across the hill head down, whilst their dog works its socks off: the handler learns nothing and hasn't got a clue what's going on. Similarly, dogs learn about their handler,

JAMES COLES AND 'BLUE PETER SEARCH DOG' CORRIE © PETER SANDGROUND.

picking up subtle clues without the handler even being aware they're being monitored! It's the two-way process once more where the handler communicates what he or she wants, and their dog understands this.

At some point in training, dogs begin to understand the difference between work and play. They may not have a concept of work, but their behaviour and urgency suggests they are task oriented and purposefully working towards a particular goal. They know they are 'at work'. Certainly, experienced handlers report that once a dog is wearing a jacket or harness they appear to behave in a more workmanlike manner. When things do go wrong, in training or operational work, it is more likely the fault of the handler and not their dog. It's even been suggested the handler gets the dog they deserve! Handlers may like to think they're faultless but research has shown that when dogs fail to make a find (when a body is located in the search area) or clear an area successfully, handlers are at fault on over 75% of occasions — but more about this point when we talk about assessment.

Searching with a dog is not entirely an objective, predictable science. Some would argue it's more an art than a science. There are very many good dog handlers, but only a small number of excellent ones. Unfortunately the very best handlers often find it difficult to communicate their skill to others, probably because they're not too sure themselves exactly what it is that makes things work. If only we could determine the chemistry and bottle it! Whatever it is, we know that the bond between some handlers and their dogs makes them extra special and exceptionally good at what they do.

Dominance

History shows that humans have largely been regarded as the 'master' of dogs – a term still widely used and adopted by many dog trainers as the desired relationship between dog and man. The idea has been promoted that the well-behaved dog must have a subservient role in the relationship and, if this does not occur, then the dog will become the dominant partner and bad behaviour will result.

Recent research questions the validity of this stance. Over the last few years, a better understanding of dogs and their actions is emerging, from research by academics taking an ever-increasing interest in all aspects of dog behaviour. That research is increasingly questioning the view that owners/trainers must dominate their dogs in order to create the right kind of behaviour.

Dogs and wolves, undisputedly, have a common ancestor. But their separate evolution has resulted in two very different animals, which cannot be directly compared. In the past, the scientific study of wolves has, mainly, been restricted to captive packs, which has led researchers to a questionable conclusion: that wolves, and hence dogs, live in a society lead by a dominant individual or pair. More recent work has shown that this type of social behaviour does not exist in wild wolf packs, feral dog packs that live around villages, or even in domestic dogs brought together at random and in fairly large numbers. It is suggested that recurring conflict situations, which lead to one individual dominating another, only occur when confinement to a restricted area does not give the opportunity for one individual to move away.

One of the great attributes of social carnivores is their ability to weigh up the worth of a conflict situation. Is the possession of food, a female or a toy worth serious injury or, perhaps, death? The current research is suggesting that groups of canids, of all types, are able to live, in harmony, without the need for a dominant individual. As the new research progresses it may have a profound effect on the way in which we look upon and train dogs in the future.

How do dogs learn?

A new born puppy is a blank canvas, ready and waiting to be scribbled on by the people it comes into contact with. By the time it arrives at SARDA's door — some weeks later — it may already have acquired some behaviours which have to be changed or eliminated. The question is, where do you go from there? The answer lies partly in understanding how dogs and people learn. If you want to teach a person something new (say to learn a foreign language or how to play badminton), you need to consider what it is that motivates them or guides their needs. Generally speaking, people only learn if they have the desire to do so, although there are many other reasons why people learn new things. The key is finding a strategy that appeals to their needs and this can be rather complicated because of the vast number of factors involved and the way in which they might interact.

Dogs are motivated by three primary drives: food, prey and sociability. We all know dogs love food. Giving them a tasty morsel is a simple way to encourage them — particularly young puppies — to learn a new skill such as sitting on command. Some handlers use tit-bits as a reward throughout training but withdraw this randomly so as not to create an over-reliance, sometimes called 'jackpot training'.

The prey drive is very powerful. Many dogs are excited by toys or other objects and will invariably attempt to pull them apart, chew them or find a place to bury them. Dog handlers use toys to reward their dog when it makes a find. The exact nature of the toy will depend on the dog but it is always kept as a special reward and only revealed when the dog is successful. The dog learns that, when it finds a person, it will be rewarded with its favourite toy.

In addition to food and prey, it's well known that dogs, as social animals, are eager to please. In this case, it isn't necessary to give a dog a physical reward — a pat on the head, a few words of praise or a cuddle are sufficient in their own right. This is a point well illustrated by Martin Clunes in his book *A Dogs' Life*. He describes his meeting with a Cumbrian farmer — a very experienced breeder and trainer of Border Collies. The farmer tells Martin that he starts working dogs between six and eight months old, when they begin to want to chase and round up sheep. 'I usually get some quiet sheep and let the dog play with them. Right away you'll see whether you've got a killer or more of a herding dog. All I do is protect the sheep, staying with them, using a hard voice and trying to block the dog to defend the sheep until the dog realises I don't want him to attack them.' The farmer explains how he uses a harsh voice when the dogs aren't moving well and a nice, warm voice when they do as he wants. He reckons dogs love praise, and work in order to be rewarded by the note of approval and encouragement. 'If they don't stop on command, they hear an angry voice. The minute they stop, they get a calm voice. The more they obey, the nicer the voice gets.'

Few dog owners would argue with this but it doesn't always work. A good way of understanding how dogs learn is to examine some of the theories, which underpin canine behaviour. Theories are generalities about the way things work. They are broad statements based on observations, research and experience; educated guesses that describe how or why things work. Theories are valuable because they make it possible to make reasonably successful predictions about what might happen in the future. So, when training a dog, it helps to know that if certain training procedures are followed (based on a theoretical underpinning), the dog can be expected to perform in a particular manner. The general nature of theories makes them applicable to different breeds of dog and different dogs within a particular breed. They also — potentially — work for different trainers and different environments: a panacea!

Much of what is known about how dogs learn and the theories underlying the learning process stems from research carried out around 100 years ago. The principles of learning and training established by the scientists of the day apply as well now as they did then, and are used by everyone involved in training dogs for search and rescue. Central is the principle of association and the linking of stimuli with responses. A simple example is the command 'Come!' (stimulus) followed by the dog's return to its owner (response). Dogs are very quick to make associations that benefit them. One of the authors has a Border Collie which, at just sixteen weeks old, had already made the link between the author donning his shoes and the morning walk. Unfortunately, the association doesn't always apply and the dog is sometimes left with a puzzled look on his face! But it works often enough to have become a well-established behaviour pattern.

Ivan Pavlov, a Russian physician and psychologist, and Burrhus Skinner, an American psychologist, devoted a great deal of time and research to exploring this kind of behaviour.

Pavlov is widely known for first describing the principal of classical conditioning. As a physiologist, he was interested in studying the chemistry of saliva in dogs. He noticed, quite by chance, that dogs tended to salivate before food was actually given to them. He'd expected them to salivate during the process of eating, but not before the sight or smell of food. Pavlov went on to examine this process in more detail by adding another event just as a dog was about to be fed, specifically sounding a bell at the same time the dog was presented with food. He repeated this many times and, after a period of time, discovered the dog would salivate on hearing the bell alone. Through training, he had linked an existing response with a new stimulus. In technical terms the sight and smell of food is called the 'unconditioned stimulus' and salivation the 'unconditioned response'. In terms of training, the bell is termed the 'conditioned stimulus' and the salivation

response to it the 'conditioned response'. We say that the dog has been conditioned to associate the bell with food. Classic conditioning is seen as an automatic form of learning where there is no understanding or cognition on the part of the dog involved.

This is learning at its most basic but it can apply to humans too. When we learn to drive a car, we learn to move our foot from the accelerator to the brake (unconditioned response) when approaching a red traffic light (unconditioned stimulus). We quickly transfer this response (conditioned response) when we see the brake lights of the car in front of us (conditioned stimulus). Conditioned responses are common where survival is at stake.

The key principle of classical conditioning is the establishment of associations between certain things. So when a dog learns to return to their handler having found a body, what they have done is associate this behaviour with the pleasure of a reward (their favourite toy, food, cuddle or word). The association is established because the desired behaviour is followed by something favourable to the dog. A key factor is that the reward must follow immediately after the behaviour with no delay. If the reward (such as a toy) is taken away, then in time, the dog's behaviour also ceases. So, during training, handlers never fail to offer a reward. Once the behaviour is embedded, the reward can be downgraded and given intermittently but it is good dog handling to reinforce the behaviour from time to time with a massive reward — the jackpot we mentioned earlier.

Skinner went on to develop Pavlov's pioneering work. Working primarily with rats and pigeons, he was interested in finding ways to make animals behave in

particular ways — a specific action or pattern of actions — by introducing some kind of reward or punishment as reinforcing agent. He worked on the notion that an animal would tend to repeat an action if rewarded and tend to stop the action if punished. Through his experiments he showed that certain behaviours could be increased in frequency through reward and decreased through punishment. Skinner was particularly interested to determine the circumstances under which a rat could be 'taught' to press a lever in order to obtain a pellet of food. He placed a rat in a box, which contained nothing but a tiny lever. Rats do not naturally press levers in boxes, but he waited until they would, quite by accident, press the lever. As soon as they did, he rewarded them immediately with a pellet of food. He repeated this many times — whenever the rat pressed the lever, a pellet of food was given to the rat. In time, he discovered that rats began to press the lever with increasing frequency. It was as if they knew that, as soon as they pressed the lever, they'd receive a pleasant reward. Skinner called this kind of learning 'operant conditioning'. Whereas classical conditioning is concerned with associations between stimuli and responses, operant conditioning describes the association between responses and their outcomes. The significant feature here is that the response or desired behaviour occurs first and the reward is given next.

Skinner went on to show that complicated patterns of behaviour can be taught using the principle of operant conditioning. What he did was wait for the first part of the behaviour to occur and reward it, then repeat this until the animal learned to associate the behaviour with the reward.

ABOVE AND FACING PAGE: SARDA WALES DOGS IN TRAINING © SARDA WALES.

*'Train the dog at a very early age to the Big Four: 'Sit!',
'Stay!', 'Come!' and 'Walk to heel!' – once the dog's
bombproof to this, Son, you'll be able to do what you
want with it.'*
Darryl Urquart-Dixon, SARDA Southern Scotland.

Next, he waited until the animal produced not just the first part of the behaviour sequence, but the first and second together, then he rewarded the animal. He repeated the procedure until the animal successfully carried out the entire chain of behaviours before being rewarded. This procedure is 'behaviour shaping' and reflects, in part, how search and rescue dogs are trained in the entire find sequence.

A key to operant conditioning is that the reward not only has to be pleasurable to the animal but, more importantly, must be administered immediately the animal behaves in the desired manner. Any delay and it doesn't work. This principle of immediate feedback is absolutely vital in dog training — for both reward and punishments. If there's a delay, the dog will think it is being rewarded for the last thing it did — which might not be the desired behaviour. Consider, for instance, a dog that runs away to play with another dog, and then finally returns much later. If it is punished upon its return (through an angry remonstration or even a slap) it will associate the punishment with the last thing it did — the return. Getting the dog to return on subsequent occasions will be even more difficult as the dog will think it is going to be punished when it does return. So, the reward has to be given immediately the animal carries out the desired action. It also has to be meaningful to the animal and administered consistently.

Operant conditioning is central to dog training. It demands great patience and discipline on the part of the trainer, because it takes an inordinate amount of time, waiting for the right behaviours to happen, and precise timing before the right associations between commands and actions are established. At all times, the dog is actively involved and volunteers the desired behaviours. In no way is it constrained or forced into behaving in a particular manner.

Classical and operant conditioning principles are very robust. Dogs will always learn to make associations between stimuli/rewards and actions. Once learned, they last a long time, but their effectiveness varies from one dog to another, so there will be variation in the kind of rewards that work (food, toys, praise) and the time required for these associations to become established. There are also differences in how dogs transfer their learning from one situation to another. Dogs tend to be contextual learners, so what is learned in one context may not transfer easily to another. For example, a dog might work well on a lead inside a home or hall during obedience classes but then pull immediately it gets outside! A training regime that works well for one dog and handler may not work for another. Finding the best approach is all about the handler getting to know their dog very well. It's been said a handler will only get the best out of their dog if they think like a dog! This is one reason why trainers can only advise aspirant handlers how best to train their own dog — it's impossible to dictate exactly how it should be done.

It's important to add that physical punishment has no place in training. Its use says a great deal more about the handler than the dog! Whilst punishments can be used to diminish or extinguish undesired behaviours, there are better ways to reduce unwanted behaviours than pure physical punishment. Removal of eye contact, turning your back, change in tone of voice or putting your dog back in the car are always effective. Dogs do not like to be ignored! Rewards are easier to administer. Toys, food, encouraging tone of voice, stroking and play are much more positive. Dogs, like humans, switch off if they expect punishment or if they're not sure what is wanted of them. In the end, training a dog for search work is largely about harnessing the dog's natural instinct to hunt.

Skinner's work, incidentally, wasn't confined to animals. His research and thinking had a significant impact in the world of education and the teaching of children. Much of what he theorised is highly relevant today, not only in regard to human learning but also the training of search dogs. Few trainers would disagree with the key principles he established:

- Learning is best undertaken in a positive, rewarding environment.
- Positive reinforcement is more effective at changing and establishing behaviour than punishment.
- Learning should be goal directed and instructions regarding those goals should be clear.
- Complex behaviour should be broken down into small steps.
- Feedback should be given immediately.
- Practice should be repeated many times.
- Complicated behaviour should be taught by working from simple to more complex tasks.

Canine intelligence

Quite apart from nature versus nurture and training aspects, canine intelligence inspires heated debate amongst professional and armchair commentators alike. Many have strong views about the intelligence of different breeds, not least of all their own dog — invariably the brightest on the planet!

Unfortunately there are few clear answers. In fact, the meaning of intelligence in general, not only in reference to dogs, is very hard to define. There was a time when human intelligence was measured and decisions made on the basis of intelligence tests, assessed through a single set of written questions.

The 'Eleven plus' exam, created by the 1944 Butler Education Act to test a child's ability to solve problems using verbal and non-verbal reasoning, mathematics and English, no longer exists and it's now widely recognised that people possess a number of specific kinds of intelligence rather than an overriding general level of intelligence. This makes sense because there are few people who excel or are weak at everything. Rather, they tend to be very good at some things and not so good at others. In other words, they possess a profile of different kinds of intelligence.

When it comes to canine intelligence, the problems of definition and measurement are more pronounced. Certain intelligence tests involve a dog's ability to recognise and respond to a large vocabulary of commands whereas others involve their ability to respond to different situations or tasks. Indeed, dog trainers, owners and researchers have as much difficulty agreeing on a method for testing canine intelligence as they do for human intelligence. Sometimes, judgements are based on anecdotal evidence and often, on very limited numbers of observations. Some people align intelligence with obedience and advocate that a dog, which readily learns to 'Sit!', or 'Lie down!' is intelligent. Others say that intelligence is a measure of thinking and problem-solving ability, whilst some people interpret genetically wired-in behaviour as a sign of intelligence. For example, sheep herding breeds such as the Border Collie are expected to learn how to herd sheep very quickly, but they only do this because they have been selectively bred over many generations for this particular quality. Is it correct to say that a Border Collie is intelligent when, in fact, it is merely displaying a genetic pre-disposition to herd? Certainly, if you tried to train a collie to point and retrieve game it would find this a real challenge. Another way to view intelligence is through a dog's drive or enthusiasm. Some breeds of dog are highly willing to please and extremely persistent in trying things. A dog that is highly driven to solve a problem — such as find a hidden toy — is more likely to reach a solution through accident than another dog that doesn't try. But does this make it more intelligent?

It's clear that dogs are capable of learning and that different breeds pick up solutions to problems more quickly than others. It also seems that dogs — like humans — do possess different kinds of intelligence. Some breeds show a type of conceptual understanding not unlike that of humans. In one study, a dog was shown a picture of a toy then went on to locate the actual toy amongst a number of others. It made the perceptual transition from a two dimensional shape to a three dimensional object. It's also well known that some dogs respond to human pointing by directing their gaze to the object rather than the pointing finger. This suggests they can think ahead and make predictions about the location of objects.

One highly respected authority on canine intelligence has attempted to categorise the various kinds of intelligence possessed by dogs. Stanley Coren suggests there are three kinds — adaptive, working and instinctive. Adaptive intelligence reflects a dog's capacity to solve problems that makes its behaviour more efficient. Examples would be the way a dog learns to track down another animal for food, or learns that its owner is more likely to give it food if it pushes its food bowl closer to the owner. Adaptive intelligence permits a dog to adapt to its environment and provides it with skills to modify that environment to suit its needs. It's a measure of what a dog can do for itself.

Working (or obedience) intelligence is a measure of what a dog can do for humans. It's reflected in the way a dog responds in a specific manner to particular human commands such as when a farmer calls 'Come bye!' and the dog moves to the left. Similarly, when a handler calls 'Show me!' and the dog takes him back to the casualty, it demonstrates working intelligence.

Working intelligence is partly problem-solving as it requires the dog to work out which behaviours are expected of it when it receives a particular command. Tapping into this kind of intelligence is not easy. The task to be learned may not be difficult (for example, running back to the handler to indicate), but getting the dog to understand that it has to do this when it locates a body is the challenge. Problems like this are solved by breaking them down into smaller parts and rewarding the dog when it is successful and ignoring it when it's not. The exercise is then repeated a large number of times until the dog figures out the problem, recognises the solution and is able to use it repeatedly on subsequent occasions. A large factor here is the influence and skill of the handler — some dogs learn quickly because their handler is able to provide better clues. Coren also believes that working intelligence reflects a dog's desire to perform learned activities — in other words, their persistence, resistance to frustration and flexibility to try other strategies.

Instinctive intelligence reflects the behaviour that dogs inherit as part of their genetic programming. It accounts for a sizeable portion of their abilities and, for some breeds, the particular behaviours inherited from their parents are clear to see and also helpful to people. Indeed, one of the major purposes of selective breeding is to enhance and refine some of these behaviours such as retrieving, herding and guarding. A good example of how the biological mechanisms of inheritance are developed through breeding is seen in bloodhounds, which tend to bark — a wired-in behaviour — when tracking a scent. Over the course of time, a few bloodhounds that did not bark were bred to produce a strain of silent-tracking bloodhounds. Today, many breeds of dog are bred to enhance physical features as well as behaviour patterns suitable for obedience testing and working function.

Coren discusses how the three kinds of intelligence relate to one another, suggesting that there is an interaction between all three, the complexity of which depends on specific breeds. He takes two contrasting examples. Poodles have few pronounced instinctive abilities but score high on working intelligence which would make any attempts to train poodles to herd sheep, for example, very demanding if not impossible. On the other hand, collies have very pronounced instinctive abilities, much of their behaviour dominated by genetically determined intelligence so collies are relatively easy to train to herd. Indeed, as collie owners will be well aware, they are natural herders, often going out of their way in the search for opportunities to herd, even if this means inappropriately circling a group of people to keep them as a group!

JOY GRINDROD AND EINICH ON AVALANCHE TRAINING WITH THE LAKES DOGS IN SCOTLAND © DARYL GARFIELD.

How does all this fit in with the training of search dogs? Well, the three kinds of intelligence defined by Coren all play a part and are recognised by handlers. A dog will learn very quickly that if they do what the handler requires (for example, return having found a body) they will be rewarded with their favourite toy or food. The speed of learning and consistency of their behaviour is a measure of their adaptive intelligence. Their ability to behave in particular ways to their handler's commands is a measure of their working intelligence and their ability to 'quarter' as they search an area of ground is a manifestation of their instinctive ability to herd — instinctive intelligence. So, in Stanley Coren's terms, a successful search dog will display all three kinds of intelligence.

But which is the most intelligent dog? Now there's a question. There are certainly differences between breeds in levels of intelligence. Some can be trained to be very obedient compared to others. Some are better able to obey commands and solve simple problems. It is also true that differences in intelligence between dogs of a given breed can be larger than differences between different breeds. The intelligence of a dog may also partly reflect their owner's ability to train them — but take a look at the breed predominantly featured here. It's the most popular amongst dog handlers and top of Stanley Coren's 'Ten most intelligent dogs' list for both working and obedience intelligence: (from the top) Border Collie, Poodle, German Shepherd, Golden Retriever, Doberman Pinscher, Shetland Sheepdog, Labrador Retriever, Papillon, Rottweiler, Australian Cattle Dog — but you didn't hear it from us...

Stages in training

The purpose of training is identical for each association: to train dog teams to find missing people. For the dog, the overall task comprises a number of related ones.

● Seek the source scent of the missing person.
● Ignore other scents that may be attractive.
● Locate the source ie. the missing person.
● Communicate their find to the handler.
● Guide the handler back to the source.

When combined these tasks define the find sequence. Achieving this requires the dog to use its senses, make decisions, respond to commands and execute specific actions whilst working over a large expanse of ground. But how do you train a dog to do all this? Each association has methods and approaches that differ in some ways. SARDA Wales, for example, uses a system in which dog teams are required to meet a number of precise objectives as they work through the training programme. Other associations adopt slightly different procedures but, to avoid confusion or duplication, we will focus on the system adopted by one association.

SARDA Southern Scotland adopts a three-stage approach to training and assessment and awards a grade at the end of each stage. By the end of the third stage, successful dogs can complete the find sequence effectively and consistently and search large areas of ground. At this point, they move on to the call-out list as a Novice Search Dog.

Southern Scotland takes the view that the end game — the find — is taught first. This is then used as a reward for which the dog learns to hunt. Psychologists call this 'antecedent learning' and it's a technique often used by sports coaches, particularly when teaching skills that comprise a sequence of linked parts, such as you'd find in a gymnastic routine. The key point is that whatever is learned first, is the last part of the behaviour sequence. Training then follows a step-by-step progression through three linked stages. The entire process of training to the highest grade can take up to three years. The association has found that if training goes on for longer then, unless there is a good reason — such as the illness of dog or handler — the chances of producing a good dog team is very slim. For this reason, a time limit of three years is introduced into the association's guidelines.

Stage One

This may take several weeks to become thoroughly ingrained. There is then a formal assessment which requires the dog team to demonstrate the find sequence in a minimum of five small areas. Each area includes some kind of challenge, for example, to search a small forest or cross a river or wall. Or the body may be on the wrong side of a deer fence or in a difficult position such as up a tree (dog teams are often called to find suicide victims). During assessment, 100% success is required with very clear indications and evidence of shuttling behaviour – considered essential behaviour when the dog team is working at night or in poor visibility – and the dog continues to lead the handler in to the body.

The first stage focuses primarily on the dog and comprises a series of gradually increasing steps, which test the dog progressively in regard to both difficulty and extent — a classic example of behaviour shaping.

The find sequence is taught over a very short distance of 30 to 50 metres, and on very easy ground. This involves stringing together several responses which the dog should have been taught during basic training such as curiosity, recall and so on, and repeating them over and over consistently until the total sequence is seen as one response by the dog.

At this stage, the dog is allowed to see the body going to their 'hidden' location, perhaps just a few metres away. Most associations call this a 'run out'. The commands 'Find!' or 'Away find!' and 'Show me!' are introduced at this stage. This is a most important phase and any attempt to complicate it, or carry it out under difficult circumstances before it is firmly implanted, may lead to problems later. The whole process is made as exciting as possible for the puppy and repeated over and over again. The dog is encouraged to shuttle, repeatedly moving between the body and handler. A clear indication is required during this stage. Barking at the handler is the most common. In the Lakes, in contrast, the dog is taught to bark at the body before returning to the handler.

The distance over which the find takes place is extended, but still on easy ground and still letting the dog see the body going to hide. Ranging is the term given to the distance a dog works from a handler in any free direction. Dogs have to be encouraged to leave the handler's side and eventually range out of sight, or else they will never succeed in practice. The dog is allowed to see the body go away, but then the body moves upwind, away from the point where the dog sees him go down. This encourages the dog to hunt for the body and begins with short distances.

Obstacles such as walls and gullies are put in the path to build up the dog's tenacity in reaching a source of scent. At first the distance is reduced when the obstacles are introduced.

Once this objective is achieved, the distance is extended over difficult terrain. The dog still sees the body set out but loses sight of him or her long before being released to locate the scent.

Next, the dog is put onto a scent without seeing the body set out. Again the scale is reduced initially and then extended. This step differs from previous ones as, for the first time, the element of hunting is introduced. However, it may last only one or two minutes.

At this stage, the handler works towards:

- Completing every search with a perfect find sequence.
- Increasing the duration of the search, slowly and steadily, to a maximum of about 30 minutes.
- Learning to read the dog as it progresses through its task — it's very easy for a dog to detect and follow a scent trail. What is more difficult for dog and handler is how they communicate with each other about what they want and need.
- Encouraging their dog to work independently, including quartering. Quartering refers to a dog's natural way of working without specific guidance from the handler and invariably involves the dog systematically working first left and then right (or downhill and uphill) of the handler, thereby sweeping a wide area ahead of the handler.
- Learning to direct the dog successfully when required, putting it into a position where it is at best advantage to lift a scent is a very important handler skill.
- Becoming familiar with the fickle nature of wind movements in differing terrain.
- Experimenting with various methods of working an area under different wind conditions.
- Acquiring knowledge of their dog's scenting ability and distance under varying conditions.
- Ensuring the dog never works beyond its capacity to maintain interest, whilst also extending the interest time factor.

Stage Two

This stage comprises two key changes. Firstly, the working capacity of the dog is steadily increased and, secondly, handler skills begin to play a part in the overall equation. Basically, this stage marks the point where the handler begins to learn their craft. Also, the majority of searches are blind for the dog but not for the handler. The handler always knows where the body is located in order to help them read the dog's indications, and to begin to understand the vagaries of wind on scent.

Knowledge of the exact position of the body at the beginning of this stage ensures the dog never makes a mistake during its first few months of training. It also ensures handlers learn their own part in the search

TOP: WANNABE SEARCH DOG GLEN TRIES THE JACKET ON FOR SIZE © BILL BATSON.

mode faster and more reliably. Without this, handlers tend to learn more slowly and their dog can be led into making mistakes that cause problems later. As the team progresses, blind searches are introduced. It is vitally important at this stage that the dog is made to use its nose at all times. Ground tracking is actively discouraged.

The formal assessment consists of the team working three areas of about 400 metres square. The handler doesn't know the location of the body and articles may be used instead of bodies. At this stage, the dog team should be able to:

- Formulate an efficient workable search strategy taking into account wind direction.
- Demonstrate adequate ranging where the dog is able to work up to 150 metres away from the handler.
- Demonstrate directional control.
- Demonstrate the find sequence.

The handler must also be able to justify the actions and performance of the team at the end of the search in a review session. As with the assessment in the first stage, 100% success is required for each search.

STEPHEN AUSTIN (SARDA SOUTHERN SCOTLAND) AND SKY © DAVID NICOL (OBAN MRT).

Stage Three

During this stage, the dog continues the challenges set in the previous stage, with no further developments. By now the dog, should be about eighteen months old and mature enough, both mentally and physically, to work over very difficult ground for long periods. The team now works blind which means that, from this point onwards, handlers need to develop special confidence in the ability of their dog.

Specifically, they are required to:

- Work, for up to two hours, in any search over moorland, forest, steep ground and crags.
- Work areas containing multiple bodies.
- Assess the thoroughness of their search.
- Report back on coverage of the area given to them.

At the end of stage three, teams are invited to take part in a three-day formal assessment, under the scrutiny of assessors from sister associations. Over this period, the team is required to undertake five searches in areas no greater than a square kilometre for a period of about two hours. A variety of criteria are used and we discuss these in the next chapter. Success here gives the team call-out status and the dog is referred to as a Novice Search Dog. However, achieving call-out status does not signify the end to training and assessment. All the associations have at least one other grade to achieve, that of Full Search Dog. SARDA

Southern Scotland has an intermediate grade (Grade 4) between novice and Full Search Dog (Grade 5). The assessment, in front of external assessors again, has the same number of runs and the same size of areas, but the team and, the handler especially, must demonstrate a much more efficient way of using their dog to search an area. Both the dog and handler should have gained experience and learned their craft through a number of actual searches and should now be a highly efficient team. The handler, at this stage, should also be experienced enough to take charge of a number of dog teams involved in a search and plan their search strategy with the search managers.

Although SARDA Southern Scotland identifies three stages between initial training and Novice Search Dog status, each containing a list of increasingly challenging tasks, there is degree of flexibility in order to eliminate any problems that occur and also to experiment with new ideas. So, it might be necessary to go right back to an earlier stage and work forwards again, if a serious difficulty occurs. Once a dog becomes a Full Search Dog, the team is not assessed again for three years providing the handler has attended over 70% of all training sessions. Anything less, then the reassessment period reduces to two years.

In terms of intensity of training it has been shown that dogs benefit best from daily training sessions. Of course, this isn't always practical, but at least three or four sessions per week are considered the absolute minimum. As training progresses and searches become longer, the frequency may become less. But, whatever the circumstances, twice a week is deemed the absolute minimum. Handlers who are unable to give this level of commitment are advised to consider whether they should proceed. Most prospective handlers are determined to succeed and become qualified, whatever it takes to meet the criteria in terms of time, effort and expense but, occasionally, as with many other forms of human endeavour, the eagerness of some trainees has to be tempered. The road to becoming a successful handler is based very much on quality, not just quantity, of training. Then, when the dog team is called out — which might be very soon post-assessment — everyone can be assured they are well up to the task.

In time, and with experience, frequent training may not be needed, as well-trained search dogs tend not to forget their basic training — although their capacity to perform over long periods is seriously affected. This is one of the main reasons why some are put forward for re-grading earlier than required.

TOPTIPS
TRAINING YOUR DOG TO BECOME OBEDIENT

Obedience training takes time – it is unreasonable to expect a puppy to learn overnight.

Don't assume that if dog obeys a command once, that command is learned. It has to behave properly on command many hundreds of times correctly, consecutively before the command-behaviour bond is established. Patience is the password to success!

Training should begin at the puppy stage.

Older dogs can be taught new skills but early learning is often faster and easier. Moreover, with the older the dog, it is likely there will be more bad habits to 'unlearn'. Preventing a problem in the first place is far less challenging that trying to cure it.

Puppies have very brief periods of concentration.

Training sessions should therefore be short and frequent — perhaps five to ten minutes, three times each day. That said, every time an owner interacts with their puppy, it is learning something about life in that household!

Training should be moderate and enjoyable using positive, non-adversarial, motivational methods (eg. games such as 'Go find!' and retrieving).

Obedience sessions should be upbeat so that the training process is enjoyable for everyone involved. Training before meal times means the puppy associates it with something pleasurable. Always praise successful behaviour and don't tell a puppy off for behaviour it can't possibly have learnt yet.

Whenever feedback (words, toys or food) is given to a dog, it should be given within three seconds.

Good timing is essential. That way, the dog associates the reward with the desired behaviour and not something it did subsequently.

Drive is an essential part of training a dog and without it, training becomes hard.

Building a relationship with a dog and enhancing its motivation (eg. toy drive) is essential.

Giving immediate praise when a dog behaves as required, reinforces the bond between the behaviour and the praise, and therefore increases the likelihood of the good behaviour being repeated.

Good behaviour can be shaped by rewarding it whenever it occurs, even when not elicited. The reward must be rewarding... don't use boring bits of the dog's dinner or a toy it isn't particularly keen on.

Punishment is an ineffective teaching technique. Praising a dog when it does something successful is far better than punishing it when it does not.

For example, if a dog runs away and is then punished on his eventual return, it will associate the return (the desired behaviour) with punishment, which makes it even harder to train. A confrontational approach undermines the relationship between a dog and owner. It's far better to ignore a dog when it displays unwanted behaviour and praise it when it behaves well. Dogs are not capable of learning from punishment and cannot think retrospectively.

Dogs should not be given commands that have no chance of being enforced.

Desired behaviours should be broken down into manageable stages that are achievable by the dog. Dogs only learn when they are successful. Further, every time a command is neither complied with nor enforced, the dog learns that commands are optional and turns off. Always set your dog to succeed, and when it has succeeded... quit! This is the point to which you return on the next training session. In other words, always end a session on a positive.

One command should equal one response. Repeating commands suggests to the dog that the first several commands have been a bluff.

For instance, telling your dog to 'Sit, sit, sit, SIT!' is neither efficient nor effective. Better to give the dog a single 'Sit!' command, gently place or lure it into the sit position, then praise or reward. Further, dogs only respond reliably to commands out of doors if they respond to them indoors. If a dog doesn't respond reliably to commands at home (where distractions are relatively minimal), it won't respond properly outdoors when tempted by other dogs, people, etc.

more TOPTIPS
TRAINING YOUR DOG TO BECOME OBEDIENT

11

Avoid giving dogs commands comprising several words. Combined commands such as 'Sit-down!' are unnecessary and may lead to confusion – particularly if the individual words are used to mean something else.

Also, use the same word with the same meaning at all times and ensure family members follow suit. For example, when using the command 'Come!' do not switch to 'Come here!' or 'Come boy!' The well-worn expression 'KISS' (Keep It Simple Stupid) may sound patronising, but it works.

12

There is no need to use a loud voice.

Even if a dog is unresponsive, the tone of voice when issuing commands should be calm and authoritative, rather than harsh or loud. Shouting at a dog when it doesn't respond to a command will not help the dog understand better what is required and may simply add to its fear, stress or confusion. Using a quiet voice also makes the dog work harder as it has to listen to you. Tone of voice is very important when it comes to giving praise and for motivation.

13

A dog's name should be used positively, and not in conjunction with reprimands or warnings.

In this way, it begins to trust that when it hears its name, good things happen. Dogs have no concept of identity so a dog's name should be trained as a command that means 'look at me' and always be a word it responds to with enthusiasm, never hesitancy or fear.

14

Be wary of inadvertently reinforcing your dog's misbehaviour, by giving it lots of attention (albeit negative attention) when it misbehaves.

For example, if a dog receives lots of attention and handling when it takes food from the table, that behaviour is being reinforced, and is therefore likely to be repeated.

Reflections on training

So, that's the theory, but what about the practice? How does it all work for real? Stephen Austin is a member of SARDA Southern Scotland. When he lost his dog Harvey, he hadn't planned a replacement straight away but, two months after Harvey's sad departure, Sky — a tri-coloured collie — bounced into his family's life. Stephen confesses he was 'collared' by Sky when on a social visit to a local animal rescue and rehoming centre. He went in for a cup of tea and left with a dog! Here, in his own words, is the story of their progress through training and assessment.

'Training a search and rescue dog had been on my agenda for a while but I really wanted to be fully settled with Oban MRT before exploring that further. Ideally, I wanted to spend time bodying for trainee dogs and their handlers, exploring the kind of commitment involved and looking into what makes a good search and rescue dog. I knew that several breeds were used, that a dog's physical characteristics are important and that a strong food or toy orientation was important to aid training but I was still a little unprepared when Sky entered our lives unexpectedly. Still, sometimes dogs choose you for a reason and it turned out she was totally obsessed

LEFT: DIAGRAM DEMONSTRATES A TYPICAL A SEARCH PATTERN WORKED BY DOG AND HANDLER © BOB SHARP/JUDY WHITESIDE.
RIGHT: STEPHEN AUSTIN AND SKY © STEPHEN AUSTIN.

KENNY HOLDS THE 'SMOKE' TO DIRECT THE APPROACHING HELICOPTER TO THE INCIDENT SITE © STEPHEN AUSTIN.

with play — a good thing — and, as we weren't in a position to get another dog, her arrival brought all my plans forward. We decided to go for it. My journey into training a search dog had begun!

'As Sky was fast approaching two years old I needed to get the training basics in place sooner rather than later. This required a series of planned steps. The point about training in steps is that each builds on the strength of the previous one then, if something goes wrong, things can be unpicked to a previous stage and work resumed from an earlier level of success. This makes for efficiency in training and ensures the dog's confidence remains high. Sometimes, there's a temptation to train a dog too quickly or omit particular steps. Shortcuts rarely work. When things go wrong — like the dog forgets what it's supposed to do — there's no systematic way to get it back on track. So, progress should follow recognised steps and proceed slowly.

'Sky and I train with SARDA Southern Scotland. The association has two training objectives, which the handler and dog have to achieve before proceeding to the call-out list. First is the 'find sequence' which entails the dog finding the casualty, returning to their handler, indicating — normally by barking — and then taking their handler back to the casualty. The second objective is for the dog and handler to cover the ground in a thorough but efficient manner. Sky's obsession for play and fondness of people at least gave her a fighting chance of learning the find sequence, although there was a small problem at the start — no bark! At this time she was the quietest dog in existence. Not a squeak, not even a whimper. I tried all the normal tricks of putting her toys out of reach, trying to wind her up as much as I could. This resulted in a lot of jumping and tail wagging but no bark. How was I going to solve this?

'Well, one evening I started my motorbike while Sky was sniffing around the back wheel and she barked in surprise. Inadvertently, I had stumbled across the key to the barking dilemma. Much to the amusement of my neighbours, Sky and I played a new game every evening for the next few weeks. This involved me giving the command 'Speak!', starting the bike, her barking, followed — much to her delight — by being thrown her favourite toy. If I was writing a scientific paper it would be called the 'Speak, bike, bark, play with toy' sequence!

'From this, we graduated to the shorter 'Speak, bark, get to play with toy' sequence. Initially, she looked somewhat bemused when hearing the speak command without a motorbike noise, but she still gave a restrained bark and got her toy as a result. You could tell she thought something was missing but such was her drive just to get her toy, she played on and evolved the sequence herself. So I now had a command — 'Speak!' — which I could use to train Sky to bark as part of the find sequence. This was the first of many challenges which Sky and I would overcome in the course of her training where a little bit of lateral thinking went a long way. However, other challenges would prove more exasperating and take longer to solve.

'Crucial to a dog's training is socialisation and becoming a key part of the mountain rescue team. It was my expectation that Sky, once fully qualified, would play a full role assisting my own team in its many searches. To do this she would need to get to know team members and be controlled in their presence. Oban MRT has been very supportive and Sky has attended many training sessions. At times this involves a search but, more often than not, she has had to be tied to a rucksack with only inaccessible sandwiches for company and ignored for a couple of hours whilst everyone focused on first aid, casualty handling, technical rescues and so on. At first she didn't appreciate being left alone with just a rucksack but, as her whimpering failed to generate any response from me, she soon settled down and is now as quiet as a mouse. I think it's crucial trainee dogs are exposed to experiences like this, because handlers don't spend all their time searching with their dog. Once a missing person is found, handlers typically resort to becoming a regular team member and dogs play no further role. Rescue situations are stressful enough without a dog howling or barking in the background!

'Over the next few months, things went well with Sky's training. The basics were falling into place and the dark winter evenings spent trudging up Ben Lora after work to reinforce the find sequence, seemed to be paying off. On a clear night, the reward of the brightly lit village of Connel guarding the entrance to Loch Etive down below with the mass of Mull's extinct volcano, Ben More, slumbering on the horizon, made it doubly worthwhile. However, more often than not, we were either caked in swirling cloud and refreshed with a fine drizzle or drenched by rain.

'At first, these rainy conditions seemed to impede Sky's abilities with a much reduced strike range but, as training progressed, her find rate under these conditions picked up to the same level as in dry conditions. The whole science of scent and scenting can appear a bit of a mystery. It's thought that dogs sense the by-products from bacteria on a person's skin and are capable of doing this from great distances. However, I'm not totally convinced that bacterial waste products are the sole scent a dog picks up on. Looking at the subject from a doggy basics point of view, Sky is solely interested in playing with her toy and constantly trying to maximise the frequency with which she can achieve that by finding a person. I think it's likely that as a dog becomes more experienced at playing the game, it adds more and more to its 'smells to look out for so I can get to play' data bank.

'For example, if when following a familiar bacterial smell associated with humans, the dog also picks up the smell of synthetic products used in, say shampoo, then that shampoo smell will get logged in the dog's memory. The next time they are out searching they might not pick up the bacteria scent first but instead get a whiff of shampoo and make the link to humans based on previous association. With further experiences of similar situations the dog increases the spectrum of scents it catches on the air, which it associates with humans and playing the game. I also suspect that humidity, temperature and such, impact on the dispersal of these scents through the air. Which would explain why, with experience, Sky became better at finding people in the rain — maybe the initial spectrum of smells she associated with humans didn't travel well in the wet and she needed to extend her databank of 'I get to play' smells before she could perform under those conditions. This illustrates why it is so important to train with a large number of volunteer bodies, in all weather conditions, as each of them will be adding their own personal and synthetic chemical smells to that all-important doggy scent data bank. Seeing a dog strike at close to half a kilometre and run into the body is a sight to behold. It makes you realise, irrespective of how they do it, that a dog's nose is a fantastic bit of mountain rescue team kit.

'After about six months of excellent progress Sky decided to change the rules of the game with no prior discussion! She started coming back to me as soon as her nose went up having picked up the scent of a human and indicating. An experienced dog might do this to let the handler know they were onto something, but then carry on and find the person. However, at this early stage in Sky's career it was not acceptable. She was just trying to get her toy prematurely and skip out the bit where she takes me to the body — a rather crucial step for a search dog! To sort this out we went back a number of steps to 'happy run aways', where the dog sees the person run off — and is restrained before they go — and then finds them to complete the sequence. We did these for a number of sessions to really get her confidence up as I didn't want to expose her to a full search training scenario again before feeling reasonably confident she had forgotten about short cuts.

'I then gave Sky no playtime at all for a few days before setting her up to see if she was back on track. I put her in a situation for potential play where she would have to evolve the whole process herself to get her toy because, as far as she was concerned,

I did know we were playing the game, so there'd be no point in her short-circuiting it. We set off on a walk, but with a friend hiding close by. I treated the session as a regular exercise walk where she had the freedom to wander and smell the countryside without her search coat. Having missed play for three days, she was hyper. I purposefully took a route about 20 metres downwind of where my friend was hiding. As we passed her location, Sky's nose shot up, she went in and found my friend, then came back to me, barked and completed the sequence by taking me back to the body. Immediately, I gave her the toy. This gave me confidence to put her back on training full search areas and the short-circuiting stopped. This whole diversion took about a month to work through and really emphasised the importance of working in a step-like manner. It also demonstrated that glitches can be worked through, but they take time and have to be tackled from the dog's perspective.

'As Sky and I continued training, I quickly began to understand the challenges that face a dog handler on a search. Searching an area has to be undertaken not only thoroughly but also efficiently, as time is of the essence and can make the difference between life and death. There are so many things to consider. As you walk across the hillside, you have to look to your own safety as you may be traversing very steep craggy ground whilst keeping a watchful eye on your dog's location, movement and general demeanour. You need to note wind direction and make a mental record of where your dog has been and which areas its nose has covered. How you search an area will vary depending on landscape

features, blocks of vegetation, streams that might translocate scent to other areas and knolls or stands of trees, which might generate very localised air currents. Large sections of steep hillside require relatively straightforward strategies for moving between boundary lines but areas with a variety of features often need quite complex approaches. All of this is not an exercise you can just amble through. As such, it's essential to think through a search strategy for the area before starting off. I soon learned that five minutes spent drawing a sketch and developing a search strategy before taking a single stride up the hill is a very important part of the overall search process.

'The more I trained with Sky, I began to understand how a dog's brain works and its physical capabilities. For a dog to perform it has to have confidence and a strong bond with its handler, enabling it to work many hundreds of metres away whilst still being aware of its handler's input and taking directional commands. If this bond and confidence is there then best use can be made of a dog's nose and its four-legged capability to run up and down the side of a hill numerous times, driven by its zest for life.

'Whilst the handler works the dog through an area, it is essential they are clued into the movement of their dog and also work in tune with the dog. If the dog's nose is up and 'on air', a competent handler will recognise this and inform the dog to carry on, even if it means going off the search strategy. This can be communicated just by taking a step in the direction of the dog. The more you work with your dog, the more you learn how to read their thinking. In my case, if Sky is on air but not sure whether she should carry on in the direction she is going, she will turn to look at me but maintain her body in the direction she was travelling. In this situation, I will support her and take a step in her direction at which point she will carry on. If she stops and turns her whole body to me, then, through hundreds of hours of training, experience tells me she has lost the scent and it's a case of — 'What now guv?' In this scenario I will give a hand signal to direct her back onto the search strategy plan. Her manner when she has locked onto a scent and strikes is to run with little intermittent jumps (presumably to get good reaffirming scent) and her tail starts to dance in a circular motion. Needless to say, there is no backward glance to me at this point — her brain has locked into 'I am going to get my toy' mode and she will only think of me when coming back from the casualty.

'A key part of training is working with helicopters. Sky's first helicopter ride took place during team training in Knoydart. The crew were great and made a real fuss and let her have a good sniff around the helicopter before taking off. She was pretty relaxed and seemed to enjoy the views from the opening. The most stressful part was when Oban team member Kenny Harris let off a smoke flare before the helicopter landed. It was the biggest firework she had ever seen — and there was no sofa to dive under! Entries into the belly of huge birds, which rattle and shake before lifting off the ground are still a little nerve racking but a doddle compared to smoke and flares.

'A year following the start of training, Sky and I had our first assessment. It was a blistering hot weekend in the Borders. This was it, the pressure was on to bring all we'd learned over the preceding year together and show the assessors that, as a team, we could do the job and get on the call-out list. With some trepidation, I went through the first of our search areas. We had to succeed on four of these with only one failure permitted. When I first saw my assigned area, I realised this was far from a simple walk in the park! The area seemed huge, with all manner of features and steep ground. To top it all, there was hardly any breeze — and with such high temperatures, I knew we'd have our work cut out! But Sky performed brilliantly. She found all the bodies and covered the areas very well — unfortunately, her handler didn't perform quite so well! It soon became apparent to the assessors that I needed more training in efficiently covering the ground.

'At the end of two days' tiring assessment I was informed that Sky was fantastic but I had more work to do! Not an easy thing to be informed by your friends and colleagues when they have been with you every step of the way during all the training. Having come so far, failing assessment was quite a knock and one I'd not expected but the experience really bought home to me that dog teams are just that — equal partners — and the human partner has to be as good as the canine one. At least I was in good company as many teams fail their first assessment through handler limitations. It also confirmed the point made to me, before starting out, that there would be highs and lows, frustrations and disappointments and sometimes I would have to dig deep, but when it all comes together it's one of the best and most rewarding things you can ever do. I still had a while to wait for that!

'At the time of writing, we are still to qualify at call-out grade, but the fantastic journey continues as we grow as a team. Initially, I thought training was all about the find sequence but, whilst this is at the heart of a successful dog team, there is much, much more. Learning to work as a team and knowing your dog's capabilities as well as your own strengths and weaknesses are important. And moving to a level where both parties take the lead, modifying the search pattern as it unfolds, is the ultimate goal. As mentioned before, Sky will tell me what information she has through her movements and she will turn fully and look to me when she has nothing to go on. Experience has taught her that if she subsequently follows my directions I will help her find her beloved toy. The most important lesson for me has been to always trust my dog. This is a common cliché used by dog handlers and yet everyone makes mistakes whilst learning, simply because they fail to trust their dog. Whenever Sky and I have failed to find a body in training it has always been a mistake of mine. It's the teamwork of dog and handler supporting and reading each other as they traverse the hill, along with the find sequence and search strategy that assessors look for when grading.'

Since writing their story, Stephen and Sky have joined the call-out team. From setting out as a novice dog team in 2008, they achieved Grade 5 at assessment in October 2010, happily joining the privileged group of fully qualified dog teams.

The faithful dogsbody

We can hardly talk about the training and assessment of search dogs without mention, in some detail, of the band of dedicated 'dogsbodies' who make it all possible! Who are they and what's their purpose? Apparently, the term 'dogsbody' originated in the Royal Navy, during the early part of the nineteenth century, where sailors described their staple food of dried peas and eggs boiled in a bag as 'dog's body'. Today, the word is more often used to describe anyone involved in some kind of drudge, menial or disagreeable work. In TV's *Blackadder*, Edmund Blackadder's long-suffering and much put-upon servant Baldrick, despite initially being the more intelligent of the two, is the classic dogsbody. However, SARDA dogsbodies are categorically not 'Baldricks', quite the opposite in fact.

In a nutshell, dogsbodies (bodies for short — or 'bravos', as they are referred to by SARDA Scotland) act as the person lost or injured on the mountainside. This small group of very committed individuals assist training in all weathers, in all kinds of terrain, for no direct benefit to themselves. In fact, training and assessment couldn't take place without their involvement. Because all search dogs are trained to find live people on the hills, the only way to teach them is for volunteers to hide in the hills and have the dogs look for them. In practice, the person working as the body is directed to a specific place on the hillside, which may be unknown to the handler and dog.

Once they're in position and hidden from view, the search area is described to the handler who, with their dog, has to cover the area in which the body is hiding. Obviously, the body must ensure they're not easily seen or heard so they wear clothes that match the terrain as best as possible and position themselves out of sight behind a small mound, in a gully or over a rise in the terrain, even buried under the snow in a prepared snowhole to simulate an avalanche scenario. Once in position they may have to remain in place for a long time, sometimes hours, simply waiting for the dog to find them.

Some associations train their dogs to bark when they find the body and then bark to indicate to the handler (barking at both ends!) but others simply require the dog to take note of the body and return to indicate by barking at the handler. Unless bodies are asked to interact with the dog, by encouraging it to bark for example, they are required to do nothing and not react to any attention from the dog — sometimes this proves difficult. It has been known for young dogs to take hold of the person and attempt to take them to their handler, and bodies have sometimes been nipped! It's much more likely a dog will walk on, roll on, lick or, it has to be admitted, pee on a body. (If the handler licks the body, pees on their rucksack or steals their sandwiches then the advice of a behavioural psychologist is definitely required!) There is one exception to the general rule about doing nothing.

Dogs are obviously playing a game they love and always enjoy winning. But if events drag on and the dog or handler begins to flag, bodies may be asked to show themselves briefly or make a noise to attract the dog's attention. This way, everybody achieves some success, albeit in a slightly artificial way.

Once the handler returns to the dogsbody with the dog, they instruct the person what to do. Some dog handlers require the body to play and make a fuss with their dog but, whatever happens, either the handler or the body will give the dog its favourite toy or reward. This might be a ball, ring, tuggy, food or even a plastic pterodactyl but it's critical the dog receives the reward immediately and learns to associate the find with its toy. This is absolutely crucial to training the dog to find. As far as the dog is concerned, it searches out the body simply to receive the reward of its toy. The fact it found someone who may be missing is quite irrelevant. Needless to say, if the person acting as the body isn't found, they would follow instructions and bale out after a given period of time.

Bodies kit themselves out to keep safe and warm, such as sleeping bags and hot flasks. And they're given a radio to enable them to keep in touch through the search. An equipment checklist for a body would include the following items:

- Rucksack.
- Warm sleeping bag.

- Waterproof bivvy bag big enough to house the body and all their belongings.
- Radio — most likely tuned to a different channel to the handlers, so instructors and assessors can communicate with the bodies without the handler hearing.
- Insulating mat to give protection from the wet/cold ground.
- Thermal/base layer clothing.
- Additional warm clothing.
- Shell/waterproof clothing.
- Midge repellent, sunscreen.
- Plenty of food and hot drinks.
- Entertainment (newspaper, book, mp3 player, mobile phone, homework).

The individual provides most of these items but all associations have a cache of equipment and clothing to ensure the safety and wellbeing of their bodies. Indeed, dogsbodies are looked after very well by the associations and always fully briefed on key matters. That said, there are bound to be a few questions the first-time dogsbody might want to ask...

Am I told exactly what is required of me? Where are you going to locate me on the hillside? How do I get there? What equipment do I need? Do you provide food and drinks for the day? What equipment will you provide? Will you know where I am as the day progresses? Does it matter how fit I am? How do I keep in touch with you? Will I be kept informed about what is happening? How long will I have to lie on the hill? Will I need to change location through the day? What happens if I get wet or very cold? What happens if I need assistance or first aid on the hill? What happens when a dog finds me? What happens at the end of the day?

Whatever the query, it will be dealt with fully and properly as it arises, and all the associations have developed procedures, documentation and insurance to keep everyone informed.

Bodies assist from the very start of a dog's training and continue all the way through to assessment. When they work with puppies, they're not just the 'lost person' but also help with the pup's socialisation with strangers and encouraging them to bark on command. Typically, the more experienced bodies are used at the very beginning of training, as teaching the find sequence is a complex procedure with a young dog. The interaction between dog, handler, body and instructor is important. The whole focus of the dog must be directed towards the body, who must be regarded by the dog as a very fun person to be with.

Many dogsbodies are non-team members, looking for a satisfying, if slightly different, way of spending their free time. Others are full team members or friends and relatives of handlers who enjoy working with dogs and their handlers. A key factor is that they are physically fit and, of course, enjoy working with dogs. For many people, it's an excellent way of experiencing and sharing in all the hard work that goes into training a search dog team. It's very rewarding to watch a young dog progress through the various stages of training, gaining experience, getting better and better until it becomes a full search dog, knowing they've been part of that dog's training. Even more so when that dog, and its handler, become instrumental in the saving of lives.

If your average search dog handler is often accused of, how shall we say, a certain level of eccentricity, their dogsbodies must be equally so! Why else would otherwise perfectly sane individuals spend hours alone wrapped up in layers of clothing lying in some unforgiving, damp location — or buried in snow — and growing colder by the minute, for the dubious pleasure of being found by an overexcited bundle of hair intent on showing its affection? We know of one couple that, on retirement — and having no previous experience of search dogs, or even mountain rescue — decided to buy a caravan and offer their services to SARDA. Throughout the year, weekend after weekend, come rain, shine, hail or snow they criss-cross the country, hiding in holes for fun, loving every minute of it!

It's not unknown for the experienced dog handler to comment that he and his dog have become a very proficient team over the years because of the massive amount of practice and training they'd undertaken. This may be so, but it doesn't always follow that extensive practice leads to efficiency and success. It's vital to practise the right things else you might become very good at doing things very well — incorrectly! The key to success is the use of feedback through monitoring and assessment. Knowing what you're doing wrong — and doing it correctly — are vital to progress, which is why assessment is such a vital part of the training process for dog teams. It's also a process which varies across the associations, despite there also being many similarities.

Top dog!

'You get on the radio and tell the assessors you've found a body. Then you give them the plan for the rest of your area. At the end of two hours, you walk out having found nobody else. You think you've covered everything, you've put the dog in all the right places and now you've got to face the result. But it's a pass! Then they tell you to get yourself ready to do another area, and you go through it all again!' Kaz Frith

One of SARDA's greatest strengths is the fact that dog teams must present themselves for assessment — and continue to do so every two or three years. Assessment is absolutely critical. It's the stepping stone to the call-out list, the culmination of years of hard work.

Co-author Bill Jennison set out on his career with SARDA over 30 years ago. Here, he reflects on one part of the overall assessment process: the nerve-wracking experience of the mandatory stock test. No handler can allow their dog to take off after sheep or cattle when on a search and failure to pass the stock test means all the hard work of several years' training could come to nothing in an instant — a critical and intimidating time for most handlers.

'It was 7.00am, one winter day in February and I was driving along the side of Derwentwater in the Lake District. This was the first day of an event I'd been training towards for two and a half years and, already, things weren't going well. Where were the sheep? I needed some sheep to convince myself Jay was safe with them! Lodged in the back of my mind was the

thought you could never be one hundred percent sure your dog would not take off after sheep. German Shepherds are not held in the highest regard in this area and I was the only dog team with one. My nerves were getting to me. I felt agitated and had to calm down. Eventually I spotted half a dozen sheep in the woods by the roadside, found a parking spot and let Jay out for a pee. With much relief on my part, she just wandered around and ignored the sheep. Fifteen minutes later I called her in and went back to the car, somewhat happier. I had to smile, as we headed back into Keswick, when I spotted another trainee, also up for assessment, heading off down the lakeside. Clearly I wasn't the only one with similar worries!

'After breakfast, everyone set off down Borrowdale, to a farm owned by Charlie Relf, for the stock test. This was a totally new experience. We hung over the dry stone wall watching proceedings. One by one we were called in and told to walk around with our dog then Charlie used his dogs to move the sheep around the field. I had never felt so nervous in my life! Up to

this point, everyone before me had passed. Charlie seemed to prolong the agony, probably because I had the only German Shepherd! Jay moved away from the sheep towards the corner of the field. Bad move! Charlie expertly moved the sheep so Jay was backed into the corner. Somewhere there is a photograph of me stood in the middle of the field with my hands behind my back, fingers crossed! Jay obviously became distressed as the sheep pushed in closer. There was nothing I could do if she decided to fight her way out, but she just stood there.

'Charlie was obviously satisfied she wasn't going to do anything and moved the sheep on, at which point Jay saw her escape and darted away — right after one of Charlie's dogs! This was a huge relief for me although it wasn't quite all over yet. Charlie exclaimed that German Shepherds are only good for one thing — guard dogs. 'Got one mesel,' he said. 'And by the way, NEVER let your dog chase owt!' But I'd passed and, just then, that was all I cared about!

'The next three days passed without

FACING PAGE: **SEARCH DOG CORRIE** © PETER SANDGROUND.

major incident. There were two assessment runs each day, and it was comforting that I knew most of those involved. As each assessment progressed, I began to feel things were going okay. Then, on the final day, it was announced that another handler, Bob James, and I were to have a 'run off' for the shield awarded to the best novice dog. Two similar search areas had been set up on the sides of a valley. The bodies were in approximately the same position on each side. We set off at the same time and both found 'our' body within about ten minutes of each other. The exercise was too close to call so the assessors decided we should share the trophy. Of all the assessments I have had to endure since, this was the one I remember most clearly!'

But why is assessment necessary? As human beings, we're constantly being measured and assessed in one way or another and there are tried and tested procedures to check whether set criteria have been met. The assessment of dogs and their handlers is no less rigorous than in any other walk of life. Every association needs to know that their dog teams are capable of meeting agreed criteria and competent to work straight away. The police who call upon the services of dog handlers also need absolute assurance that newly qualified dog teams can work effectively. There's no room for wavering on standards — teams must be ready to operate effectively and immediately.

The way assessment is carried out varies between the associations, but all of them require candidates to search specified areas under the scrutiny of their peers, as well as members of other associations. Those members responsible for assessment have lots of operational experience. With SARDA Southern Scotland, for example, they're required to be handlers who currently have, or have had, a fully graded search dog, and have been reassessed at least once. They are then elected by the membership to serve a one-year probationary period as a trainee assessor before they can become an external assessor with another association. The presence of external assessors allows parity between associations and ensures that any police force in the British Isles which asks for the assistance of a SARDA air scenting dog will get a dog team that is able to perform to a known minimum standard. It's a measure of credibility should a dog team's qualifications ever be called into question.

Each association has a number of preliminary assessments of obedience and stock safety, prior to formal assessment although the exact details and timing vary. Some are integrated within the training programme, whilst others separate assessment from training. Some tests have a subjective element, others are more formal and objective. Either way, the stock test is a deal-breaker — small wonder it's so nerve-wracking!

Potential search dogs must demonstrate that they can work safely in the presence of livestock, under any circumstances. Many searches take place around farmland or in wild areas where sheep roam throughout most of the year. In some parts of the UK — Scotland in particular — deer roam free across the year. Dogs cannot be allowed to let natural hunting instincts interfere with their working ability. No association could allow a dog that was suspected of being distracted by livestock

to begin formal training or continue working once qualified. The procedures for stock testing may vary but most associations use some kind of initial internal assessment, followed by assessment by an outside person such as a local farmer or shepherd. Dogs must also demonstrate a basic level of obedience, and be able to walk to heel and obey standard commands such as 'Heel!' 'Stop!' 'Stay!' and 'Come!' A dog that doesn't understand these commands cannot hope to be trained successfully. NSARDA has devised a procedure where dog and handler are required to perform a number of exercises on varied terrain, at a pace directed by an assessor. Specifically, the dog is required to walk to heel both on and off the lead, remain in a down position for up to ten minutes, and stop on command when both close to their handler and at a distance.

It goes without saying that any search dog must be fit and agile enough to work effectively in the terrain, able to negotiate small stone walls, boulder strewn ground and other natural obstacles. It should also be evident they have the right kind of temperament. They must have a good working partnership with their handler, a natural curiosity and show they aren't aggressive to other dogs or people. Characteristics like these are easily noted by more experienced handlers.

As for the human being in the partnership, it may seem obvious that anyone who aspires to become a qualified dog handler must like dogs, but it has been known for individuals who are not really 'doggy' people to express an interest. Apart from the few exceptions mentioned earlier, before the aspirant handler even embarks on the training process, they must already be an experienced member of a mountain rescue team — and have the backing of that team. It's absolutely essential that handlers are committed to the cause of mountain rescue and sufficiently competent to cope with the technical and physical challenges central to many rescues.

Dog handlers too must possess a good level of fitness. And be able to demonstrate that they are at one with the mountain environment — perhaps more so than their mountain rescue team colleagues. They can't rely on SARDA to teach them basic mountaineering skills! They don't need to be skilled rock climbers but they must be confident when moving over steep ground in both summer and winter conditions. They should also be proficient navigators and familiar with radio communications. A good measure of self-reliance is also a must as there are many times when handlers find themselves in extreme situations caused by the weather or terrain when they need to cope without outside support. It helps if potential handlers are happy to work alone or in small groups and have a general inclination to work unaccompanied. Peter Durst, a highly experienced member of SARDA, once commented that, 'as a dog handler you will not be asked to exceed your capabilities, but you will approach the limit of your capabilities on more occasions than the average team member.'

Probably the biggest factor, for anyone thinking of becoming a dog handler, is their willingness to invest an extraordinary amount of time, money and energy to the process — it's a decision that can seriously impact on friendships and family and not to be taken lightly.

WELL AT LEAST HE FOUND YOU!! © DAVID ALLAN

Assessment in action

Not surprisingly, the various associations have similar assessment programmes although there are variations, which have developed across the years. At their core is the search scenario, in which dog teams are required to locate a number of bodies in a prescribed area under the watchful eye of the assessors. There are differences in the number of search scenarios given to the handler in any single assessment event, as well as the monthly timing and length — in terms of days — of assessment. One programme might involve assessment on a number of individual days within a time limit — as occurs in the Lakes — whereas another might involve a three or four day assessment held either once or twice a year. The system adopted by some associations involves five 'runs' (search scenarios) per candidate in areas of up to

ASSESSMENT PROGRAMME FOR SARDA SOUTHERN SCOTLAND AND LAKE DISTRICT MOUNTAIN RESCUE SEARCH DOGS

	SARDA SOUTHERN SCOTLAND		LAKE DISTRICT MOUNTAIN RESCUE SEARCH DOGS	
Pre-training criteria.	Must 'body' for three months. Member of recognised MRT. Reference from team leader.	Up to three months.	Member of a recognised Lake District MRT. Reference from team leader. Initial assessment of dog. Mandatory obedience test (basic skills required for effective training).	Up to three months.
Stock test.	Carried out annually: Farmer or shepherd serves as examiner.	Every twelve months.	Continuous through dog's working life.	Ongoing.
Training stages.	Indication test. Small area test. Log book.	Up to two years.	• Stage 1, Develop sound indication, leads up to blind searches of 10 to 15 minutes. • Stage 2, works up from end of stage 1 through to starting assessment. • Stage 3 Assessment. • Stage 4 Graded dogs, maintaining and pushing standards. • Progress recorded by assessors and training reports issued to handlers.	Up to two years.
Novice.	Five search scenarios in three days. External assessors involved.		No Novice grade.	
Full.	Five search scenarios in three days. External assessors involved.	Up to one year.	Eight assessment days, two of which must be in succession. Usually two areas per day unless large (3.5 hours plus). Have to be seen by external assessors during assessment process. Handler to hold MREW Casualty Care Award.	Up to one year.
Ongoing assessment.	Required every two years (three years if handler attends 70% of training). Two search scenarios in one day. External assessors involved.	Every two (or three) years.	'Look See Assessment' to ensure dog/handler team is still effective (1.5 hour area, overseen by two assessors). If necessary, a more formal assessment arranged to test out any weakness. Informal checking during weekly training and call-outs.	Annually. Ongoing.

Handler:	Date:	Assessor:	
Dog:	Grade:	Location:	Area No:

AREA

10 – Excellent	Initial search strategy	
9 – Very good/Excellent	Ranging	
8 – Very good	Natural hunting ability	
7 – Good	Directional control	
6 – Acceptable/Good	Coverage of area	
5 – Acceptable	General reading of dog's actions	
4 – Weak/acceptable	Handler's response to changes	
3 – Weak	Dog's maintenance of performance	
2 – Doubtful/Weak		
1 – Doubtful		
0 – Outright failure		

FIND SEQUENCE

Did handler read strike?	1	
Yes	2	
Dog unsighted to handler (UN)	3	
No	4	

Did handler read find?	1	
Yes	2	
Dog unsighted to handler (UN)	3	
No	4	

Missed body code	
Not assessable by assessor or body	1
Handler knew of missed area on debrief	2
Bad luck in very bad conditions	3
Bad luck but dubious coverage of area	4
Due to poor area coverage	5
Due to bad area coverage	6
Failure to read dog's interest	7
Failure to recognise dog has found	8
Dog has no interest in an obvious body	9
Dog failed to indicate	10

Missed body (further details overleaf)							
1		2		3		4	

Air scent strike A – Straight to body B – To body site – had to work for find C – To body site – failed to find body location D – Strike/bumped into site E – Ground scented to body location	1	
	2	
	3	
	4	

Return to handler F – Too close to return G – All the way H – Well short of handler I – Only till handler in sight J – Came out from body but no return K – Not at all	1	
	2	
	3	
	4	

Indication L – Full indication to handler M – Handler read attempt to indicate N – Handler failed to read dog's actions O – No indication P – Suspect induced indication	1	
	2	
	3	
	4	

Return to body Q – All the way back to the body R – All the way close to body site S – Well short of body sight T – Too close to return U – Not at all	1	
	2	
	3	
	4	

Follow up sequences V – Consistent handler/body returns W – Carried out satisfactory returns X – Carried out weak returns Y – Too close for follow-up returns Z – No attempt at follow-up returns	1	
	2	
	3	
	4	

Missing information? Add information overleaf

AIR SCENT TRAINING ASSESSMENT AREA REVIEW

a square kilometre with a time limit of two hours per search. In addition, some associations require handlers to maintain a logbook of their training and assessment experiences. See page 148 for a summary of how two different associations manage their programmes.

All the associations use particular geographical areas for assessment based on past experience and suitability. The areas chosen have to meet specific criteria not only in regard to their technical suitability — reflecting the kind of terrain and level of difficulty found on real searches — but also vehicle access, permission from landowners, stock avoidance and the availability of suitable accommodation. An area should allow assessors to observe both dog and handler most of the time, and test the dog team's ability to both search and clear — in a solid find sequence — over the type of ground they are likely to be called into. SARDA has examined the suitability of this approach over the years, ever mindful that it can never match the variability of the real situation. It would be very difficult, if not impossible, to set up an assessment search in a forest or in the dark, for example. The possibility of an assessor walking with the handler has also been discussed but, in the end, the standard format of a dog team working an area in daylight in full view of the assessors is arguably the best approach.

Most associations work to the assessment criteria devised by NSARDA, although it's fair to say the procedures based on these criteria are not an absolute blueprint every association follows meticulously. Each has its own approach dependent on its particular circumstances but, in every case, a precise marking

TOP: SARDA WALES DOG UNDERTAKES THE STOCK TEST — WHAT WILL THE DOG DO WHEN THE SHEEP MOVE IN? © RICHARD BEECH LEFT: WAYNE THACKRAY (SARDA ENGLAND) AND DODGE UNDER ASSESSMENT FROM NEVILLE SHARP ABOVE: BILL JENNISON AND JAY WITH THEIR BEST NOVICE DOG SHIELD.

scheme is used to assess handlers and dogs on a search. This is necessary to bring objectivity to the process and consistency between handlers. The marking scheme used by a particular association is used by all assessors whether they be internal or from other associations. On page 151 is an extract from an assessment schedule, devised by NSARDA some years ago, to identify the criteria used to check the ongoing performance of dog and handler as they work their way through a search task.

It's important to emphasise that forms like this are living documents and regularly subject to evaluation. Currently, there is discussion about the usefulness of some of the numerical systems. For example, it may not be feasible to differentiate say 'area coverage' on a ten-point scale — a lesser scale may be more practical. There's also a suggestion that specific skills such as ranging and strike distance should receive greater elaboration. Several approaches have been tried but there's still much work to be done.

At the end of each day's assessment, the team of assessors meet to discuss the progress of each dog team. The performance of each team for each run is analysed in detail and both positive and negative features balanced. This is where the marking schedule comes into its own, because it provides a factual picture uncontaminated by the fading recollection or prejudices of those involved. The details contained in the schedule, along with the views of each assessor who observed a particular candidate, are combined and a decision made about whether the team has passed or failed the day's tasks. Most important, feedback is given to the handler to help them progress the following day. At the end of the assessment event, the assessors make a final decision about whether the dog team has passed. If the team has failed, they must wait until the next assessment for the opportunity to be retested.

Although the nature and timing of a formal stock test varies between the associations, most stock-test each dog on an annual basis — an anxious experience for most! Anyone who works with dogs knows they can have, very naturally, a mind of their own. It is possible to train habits into and out of a dog, but it's never certain they'll do exactly what's required, when it matters. More often than not, a local farmer tests the dogs and they are free to carry out the test in any way they see fit. Farmers and shepherds are perhaps best placed to make judgements about a dog's behaviour in the company of sheep and cattle. It's also courteous — and good public relations — to ask those who work and own the land being used for assessment to carry out the test. That said, some associations devise and carry out their own tests, sometimes with shepherds absent.

Whatever the format, the dog's reaction to the sheep is assessed and a decision made whether that dog has passed or failed. One association starts with the dog being worked in a pen containing a small number of sheep. The dog must run to the handler and be comfortable in the presence of sheep. This is followed by the sheep running past the dogs to see if there is any possibility of chasing the sheep. The procedure adopted by NSARDA is very similar. The dog is called through a number of sheep in a confined area then given a 'Stay!' command and the sheep are herded within five metres of the dog. The dog fails if it attacks or chases the sheep. It is acceptable for dogs to break their stay, provided they retreat or return to their handler.

Of course, dogs can also cause problems when amongst other animals and birds. It's well known they can disturb cattle, although they probably cause little danger. Indeed, a dog that approaches a cow and her calf could well receive a nasty, if not fatal, kick. A problem not universally recognised by handlers occurs when search dogs are close to game birds. Young pheasants in pens are very easily disturbed and extremely susceptible to stress and disease from dogs. Pens of birds sometimes have a unique disease resistance and a search dog which moves around several may inadvertently pass on a disease from one pen to another. Pens should never be opened to allow a dog to search within as this will invariably cause total panic amongst the birds and send them in all directions and handlers are always advised to speak to the local gamekeeper when searching close to pens of game birds.

Doubtless every handler, failed or successful, has a 'stock test tale', often highly comical — the sort of tale they and their friends are happy to recount, over and again, given any sociable opportunity. One such tale involved the handler, about to subject his dog to its first stock test, who was so keyed up he'd failed to notice someone had unclipped the dog from its lead. Oblivious to his plight, into the field he marched, doing his best to look professional, trailing a dog lead. Without a dog. Needless to say, the moment he realised he was without a dog, in true comic fashion, the assembled crowd erupted in laughter. Happily, once recovered, the dog did go on to pass the test.

Less fortunate was the handler from a visiting association who came to train during the time of the home association's stock test. It was agreed he should be tested like everyone else. Nobody took much notice until someone announced that the man's dog had been in the field for a very long time. Everybody watched. The handler had been asked to move his dog around the field for a good five to ten minutes. Then, with a backward glance at his handler, the dog launched himself into the flock of sheep and began to chase. He was quickly brought to heel and none of the sheep were harmed, but the shepherd commented afterwards that he knew the dog would go for them — and he'd made that judgement within a couple of minutes. The farmer could tell the dog 'was interested' in sheep — it was just a matter of time before he showed his true colours. The dog, of course, failed the test and headed for home — but not before the shepherd had offered the handler a sizeable sum of money for his dog, believing it could be successfully trained as a sheep dog! So not entirely a failure!

From a personal point of view

Stock test tales apart — humorous or otherwise — assessment is a serious business and not just for the handler. Bill Jennison can boast long and distinguished experience as a trainer and assessor. It has allowed him to formulate a number of clear views about assessment.

'It doesn't matter whether you're an external assessor attending an assessment course run by another association or an internal assessor for your own, you have to be fair and honest. The bottom line always has to be — would you feel happy if the dog team you are assessing was out searching for one of your relatives? Any doubts at all and the competence of the team has to be called into question. As the training officer of my own association I don't like to assess our own members. Because I have responsibility for their training, to assess them as well means that, in part, I am also assessing myself! I feel strongly that the performance of any dog team should be assessed quite objectively by somebody who is detached from the operation and training of the team's own association. I also feel strongly that when assessing others, the assessor should have their own dog with them. Then, if a candidate doesn't understand or accept the comments offered by the assessor, they're in a position to demonstrate to the candidate the matter in question. Linked to this last point I feel that if an assessor does not have a current qualified dog then their credibility could be called into question.

'There are a number of practical things I have learned over the years. Assessors should appreciate any differences between their own association and the one they've been invited to assess, especially in regard to training. External assessors are asked to make comment on the performance of dog teams that have been trained by another association, whose approach may be different from their own. Therefore they have a duty to assess them within the context of the 'home' association and never offer advice about training methods to dog handlers under assessment. An external assessor may have a view about the approach adopted by another association and, if they felt it might add to constructive discussion, they should raise it at some other time — not when they're wearing their assessor's hat.

'The duration of an assessment run is something people have questioned over a number of years. Two hours may seem a long time for one assessment run, but I feel it takes this long to see if the team can maintain its performance. Dogs do become bored if they search for long periods without a find. Handlers also become frustrated and that change in mood can be transferred to their dog. The placing of bodies too is a matter for discussion. People should not be placed in ridiculous places where a dog would find it extremely difficult to find them or where the team would be placed in danger.

'I think the use of marking schemes is of paramount importance as they explain in detail what assessors should be looking for. As an additional aid, I tend to study the search area before sending out the bodies and work out in my mind how I would search the area. I then place one body where the team should get a find within about 20 minutes. An early find tends to give candidates a very welcome confidence boost. Other bodies can then be placed in positions where the dog will find if the search is carried out in a methodical way. There are occasions when the handler decides on a different way to search the area to the one I expect, but that's alright. There is never a correct way to search an area.

'I am always conscious that the first assessment for a dog team is a difficult time. For this reason they should be looked at in a slightly different way to those being upgraded or reassessed — for example, the depth of feedback given to the handler may be more substantial for those going for their first assessment — but the criteria cannot be adjusted. Assessors should always remember that if the team passes, then they become fully operational and must be expected to be responsible for a search task, as any handler would be. The main thing is that assessors adopt a positive stance and endeavour to help handlers as much as possible. Assessors are not there to fail people. They want handlers to show them what they can do and, within the bounds set by the assessment criteria, they want to pass everyone.'

Simon James and Caroline Morton are members of SARDA South Wales. They have several years' experience assessing dogs for other associations. Simon is a cartographer with the Ordnance Survey and Caroline a trainer with the Guide Dogs for the Blind Association. Both have fully graded search dogs. This is their take on what they look for when assessing.

'Our view as visiting assessors is that we assess to the standard required by the hosting association. Overall, we're not focused solely on passing or failing a dog team in a particular area, rather we need to be convinced the team is ready to operate effectively on a real call-out. We feel this is the crux of the assessor's responsibility. Specifically, we focus our attention on the following aspects.

Firstly, the indication sequence. We need to see an obvious, identifiable and specific find sequence, which is consistent across all searches. Both dog and handler must show they are committed and enthusiastic.

Secondly, we look at the area covered. At Novice level we look for a thorough coverage: the area has to be completely stitched up. Although, it's not critical at this stage, if the handler is 100% efficient in their searching.

'At Full Search Dog level we want to see what we describe as a bold approach to the search, which shows a high level of efficiency. This might mean that both dog and handler cover less ground but still manage to fully clear an area. We're also looking for thorough coverage in technical areas such as gullies and crags.

'Thirdly, we look for a proactive approach by the dog in which it shows a degree of independence and decision-making that is not dictated by a series of constant send-aways by the handler. As part of this we look to see if the dog is effective and controlled in its ranging capability. Central to this is the efficiency in what the dog does — it shouldn't move in a manner that wastes time or duplicates coverage.

'Fourthly, the handler must provide an accurate report of the search, commenting on what areas were or were not covered as well as the capability of their dog, detailing exactly what it achieved or failed to do. All of these individual factors will combine to tell us about the level of competence and professionalism of the dog team. There may be particular strengths and perhaps an area in need of further development but, if we feel the team is able to operate effectively, efficiently and safely, then we would not hesitate in awarding a pass.'

Why do some dog teams fail?

There are occasions, of course, when dog teams fail to meet the assessment criteria or stock test and the implications of this are quite significant. Failing a stock test means the team is removed from the call-out list and not allowed to resume training until the dog is retested and found to be safe. Failing an assessment requires a team to go through the full assessment process again. Hopefully, when this happens, the handler takes on board the reasons for failure to ensure the same problems don't arise again.

A unique study carried out some years ago, by Dave Perkins and Pete Roberts from the Centre for Search Research in Northumberland, examined why dog teams fail assessment. They used data from 200 assessments organised by SARDA Southern Scotland, involving twenty different dog teams and 476 potential dog finds. The actual data used was taken from the assessment sheet shown on page 151. The purpose of the analysis was two-fold. Firstly, the researchers were keen to determine how likely it is that a dog will find

SEARCH DOG ANGUS FINDS SARDA SOUTHERN SCOTLAND BODY JOANNA © PETER SANDGROUND.

a missing person. To do this, they estimated what is called the Probability of Detection (PoD). Search managers need to know the capability of the resources that can be deployed at a search incident, be they helicopters, dogs or people, so they can deploy those resources in the most effective way possible. They might consider, for example, how the terrain or weather affect the capability of different resources and what is the likely success of each resource. The study showed that, overall, dog teams are capable of achieving a PoD of 90%. In other words, from the 476 opportunities to find a person, dog teams were successful on 430 occasions. Because the study was based on a large amount of data over many years (1988-94), and obtained from realistic searches involving a wide cross-section of dogs, the researchers were confident that the figure of 90% is a valid figure for the PoD of an air-scenting wilderness search dog. In lay terms, what this means is that if a dog team is working in an area where a missing person is located and the handler uses their dog correctly, then the chances of finding that person are extremely high — a 90% success rate. This is sure testament to the effectiveness of air-scenting search and rescue dogs. One of which SARDA members can be very proud.

The second aim of the study was to look at the factors that have a bearing on the success or otherwise of dog teams. The researchers were especially interested to know why dogs fail to find bodies. Of the 476 potential finds, there were 46 non-finds, which could be examined. On these occasions, 51 reasons for failure were identified. In each case, the fault lay with either the handler or the wind conditions, which prevailed at the time of the search. When conditions are calm with no wind, it's much more difficult for a dog to pick up an airborne scent. Regardless of a dog's capability, it's been shown there is a greater potential for a failure to find under these conditions. As we've already seen, wind and its affect on the flow of airborne scent is a very complex factor. Handlers can be neurotic about the wind, particularly when being assessed. Even on call-outs, dog teams rarely have the luxury of working with the wind to their advantage but it's very important during assessment and handlers need to use it well. When there is a lack of wind, dogs have to be directed much more to ensure the search area is thoroughly covered but, in the study, there were only a few occasions when the absence of wind was cited as the reason for the dog's failure to find the body. Most reasons focused on the handler's behaviour.

Significantly, 75% of the reasons for failure were attributed to handler error such as a failure to read the dog's interest, failure to recognise the dog had found the body, or poor area coverage. Poor area coverage was found to be the most significant problem. These results show that how the handler organises and manages their search, and also how they control and read their dog's reactions, are critical to success and the latter is very important. In many cases, when a dog fails to indicate, there are subtle changes in its behaviour which, if recognised by the handler, can be used to encourage the dog to search in a particular area and hopefully lead to a find. Of course, this can only happen if the handler has sight of their dog at the time of the strike. There are occasions when a dog is persistent and repeatedly gives indications to their handler who initially fails to get the message. Eventually, the handler picks up on the dog's behaviour and reacts accordingly — situation saved by the dog! The handler's understanding of their dog's behaviour and their sensitivity to subtle movements or mannerisms are absolutely crucial in the overall search process.

This was borne out when the investigators assessed the factors, which lead to an increased PoD. Not surprisingly, they showed that the chances of finding a body increase when handlers have a good search strategy, fully cover the search area, react well to unexpected changes in the weather or ground conditions with good directional control over their dog, and read their dog's reaction well. When they are competent on all these factors, their chances of finding a body are in the order of 95% to 100%.

So far, we've said nothing of the dog itself, and the part it might play in failure, but the truth is, the study found no evidence of canine failure. As the saying goes, 'Aye, t'dog's alright but th'andler's useless.'

WE CAN ALWAYS RETAKE IT NEXT YEAR...!!
© DAVID ALLAN

Call out the dogs

'Stamina and endurance, coupled with suppleness and the ability to work things out, are part of the sheepdog's heritage. This dog is travelling at speed, looking where he is going and concentrating on his job at the same time while he is barely touching the ground.' Barbara Sykes

Operationally, there are refined and well-practised systems in place for deploying dogs and their handlers and for integrating them successfully with other agencies. Many years of practice and thousands of different kinds of searches in areas across the UK have ensured that mountain rescue teams, the police authorities and dog teams work in harmony, efficiently and effectively. And, whilst every search is specific, there's now a wealth of historical and statistical evidence that can help the police refine the search for a missing person to focus resources more effectively. The resources, clothing and equipment available to mountain rescue team members and search dog handlers, along with advances in computer and GPS technology, have had a huge impact on the way searches are carried out and the comfort of all involved — dogs and humans alike! Whilst they might take a bit of getting used to — particularly for some of our four-legged friends — helicopters enable the rapid delivery of multiple dog teams to the areas they need to search.

Invariably now, dog teams are called to assist when someone is reported missing in the mountains, hills or forests. In fact, they're often the first resource to be requested by the police and search managers if a large area has to be covered or a night time search is required. A dog team can be deployed quickly by helicopter to remote areas where they can immediately begin to start searching, whilst other search resources are being marshalled and, as we've said before, it's not just mountain incidents where dogs play a part. Increasingly, they're called to search semi-urban or farmland for missing children or old people who have strayed from a care home. In recent times, dogs have also been used to locate possible victims of crime as well as people drowned in inland waterways such as canals and lakes. Statistics reveal there are more and more incidents where handlers and their dogs respond to situations which do not involve other mountain rescue teams. But, for all this to work well, procedures have to be in place to ensure they are deployed for the right purpose — at the right time.

Typically, search dogs are summoned as early as possible, invariably the first resource requested by the police or mountain rescue team. This is for two reasons. Primarily, this gives the dogs the best chance of success because it means their ability to air scent at the scene is not compromised by the presence of other people. So, they are almost always tasked prior to the arrival of other personnel involved in the search, to avoid the risk of contaminating the search area. This also gives handlers a greater time window to travel to the incident location, bearing in mind that some may be travelling great distances from their home.

Each association has a well-honed call-out system. Central to this is a coordinator who serves as the link between the police and the handlers within the association. The control room for each police authority will have the contact details — a first point of contact and back up details — for each coordinator, to enable contact via a single phone call and/or text message. In Scotland, each of the eight police authorities has details for both the Scottish associations, with one being nominated for the first call. For example, Northern Constabulary would call SARDA Scotland first, whereas Dumfries and Galloway Constabulary would initially call SARDA Southern Scotland. The control room indicates the number of dogs required — which may just be one or as many as possible — and the coordinator indicates whether the request can be fully met. If not, they can call the other association for help. Before the police control room contacts the call-out coordinator, the local mountain rescue team may also be consulted about which resources to deploy, but this doesn't always happen.

If it's obvious a search dog team is required (and most police authorities will have sufficient experience to know when to use dogs) then the rescue team will be by-passed and a direct call made to the call-out coordinator. The rescue team may be called later and either placed on standby or called out, following discussion with the team leader. In cases where a search is required, it's more than likely the leader will advise deployment of dog teams first, followed by his or her team members. Whatever is decided, the main thing is that dogs are given an opportunity to search an area before other people contaminate it with their own body scents.

Once a call-out coordinator receives the green light from the police, handlers are alerted by phone or text message. In some cases handlers continue to be contacted via pager, although this technology is now considered somewhat dated and not always used. The call-out coordinator will decide which handlers are required and, if only a few are needed, will contact those who live closest to the incident location. In situations where there are several people

missing or the search area is expected to be very large then many handlers, if not all those available, will be tasked to attend. In these instances, it's likely that handlers from adjacent associations will also be requested, as was the case with the Cumbria shootings in June 2010 or during the Lockerbie disaster, when dog teams from both sides of the border were tasked. In the case of Lockerbie, some handlers travelled hundreds of miles and were involved for many days.

Once handlers and their dogs are on scene, their involvement and what they do is managed by the search coordinator with overall responsibility. This may be a police officer, mountain rescue team leader or other qualified person, and he or she is guided by a number of key principles.

There's absolutely no point in summoning search dogs after all else has failed. Calling in the dogs on the second or third day of an operation, might tick some boxes but it's hardly an exercise in search effectiveness. Neither should the time of day be an issue. Dogs can work anytime, day or night, in most kinds of weather. If there is a limitation, it's that dogs shouldn't be deployed during the heat of the day in still, hot conditions when they're not only at risk of suffering hyperthermia but also, because scent tends to rise when the weather is hot and still, it is very difficult for them to detect. Basically, heat makes scenting difficult, saps a dog's energy and places them at risk of heat exhaustion.

Search dogs are always used before large parties of people move into an area, and while there is still a chance of finding the missing person alive. If helicopters are available, consideration is sometimes given to airlifting dogs from their home areas to

speed their arrival at the scene of the search. Dogs always work better away from other parties and certainly upwind of any other search team operational in the same broad area. If a dog does indicate on someone who is involved in searching, the dog is merely rewarded and sent off again to continue looking for the missing person. However, experienced dogs learn to ignore the scent of other searchers in the very near vicinity, and are therefore sometimes capable of working alongside others in a line search.

Dog teams work very effectively in the dark and in cloudy conditions when it is impractical or difficult to continue with ordinary search work. They are extremely effective in the very situations where human sight is most limited: in the dark, in dense woods, thick cloud, heavy brush and even under snow cover or water.

It's important that dog teams are given the opportunity to search areas where there is the best chance of finding the missing person. Neither they nor their handlers can work miracles, but a trained dog is the best search resource known to man and that should be optimised. It's rather subjective trying to compare the relative effectiveness of dogs and people but it has been estimated that, depending on weather and terrain conditions, one dog is roughly equal to about twenty searchers in a line. That's a huge potential impact on the consideration of resources.

The exact nature of their involvement is subject to discussion with the search coordinator, but this is the point where the specific skills and knowledge of the handler and dog's capabilities come to the fore. In general, dogs are deployed in either a hasty, or a more detailed search. The former is an initial, targeted response, probably before any other agencies are involved, where there may be good information about the probable location of the missing person. It may involve a path search, a search of known blackspots or a check of the missing person's intended route. The search area is agreed and then divided into logical sub-areas where practical, taking into account the nature of the terrain, wind direction, safety considerations and access points. Then, each dog team is usually assigned a segment of the search area to cover systematically.

It's important to make the point that the handler's task is exceptionally challenging. They have to direct and observe the behaviour of their dog, navigate successfully, follow an agreed search plan and look to their own, and their dog's, safety. All at the same time. So it's not surprising many handlers choose to be accompanied by another competent person who can take responsibility for navigation, leaving them free to effect the search.

Dogs can also be deployed to work in pairs or with a number of dogs in an extended line. If this has been practised, the dogs will ignore the scent of the other handlers and also that of navigators or other personnel deployed to assist in the line. The need for practice is required, not for the sake of the dogs but for the handlers. In this type of search, in addition to what has already been said above, the handler has to be aware, not only of their own dog, but the dogs on either side of him. They have to ensure that the dogs continually cross as they are moved on each side of the handler to ensure there are no gaps in the line. The complexity of this type of search is illustrated by the amount of radio chatter between handlers as they work their way through an area.

As the search unfolds, handlers will regularly update search control on their progress, especially if they choose to move out of their designated search area, come across an unexpected hazard such as a swollen river, or if their dog has indicated outside the area. They might also make a judgement about the terrain and suggest a change of plan, which they were unable to do before their search began when simply looking at the map. Sometimes a handler has a hunch about a particular location, or their dog may show unusual interest, which takes them to a feature such as a crag, small area of woodland or watercourse, which is worth exploring. Many handlers now carry GPS-enabled microphones as part of their radio communication system which allows the search coordinator to identify — in real time — their precise location on the electronic map at base. So, if the dog and handler move away from their intended search area, their movements can be recorded to provide the coordinator with an overall picture about the area covered or excluded. If technology like this is unavailable, handlers will always be required to map out the area they have covered and report their probability of detection (PoD) to the search coordinator on completing their assigned task in terms of the percentage coverage of the designated area.

The one aspect of any search at which dog teams excel is the clearing process. The level of confidence attached to the decision about whether or not an area contains the missing person is greater if a dog team — as opposed to a line of people — has searched that area. That said, the confidence attached to clearing an area is improved considerably by searching it first with a dog team or teams, followed by a sweep search with team members and possibly a helicopter. In a line search, depending on the terrain and cloud conditions, team members may be spaced far apart or very close together — perhaps as close as just a few metres. Where there is good evidence the missing person is somewhere in a given area, but they haven't been found by dog or human teams, the area will be searched again — possibly later the same day, or even the following day when conditions are better or the wind has changed direction. Searching the same area from a different direction may also give a dog the opportunity to pick up scent previously hidden by boulders or small gullies, and it may give the handler or search teams sight of small areas previously unseen. And dogs, of course, are immensely useful at night as, unlike their human colleagues, they rely on scent rather than sight.

Once an area has been identified it might be searched thoroughly by several resources — dog teams, mountain rescue teams, helicopters and others including volunteer members of the public — with increasing intensity from a rapid sweep to a fingertip search. A search might continue for several days before it is terminated. It might even be resumed several months later if there's a strong feeling the body is still located in the vicinity.

Dog teams will work as long as is required given regular rest periods but the temperature, their level of fitness (dog and handler), and the nature of the terrain will all influence how long they work. It has been known for dogs to work for many hours a day on a multi-day incident, although this is quite extraordinary. The majority of working sessions are much shorter but this is far from guaranteed. Sometimes there's little way of knowing, from the start, just how long the job will last.

Demonstration, were it needed, that a good knowledge of their local area, combined with a level of fitness and fortitude — not to mention commitment — are absolutely central to search dog handling came in early January, 2009 with a dramatic rescue on Skiddaw, in the Lake District. Elly Whiteford, Lakes dog handler and member of Keswick MRT, was at work in Penrith one Tuesday afternoon when her pager went off. 'Team call-out — four stuck on Skiddaw' was all the message read.

'I glanced out the window. The weather didn't look too bad although there had been sporadic snow showers all morning. However, I knew the weather on the tops would be quite different. With a sense of urgency, I made ready to leave when a second message indicated the location of the missing group was unknown. Humhh… bad news! A third message quickly followed, requesting use of search dogs. My own dog Mac, a tri-colour collie, is a fully trained search dog with Lake District Mountain Rescue Search Dogs. He had a poor start to life having been found abandoned on a Cumbrian beach and then transferred to a rescue centre but once I'd taken him on board I realised quickly he was a very smart dog. He's now been qualified for over three years and attended more than 60 call-outs.

'Once on my way to Skiddaw, I followed progress of the search on my radio.

Nearing Keswick, I learned the first team vehicle had left and the second was waiting for me at base. Traffic was slow and I didn't want to keep team members waiting so I radioed to say I'd meet them at the bottom of Dodd Wood. An update by radio confirmed the lost party was near the summit of Skiddaw. The quickest way to the summit ridge is from the col between Dodd and Carlside, and that was our intended ascent route. My fellow handler Mick and search dog Ginny were already on their way up Jenkin Hill from the south.

'I arrived at Dodd Wood to find the team Land Rover already at the gate, but it had to wait as the key was in the team transit van just behind. I hurriedly sorted out kit and dog, grabbing crampons and ice axe. Once the transit arrived, we all headed up the track to the col below Carlside. By now, it was snowing and the track was slippery even for the four-wheel drive vehicles. Immediately, I was ready to go and began to search with Mac as I headed up the hill. Above me, the advance party was relaying deteriorating conditions with a request we work in pairs. Fellow team member Chris was just ahead and in sight, so I carried on to join him. The snow was falling steadily and had already settled a couple of inches deep. It was quite pleasant in the shelter of the hill and Mac was very excited, bouncing and jumping in the drifts and playing in the snow. He ran ahead to Chris indicating that I was just behind. It was now about 3.30pm with daylight rapidly disappearing.

'The conditions on the way up Carlside deteriorated considerably. The higher we climbed, the wind speed increased and the temperature dropped — a lethal combination for anyone in difficulties on the mountainside. Halfway up we heard there

were five people lost on the hill and not four, as originally indicated. To make matters worse, the fifth person was independent from the group we were trying to locate, and nearer the summit.

'At this stage we still didn't have an exact fix on anyone. Mac and I pressed on beyond Carlside and upwards along the quickly disappearing path to the summit of Skiddaw. The wind was now quite ferocious, stripping the snow from the rocks and scree. Just standing upright was very difficult. Visibility was quickly deteriorating and, with failing light and thick cloud, it was difficult to see even with goggles on. I stopped to put on my crampons, but annoyingly, one broke as I tried to attach it to my boot. I struggled to put it right but my fingers were bitterly cold, the wind was fierce, and the light now too poor to see properly. So I abandoned the crampons and headed up to where Chris was waiting.

'Mac was now beginning to be affected by the weather; his coat and eyes were catching the snow and his ears were really cold. He kept thrusting his head into my legs or moving behind Chris to shelter from the wind.

'Approaching the summit ridge, the high winds made standing barely an option. Driving snow and ice about an inch thick covered the entire ground making walking without crampons almost impossible. Mac was unhappy in the high wind, crouching low to minimise its effect. I was worried he'd be blown off balance so I held on to him while crossing the summit ridge on all fours. By now the advanced team had successfully located the lost group of four, who were huddled in a stone shelter on the summit ridge. The team had quickly moved them to the north side of the summit and out of the high winds. The team's paramedic confirmed that one member was severely hypothermic and in trouble. Once other team members arrived, she was wrapped in additional clothes and a waterproof casualty bag and loaded onto the stretcher. Meanwhile, the summit area was checked for the fifth person, but there was no sign of her.

'Following a brief respite from the weather, I fitted my one good crampon. We then decided that three of us would search for the remaining missing person, whilst the rest of the team evacuated the group of four. We began by traversing the eastern side of the summit ridge in a northerly direction just below the summit, reasoning that the missing woman would head down the lee side to seek shelter. It was now dark, making it virtually impossible to see each other. To make things worse, radio contact was lost. My microphone was frozen and I had no radio communications. Shouting was out of the question!

'We traversed the summit and cut northeast down the slope towards Bakestall. The snow had drifted along the fence line so only the top couple of inches were visible, but at least it gave us a rough line to follow. We sank up to our thighs every couple of paces making it extremely hard going. Mac struggled to cope but showed a determination to continue alongside us. As we moved down, radio comms improved slightly. At one point, my radio crackled into life momentarily and I thought I heard that a lone head-torch had been spotted descending Jenkin Hill. It was possible this was the person we were looking for, but at least fellow dog handler Mick was covering that line.

'We decided to continue along the fenceline. The plan was to meet up with another search dog team on the way up, as well as members of the Cockermouth team who were scouring the north side of Skiddaw. Mac was working purposefully just in front of us and along the fenceline. Part way along the fenceline, we gathered together to check our location on the map against the grid reference on my GPS receiver. At this point I failed to notice that Mac had darted off and disappeared. I looked up just in time to see him coming down the slope behind us. He was barking urgently and then turned and headed back up the way he had come. He was telling me he'd found something.

'I turned and followed as best I could against the strong wind. Mac came back again and again barking as I headed up the slope, following him into more exposed conditions. Then I saw an orange survival bag on an exposed area of frozen grass. We'd found the missing person — about 200 metres north of the summit. She was lying with her head and shoulders out of the bag and into the prevailing wind, her gloved hand gripped around a walking pole and her head and shoulders covered in snow. She was alive, but extremely cold. She could barely speak, was confused and shaking and clearly suffering from advanced hypothermia. I knelt down to shelter her and let her rest her head on me while talking to her. Mac shuffled in beside her for shelter. She was extremely fortunate to be alive, having spent around five hours without moving more than a few hundred metres.

'Some of my fellow team members soon arrived to help. We battled against the wind to put the casualty into a survival shelter.

We changed her wet outer clothes for dry ones, wrapped her in additional dry jackets and encouraged her to eat a high-energy boost bar. Throughout all this she was unable to assist and had to be physically supported against slipping down the icy surface. It was now critical to make a quick decision about what to do; the woman's condition was failing and the weather worsening. We hurriedly discussed our options: do we use a stretcher or walk her down? It was possible she was too cold to walk and to do so would simply exacerbate her condition. We transmitted our find and grid reference to base but realised we didn't know how long it would take to get back-up. Under the circumstances we agreed it would be best to get the woman on her feet and begin to head down the hill. Two of us supported her whilst the others navigated and we made our way back to the fenceline and relative shelter.

'Initial progress was extremely slow. Our casualty was struggling to walk, even with our support, and the poor underfoot conditions made it almost impossible to move in a coordinated manner but, with constant encouragement, we made gradual progress along the fenceline towards Bakestall and hopefully, back-up. It seemed an eternity but it was probably only a few minutes before we saw torch beams of fellow search dog handler Ian, and Keswick and Cockermouth team members, heading towards us.

'We met at the fence corner where they took over the supporting role of our casualty and then followed the fence line over Bakestall and down towards Whitewater Dash waterfall. As we lost height, the wind dropped significantly and more Cockermouth team members came

SEARCH DOG MAC, HERO OF A DRAMATIC SEARCH ON SKIDDAW, JANUARY 2009 © KESWICK MRT.

to join us and help support our casualty off the hill. Thankfully, she was improving by the minute and we soon realised she was out of danger. I'm absolutely sure that, had Mac not found her, things could have been very different indeed.

'As we approached the waterfall, we saw the lights of the Cockermouth team vehicles making their way up the track — what a welcome sight! We quickly loaded our casualty into one of the vehicles which turned and made its way down the track and onwards to Keswick Hospital. By now, it was after 8.00pm and we'd been on the mountain for around five hours in terrible conditions. We were all exhausted and starving, including Mac — who had missed his dinner! However, the evening was not over yet.

'Our radios went live and we learned that the team evacuating the party of four was still on the mountain, near the top of Jenkin Hill. Two of the casualties were now on stretchers and the other two needed help to walk. Moving the stretchers across the iced scree and banks of snow, with the constant buffeting by high winds, was making progress painfully slow. More help was needed so members of the Cockermouth team sped off to the south side of Skiddaw to help the Keswick members, dropping me at my car on the way. Eventually, with their help and further support from Patterdale team members, all the casualties were safely evacuated from the hill.

'This incident had involved team members from three mountain rescue teams — Keswick, Cockermouth and Patterdale — and eight search dogs. It is to their credit that all casualties survived and no team member suffered in the process.

Mac's find that night most certainly saved the lady's life. In the conditions she was exposed to, her condition would have deteriorated rapidly and, even if found later, she would certainly have been severely hypothermic and possibly died.

'As far as Mac was concerned, it was just another walk in the hills, but he convinced everyone that dogs are an invaluable asset to a serious mountain search. His reward was an overdue evening meal and a few extra treats, normally reserved for special events. And my reward? Knowing that my dog had battled against horrendous weather and ground conditions, and saved someone's life into the bargain, was enough. Oh, and the wee dram went down well too!'

Two years after this incident Elly decided to retire Mac. As she explained to her colleagues in the team, 'With winter coming on, I'm reluctant to take him out in bad weather and away from the fire. His health has been deteriorating for a while, he has arthritis and has slowed down a lot and deserves the rest. Mac has been a fantastic dog to train and work. He came from an unknown background, mistreated and then abandoned on a beach and finally ending up at Eden Animal rescue in a foster home. It is a credit to his fantastic nature to come from such a background to become a search dog. It took me two years to train and grade Mac — pretty quick for a more mature dog from a dodgy background.

'In his time as a search dog he has attended more than 70 call-outs and had several locates, including a couple of Manchester lads on Little Stand in winter, an elderly chap in Blengdale and, of course, the brilliant find on Skiddaw in full

winter conditions where he undoubtedly saved the lady's life. I am most proud of him for that. He has seen me through thick and thin, taught me loads, is my best friend and been an absolute dream to work, which I will miss. A big thank you to all who helped me train and grade Mac and for the faith and support to train an older dog — I hope you all think it was worth it as much as I do.' Who could argue with that?

The walker rescued on Skiddaw may well owe her life to the ready availability of so many rescuers living and working very close to the incident scene. But it isn't always so. People are reported missing in very remote areas and sometimes it can take many hours to mobilise any kind of rescue attempt. The islands of the Inner and Outer Hebrides in Scotland present some of the most serious challenges to rescue personnel. With very few exceptions, speedy access by road is impossible and few rescue personnel live on the Islands. The Isle of Arran sits in the Firth of Clyde just off the Ayrshire coast in Central Scotland. A tiny island only twenty miles in length from north to south, it is home to mountains, rock faces and glens, the grandeur of which belie its size. The northern part is composed of granite dated as the oldest in the world, and features more than its fair share of classic rock climbs such as South Ridge Direct and Sou' Wester Slabs, attracting climbers from across the UK and beyond. The most popular mountain is Goatfell, a hotspot for many walkers whose navigation lets them down in bad weather.

Neil Hamilton-Bulger is a member of Arran MRT and a dog handler with SARDA Southern Scotland. In May 2007, he and his dog Briar were enjoying a leisurely walk

on Goatfell and descending towards the farm High Corrie, a preferred end point for walkers leaving via the East Ridge. Rather than heading straight down to the road end, he decided to take a shortcut and headed north along a forestry fence. After ten minutes or so, Briar ran off, without warning, in the opposite direction to Neil and a few hundred metres along the path whence they had just come. She disappeared from view but within few minutes came bounding back towards him.

'I thought this very strange,' recounts Neil, 'as she always likes to keep me in sight, apart from when she is working. She began indicating, as she would when she's working and has found a person. Usually, when we are out walking, she often picks up people's scent but just stands rigid with her nose in the air for a few seconds then continues on. When we're on a call-out, Briar wears a special jacket. It changes her frame of mind — she knows she's in working mode. I've seen this happen when we work with helicopters. For example, if a helicopter flies over my house, she'll more than likely run and hide under the bed — but, once the jacket's on, she's as eager as me to climb into that helicopter and get to the search.

'On this occasion, Briar wasn't wearing the jacket but behaving as though she was on a rescue mission. Thinking she was simply playing, I told her to stop being silly and tried to get her to walk on. But she wouldn't have it. She was barking and jumping and when I tried to move away she wouldn't let me go. So, I thought I'd go along with her indication and told her to show me what she'd found.'

No sooner had Neil given his instruction,

MISSING PERSONS

NUMBER CRUNCHING

When someone goes missing – be it a hillwalker who fails to return from a mountain expedition, a child that goes astray on a family picnic or a depressed person who leaves home unexpectedly – urgent attempts are made by the police and others to gather information that provides clues to their whereabouts.

In the case of an overdue hillwalker, questions might be asked about their route and the expected time of return, whether they had any alternative plans, where were they last seen, where did they park their car, and so on. An elderly person, missing from their nursing home, would prompt a different line of enquiry: their state of health, where friends and family live, the places the missing person lived or frequented in their younger days. A picture is built from the evidence available, resources can be mobilised and a plan devised to locate the person as quickly as possible.

Since its beginning in 2000, the *UK Missing Person Behaviour Study* has collected data on almost 1300 searches, which have been analysed to produce behaviour statistics for missing persons and there are clear consistencies in the way different groups of people behave when they go missing. To give an example, it's been shown that when an organised, formally led group of hillwalkers becomes lost, almost 40% are found on open ground and around 25% on a path or track of some kind. Information like this paints a picture of all possible scenarios, although it's not completely foolproof as it only identifies the likely outcomes for the missing person or group. Invariably, historical information can be matched with specific information about the particular incident, to help construct a search strategy.

We've talked a lot about dog teams being tasked to look for missing children and people who are depressed, as well as overdue walkers. So how can the study help in those cases? Bearing in mind that these are never accepted as definitive, that there is always room for an alternative, equally plausible scenario, there are some key characteristics a search manager can extract from any particular group.

Take the group 'Missing children aged 1 to 16 years'. Seventy-one percent of all missing children are found in buildings, the majority of which (51%) are classed as 'habitation'. A child missing in farmland is 52% likely to be found in a building — almost equally likely to be classed as 'habitation' or 'building/shelter' — and 20% likely to be found in trees. In environments other than urban or farmland, the missing child is equally likely (33% of incidents each) to be found in a building (habitation and building/shelter equally likely) or on a road, track or path (then almost twice as likely to be on a road as a path or track). A child missing in farmland is likely to be found closer to the point they were last seen than a child missing in other environments — in farmland, half are found within half a kilometre of this point whereas, in other environments, half are within 1.1 km.

In a category which covers all the forms of dementia, including Alzheimer's Disease, for incidents in farmland, females are most likely to be found on a road, track or path (42%) or in a building (26%), whereas males are equally likely (29%) to be found on a road, track or path, or next to a linear feature, or in a building (20%). In urban areas, the missing person is 36% likely to be found on a road, track or path, and 29% likely to be in a building.

Despondents are people who are thought to have disappeared deliberately, generally as a consequence of an intention to commit suicide, depression — either diagnosed or suspected — or stress/distress due to personal or domestic problems. The study suggests that the principle of lines and points is a useful guide to constructing scenarios for this group in particular. The 'points' referred to are the missing person's most likely destinations. The 'lines' are the routes they could have taken to get there. In general, the likely point

towards which a missing despondent might be heading are buildings or trees and bodies of water. Half are found within a kilometre of the point last seen and 15% are found in a place that's significant to them in some way. This might be a local beauty spot or viewpoint or somewhere they associate with particular memories. For incidents in farmland, 35% of females and 42% of males are found in a building, and 24% of females and 18% of males are found on a road, track or path. For urban incidents, 48% are found in a building, 20% in water and 14% on a road, track or path.

In the case of missing walkers, a missing male is 44% likely to be found in open ground, 22% in a building, and 21% on a road, track or path. A missing female walker is 39% likely to be found on a road, track or path, 25% in open ground and 21% in a building. At 33%, a mixed group is equally likely to be found in open ground or in a building, and 25% likely to be on a road, track or path.

Statistics like these provide an objective and targeted basis on which to plan a search. They're particularly helpful when dog teams are deployed because they allow what we believe to be the best possible search asset — and we hope you're now agreed on that point — to be deployed in the most effective manner possible.

Briar raced back in the direction she had come from. Neil followed her beyond the path they had originally been walking on and down into a gully, to a stream called the Corrie Burn.

'When I arrived, there was Briar standing next to a man who was sitting in a heap next to the burn. He was in a bad way – his face was covered in blood and he looked shocked and confused. From what I could gather he was descending having climbed Goatfell and had left the path to drink from the burn. But in climbing down he stumbled and fell face first into the burn taking the full impact on his hands and face.'

Neil cleaned him up and treated his injuries and the man quickly began to feel normal once again. In fact, he insisted on making his own way back down the remaining part of the path to High Corrie. Neil felt he didn't require to be stretchered off the mountain but insisted he accompany the man down the path. They walked slowly down the path with Briar taking the lead until Neil found a place where he could get good mobile phone reception to request an ambulance. But they decided that, as the man's wife had a car at High Corrie, it would be simple

TOP: BRIAR © NEIL HAMILTON-BULGER.

Kit fit to go

Mountain rescue teams often work in extreme weather conditions, exposed to many hours in the dark, cold, wind and snow, sometimes in hazardous locations. When others hunker down in the warm, shelter from the storm or snuggle under the duvet, rescue team members leave whatever they're doing or drag themselves from their slumbers, pop the kettle on, fill the Thermos, lace up their boots and step outside.

They must be self-sufficient and resourceful and carry appropriate clothing, food and survival gear to sustain long periods unaided. And it could be argued dog handlers need to be especially resourceful as they often work alone or in small groups of just two or three people — and they're also responsible for their dog's health and safety.

Every handler takes with them high performance waterproofs, warm clothing, hat and gloves, plus additional items in case of deteriorating weather or others in need. Other basics include a survival bag, map, compass, GPS, powerful hand-held torch, head torch and special items for winter travel: ice axe, crampons, snow shovel and avalanche transceiver.

Remember, a dog team is more likely to find a missing person than a regular search party, so it's critical they are prepared — especially vital if the casualty is injured or hypothermic, so all handlers carry substantial first aid kits, an emergency survival shelter, extra clothes and high-energy food.

All of this makes for a very heavy rucksack, and there's the dog to think about too! Fortunately, dogs are better than their handlers at coping with bad weather and usually make do with their own built-in fur coat. However, most wear a high visibility jacket which enables handlers to spot them in the dark or cloud and also provides some protection from the weather. Dog 'booties' are not popular and have their disadvantages — a dog's pads are used to rough ground so don't need additional protection. Other items might include a special harness for winching into helicopters and some kind of illumination device such as a chemical lightstick, fluorescent light collar or flashing strobe light. Add to all this food, water, a small first aid kit and, of course, the all important toy or treats as reward for finding the missing person.

enough for her to take him to hospital in Lamlash a few miles away. Neil was happy to agree to this and shortly afterwards they arrived at the path end to meet his wife and car. Both expressed their very grateful thanks to Neil and Briar before leaving. It turned out the man had suffered a broken nose and serious facial lacerations, but his injuries were not serious enough to keep him in hospital.

Neil doesn't know why Briar took it on herself to indicate as she did. Maybe she smelt blood or human scent associated with fear (called butyric acid, it's one of the components of human perspiration) but, to this day, it remains a mystery. A few weeks later, Neil received a thank you letter, addressed to Briar, with a cheque to buy her a new squeaky toy!

Come fly with me

Mountain rescue team members, and dog handlers in particular, carry a substantial amount of kit to cope with the variety of circumstances they might face, but all the kit in the world counts for nothing without the rapid deployment of dog and handler as close to the incident scene as is humanly possible. Cue the Sea King!

Mountain rescue in general enjoys a very good relationship with the RAF and RN search and rescue helicopter teams and they train and work together on a regular basis. The use of a helicopter in any search operation is a very powerful tool. Terrain permitting, the aircraft may well be able to land at the scene, delivering personnel, dogs and equipment exactly where they're needed, quickly and efficiently saving possible hours of foot-slogging for rescue team members and dog handlers. Following an avalanche, for example, when time really is of the essence — the difference between life and death for the victims a matter of minutes, not hours — dogs and handlers can be rapidly placed near to the debris and ahead of other searchers who may well contaminate or mask the scent for the dogs.

If it's not possible to land, the helicopter winch comes into play, with teams required to exit the helicopter from a 'hover' of around ten metres — which is why it is vital all concerned receive the training to confidently work with the winchman and crew. Dogs and humans need to be trained and exposed to a variety of experiences and situations. Team members undergo mandatory safety training, winching and helicopter crash drill briefings through video footage, lectures, practical drills and exercises. By becoming familiar with the protocols and drills, they can operate in a safe and confident manner without compromise to the helicopter, the crew or themselves and help alleviate any fears and anxieties. Needless to say, dogs don't tend to be as attentive or have the same ability to sit through videos and lectures as their human counterparts so the process of familiarisation, for them, is one of gentle progress and gradual desensitisation to the unusual smells and sounds and there are a number of steps involved.

PAUL MARTIN AND CAIRN APPROACHING THE HELICOPTER © PETER SANDGROUND.

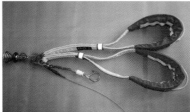

TOP: CAIRN AND CORRIE, PAUL MARTIN AND JAMES COLES — INSIDE RESCUE 177 © DAZ CRAIG.
LEFT: READY TO WINCH © DUNCAN TRIPP.
ABOVE: SINGLE AND DOUBLE GRABBIT HOOKS © DUNCAN TRIPP.

Once the handlers have received the standard briefing for all mountain rescue personnel on helicopter operations, each is presented to the crew with their dog. In case of any aggression (on the part of the dog, that is) the co-pilot is 'volunteered' to be presented first! The process begins with the helicopter shut down, on the ground. The handlers and their dogs are free to wander around, in and out of the aircraft. After a suitable period of familiarisation, a single engine is started and, once again, the handlers and dogs can wander around and in the helicopter. Then, while the other engine and rotor head are started, the handlers and dogs remain at a safe distance before approaching again to wander around and in the helicopter.

Finally, with handlers and dogs secured inside, the helicopter takes off for a short familiarisation ride. On the ground again, handlers and dogs exit the aircraft before it takes to the air again, ready to assume a hovering position. With the winchman on the ground, the winch is deployed with a static lead, two Grabbit hooks and a strop and, one at a time, each handler is called forward with their dog.

These steps are completed as often as required to the satisfaction of all concerned, and this may be a few or very many, depending on the individual dog.

For most dogs, once they've completed training, it's relatively easy to get them onto the aircraft. Often, enthusiastic dogs and handlers run to the helicopter ready to jump into it. Some fail — usually the handlers! It's far easier for handlers, once cleared, to enter the rotor disc, approach the door, hand the lead to the crew and lift the dog in. Then they can climb aboard, strap themselves in and take the lead back from the crew member thus ensuring positive control of the dogs, and also that the handler is not distracted getting him or herself in. Exiting the aircraft is the reverse procedure.

The flying of dogs is relatively unique to search and rescue helicopters so there are a number of additional considerations handlers need be aware of. Dogs can be unpredictable. Their natural survival instinct in an unfamiliar environment can be expressed as fear and aggression — more so when forced into a noisy, smelly helicopter! The prescribed rule for the carriage of any dog is that they must be muzzled but, given that dogs on search and rescue operations must have completed mandatory helicopter training, the crews generally take a more pragmatic approach. But if, during training, a dog shows any signs of aggression, the handler ensures it is muzzled.

Generally, dogs — like their handlers — are so focused on the task that crews have little or no problems with either, although it has been known for dogs to use the under-seating area as a refuge. And, once there, they can take some coaxing out! Most settle and 'enjoy' the ride — some a little too much. One dog is known to make straight for an observation window so he can get an all round view! One eager pooch had to be dragged away from its warm vantage point, having jumped into the cabin and straight onto the co-pilot's lap! Another refused to take a biscuit so his handler absent-mindedly threw it out of the door. The dog, you'll be pleased to hear, was happily caught mid-flight halfway out the door. Feeding dogs whilst in flight is not encouraged!

Dogs are not designed to be winched.

Nor, incidentally, do they generally have the desire to try! So, when it comes to winching in and out of the helicopter, there's a real need for any harness to be formally recognised and cleared for purpose. Not only does it act as a winching medium, a harness also provides the dog with a degree of security, comfort and restraint. Ideally, when dog and handler are to be winched, they are presented with the winch hook which will generally have a static discharger, two Grabbit hooks and a strop. The ideal procedure is for the dog to be attached first to a Grabbit, the handler's rucksack to the second Grabbit and the handler then gets him or herself into the strop. Once in the strop, the handler lifts the hook up into the winching position, to check that both dog and bag are still attached. With one hand holding the hook, the other hand must 'protect' the gate on the Grabbit with the dog, to ensure the dog's harness attachment hasn't 'rolled over' the Grabbit gate, which could lead to the dog falling off. Once the winch takes the weight, the handler removes his hand from the hook and the Grabbit, and turns their attention to supporting and reassuring the dog. At the door of the aircraft, the handler again guards the Grabbit gate until they are safely inside the helicopter.

This is the theory — but things don't always run like clockwork, as one of the authors found to his cost. On one helicopter training day with the Lomond MRT, Bill and Jenny were the last of their group to be boarded. Jenny was uncomfortable, to say the least, having endured the downdraught for over five minutes. Both were winched into the doorway and the winchman took hold of Jenny's working harness — at which point she spooked, backed out of the

harness and ran into the flight deck. Following a spectacular rugby tackle by one of the crew, Jenny — and by default Bill — found themselves unceremoniously dumped out of the aircraft, which quickly took off and disappeared, leaving Bill to ponder the relative costs of dogs and helicopters!

When it comes to winching from the helicopter, as with the winch in, dog, rucksack and handler are attached. Again, it is important the handler guards the Grabbit the dog is attached to. Poised at the door, ready for winching out, the handler checks the strop has not slipped whilst moving from their seat to the door and managing the dog's movement. Once on the ground, the handler first slips the strop, then removes the rucksack and, finally, the dog.

Generally a dog's survival instinct is much stronger than a human's. As such, they are generally reluctant to be winched, especially from the helicopter. It's not unknown for a dog to dig its claws into the floor seam, leaving its harassed handler to prize his reluctant dog from the aircraft, claw by scraping claw. Once on the ground they are normally glad to be alive and keen to make good their escape as one handler found to his embarrassment, having just removed himself and his bag from the strops. His dog, who'd clearly had enough of all this noisy winching business, made a break for freedom — hook and helicopter still attached. Only to find that pulling ten tons of helicopter was a futile exercise — the hoist may resemble a 75-metre retractable lead but, fed with 3000 psi of hydraulic pressure, no amount of canine adrenaline was going to overcome it!

Doggie Tales
TARAH
THE AVALANCHE DOG

Every winter there are hundreds of avalanches reported in Scotland. The Sportscotland Avalanche Information Service based in Aviemore, established over twenty years ago, provides climbers and walkers with a daily forecast of avalanche hazard in five of the major mountain areas. Thousands of mountaineers each year take advantage of the service and this is likely to be one of the reasons why so few people are actually caught in an avalanche.

Chance in a Million, the classic book on this subject, very accurately quantifies the actual risk involved. Though the risks are low, they still exist and, every year, a small number of people fall victim and, very occasionally, die. If someone is buried in an avalanche, their best hope of being located is by those who are on the spot. The chance of survival decreases rapidly. It's been estimated that, if a person is alive when the avalanche comes to rest, their chances of survival drops to 20% within an hour. Most organised searches for avalanche victims therefore tend to be exercises in body recovery.

Trained search and rescue dogs are highly effective in locating buried persons. In good conditions, they can search an area in about one tenth the time it takes a team of twenty people equipped with probes. They are also very good at detecting people buried several metres under snow. In one case, some twenty years ago, a German Shepherd called Auric found a body buried under three metres of snow. Typical times for the thorough search of a 100 metre wide square by a well trained dog is about 30 minutes for a general search, and one to two hours for a fine search. But times could be much faster than this depending on the type of snow. Compact snow, which is non-porous and icy, will limit the passage of the buried person's scent and make the use of dogs less effective. The same applies if there are distracting scents created by other people, or if the weather is particularly bad.

If a dog is immediately available, other rescuers are typically kept away from the avalanche debris to avoid scent confusion. If many people have already been searching debris, 'resting' the slope for ten minutes after searchers have operated allows many of the false scents to dissipate. However, the vital search by people on the spot is never delayed by the expectation of the appearance of a dog. Handlers searching an avalanche always carry an avalanche transceiver to aid their own detection should there be a further avalanche.

A very large avalanche took place in the Scottish Borders in 1995. Steve Penny, team leader of the Tweed Valley MRT was a member of SARDA Southern Scotland at the time, with his dog Tarah.

'In the early hours of a Monday morning, in the spring of 1995, I was asked to join a search for a missing walker in the hills near to Moffat in the Scottish Borders. Heavy snow had fallen in strong winds, a couple of days before. This was followed by a rise in temperature and low level snow melt. The walker was reported missing on the Sunday evening after failing to return home, his car located at a popular car park. The weather that evening was windy with blizzards and the initial search teams could find no trace. As darkness descended, the search was abandoned but scheduled to resume with the assistance of dog teams the next day.

'The morning was clear and cold. Five search dogs were deployed into the search area, tasked to search the area around White Coomb and Loch Skeen. In particular, we were to concentrate on areas of potential avalanche activity. Although the weather overhead was good at the start, conditions underfoot for both dogs and handlers were difficult. The snow was soft and lying deep in the peat hags. On more than one occasion we floundered as we unwittingly walked off harder ground into waist deep snow. Several hours into the search, three of us identified a significant channelled avalanche.

The dogs showed a degree of interest in this area but nothing positive. As we continued to move around the hill, a helicopter from RAF Boulmer was deploying ground teams onto strategic points.

'In the corrie to the north east of White Coomb, we came across the debris of a huge avalanche. (We later estimated the width at the crown wall to be around 500 metres.) I was with two other dog handlers. We split up and started to move across the debris. The snow was in blocks but not too difficult to walk through. Within minutes of starting, I could see that Tarah was showing some interest. This was more positive than on the avalanche we'd crossed earlier. She made for a point some 20 to 30 metres ahead of me and started to dig at the snow. Very quickly, she came back to me, indicated strongly, and dashed back to the spot where she had been digging. As I approached, I could see a mitt lying at the bottom of the hole she'd scraped. The mitt was not empty! I called the other handlers down and alerted the base. Within minutes we were digging to clear the snow and it became clear the casualty's arm was raised and outstretched and his body over a metre deep in the snow. Tragically, there was no sign of life. The casualty was airlifted by the helicopter and taken to the base location where a doctor was present to confirm death. Back on the hill, the weather was beginning to deteriorate again and we started to walk back down to the base.

'I had very mixed feelings about the incident. I felt extremely sad on account of the tragic loss of life but, at the same time, a sense of exhilaration because the dog I'd spent the past two and half years training had made the find on her second call-out. The avalanche was so large, it would have taken days to search with human teams equipped with probes. The fact that Tarah was able to locate the casualty lying over a metre below the surface within minutes is testimony to the tremendous benefits a search dog can provide in any search. All of her training was worth that one find alone. All dog handlers feel a very special relationship and sense of teamwork with their dog, which is heightened when the training comes to fruition on a real incident. Needless to say, Tarah was given an extra helping of supper that evening and a special spot by the fire!'

FACING PAGE: BILL JENNISON'S SECOND DOG JAKE AT WORK IN THE AVALANCHE DEBRIS © BILL JENNISON. ABOVE: DEEPEST AVALANCHE HEADWALL EVER RECORDED IN THE UK © OCHILS MRT.

STEPHEN AUSTIN (SARDA SOUTHERN SCOTLAND) AND HIS DOG SKY UNDERTAKE HELICOPTER TRAINING © DAVID NICOL (OBAN MRT).

In action

It isn't often an incident demands the involvement of more than one helicopter at a time — even were they available — although there are exceptions. Television screens were buzzing in November 2009, as flood waters engulfed the Cumbrian town of Cockermouth, and multiple Sea Kings assisted mountain rescue teams in the evacuation of flood victims from the roofs of their homes and work places.

Sometimes there's an incident so serious it involves every resource, every agency, every ounce of endeavour an organisation has to offer. It has such devastating and far-reaching consequences that the effects reverberate for many years after the event and mark forever the minds of those who were there. Indeed, the shockwaves from an ill-fated evening on 21 December 1988 — when a terrorist bomb exploded on board a passenger aircraft, in the air above the village of Lockerbie in Scotland — have continued to echo around the world ever since. In 2009, Abdelbaset Ali al-Megrahi, the man convicted for his part in the bombing, was released on licence from a Scottish prison, on health grounds, expected to die within weeks. He lived out his final days at his home in Tripoli — as debate about his guilt or otherwise, rumbled on — surviving for almost three

TOP: IAN BAIRD, SARDA SOUTHERN SCOTLAND (LEFT) AND HEATHER MALLING, SARDA WALES (RIGHT) AT THE SCENE OF THE LOCKERBIE AIR CRASH © PRESS ASSOCIATION.   ABOVE: THE NOSE CONE © DAVE WHALLEY.

years, until May 2012. During that time — fuelled, no doubt, by his longer than expected survival — there were many calls for his return to jail in the UK or even extradition to the US. No doubt, long after his death, the late night debates and legal wrangling will continue.

Lockerbie was unique — a steep learning curve for the emergency services and mountain rescue alike. It was the perfect example of search and rescue dogs and search and rescue helicopters working together in a crisis.

With only a few short days until Christmas, people everywhere were returning home to their loved ones, making their last minute preparations, looking forward to a break from work, a chance to relax and party. But, for residents of the quiet market town of Lockerbie, the 259 passengers aboard Pan Am flight PA103 bound for New York, and emergency services personnel across the UK, all that was about to change. At 7.02pm, a terrorist bomb exploded aboard the Boeing 747, killing everyone on board and eleven local residents of Lockerbie. Thirty-eight minutes after take off from Heathrow, the plane had reached an altitude of 9,500 metres.

At Shanwick Ocean Control, first one blip appeared on the radar screen, then three more, then five as the shattered pieces of the airliner fell from the skies. The impact of the crash was so strong, a blast of 1.6 on the Richter scale was registered at British Geological Survey stations in the south of Scotland. Minutes later, eye witnesses described a 'fireball' falling from the sky. The plane had broken up in mid-air so suddenly that the crew were unable to send any message, and so dramatically that wreckage and debris were scattered for miles — across the border as far south as Kielder Forest.

In the cold light of the morning following the crash, the full horror of the devastation became apparent. The wings of the 747 had struck the A74, engulfing cars in flames. The fuselage had landed on a housing estate demolishing several homes, the four engines fell onto the village and there was a gash 47 metres wide and 60 metres long slewed between two rows of houses. Twisted fragments of metal littered streets and gardens. Bodies lay strewn around the towns and fields, many mutilated beyond recognition. At times like this a contingency plan swings into action which brings into play every possible appropriate resource. All the agencies — the emergency services, local authorities and voluntary organisations — involved in dealing with the incident come together in a common cause. As with any aircraft incident, the Aeronautical Rescue Coordination Centre deploys search and rescue helicopters and RAF mountain rescue teams to the area. Mountain rescue teams were tasked as fast as possible on arrival, to search for and recover survivors, provide specialist advice to civil emergency services, assist with the cordoning off of the crash site and the provision of communications. A temporary restricted air space was established — a radius of five miles and height of 600 metres. The fire services specialised in the immediate area of the crash site to deal with fire and toxic hazards and a press centre was established for relatives and journalists wanting information.

On that fateful evening in 1988, Dave 'Heavy' Whalley, team leader of Leuchars MRT, was just beginning to enjoy a spot of well-earned leave. With more than a hint of irony, he recalls his parting shot to colleagues: 'Don't call me unless a jumbo jet crashes in the mountains.' It's the sort of thing you might say, never imagining for one moment it will happen. It was the first day of his break, just as he was making plans with his girlfriend, when the call came through. At first, he assumed it was a wind-up, his deputy having a laugh. But then 'Raz' suggested he turn the telly on and see for himself.

'I switched on. It was like a dream — a nightmare. I quickly sorted my gear, left my girlfriend and shot down to base. The troops were dashing about — the usual organised chaos before the brief. What do you say at times like this? How do you cope with 250 casualties? Never in our history had we to deal with something like this. Already, troops from RAF Leeming were airborne for Lockerbie with RAF Stafford in hot pursuit. Raz left with the team whilst I followed behind. Before leaving I phoned the police as the motorway was closed. Very kindly, they escorted me all the way but we travelled so fast that my dog Teallach, who was in the back of the car, was even more terrified than normal! It was a weird experience driving down the M74 with no cars in sight. As we approached Lockerbie, the police had blocked all entrances and the press were everywhere. There was wreckage all over the road and the sky was illuminated with reflections from burning fires. It was also full of helicopters — it could easily have been a war zone. An engine had impacted into the road, aircraft panels had landed on roofs, there were open suitcases and Christmas presents spread about. Quite an incredible scene. The smell of fuel was overpowering — a smell that will remain with me for the rest of my life.

'The police took me to where the troops were located, held back whilst Leeming MRT carried out an initial search. On their journey up, they'd been listening to the radio and hoping to save lives or help casualties. But there was little to do. The scene was utter mayhem and confusion with a real danger from the uncontrollable fires. But very quickly and with quiet efficiency the head of the RAF MRTs, together with the Inspector of Land Rescue, set up control.

'I was told to keep the teams happy, find a base and control the helicopters to avoid the real chance of a mid-air collision. Communications with the outside world were non-existent. The satellite phones had broken down and landlines were severely damaged by the crash. Somehow, we managed to set up a landing site for the choppers and gained some type of control into search areas — extremely important for flight safety. Eventually, the police gave us a briefing in the school, which was to become the coordination centre for the disaster. There were over five hundred people present including ambulance, fire and police personnel, coastguards, voluntary services and RAF and civilian teams. There was, as you'd expect, chaos.

'The civilian teams from the Borders looked to the RAF teams for guidance. As luck would have it, we'd just carried out exercises in the Borders a few months previously when the scenario was an aircraft crash. Through this exercise we had made key contacts, which were to prove invaluable in the days ahead. It was decided at the briefing to wait until first light, as it was too dangerous to search in the dark with the fires still raging. Frustrating for the troops who were keen to go out and help, but they accepted they had to sit and wait — few slept.

'Information was hard to gain and I decided to recce on my own. Lockerbie is a small town, situated just off the motorway near the Borders. It has the smallest police, fire and ambulance authority in Scotland, which was completely overwhelmed. A local policeman and myself went around the crash site in the dark. It was a scene from hell — bodies, wreckage, Christmas presents and clothes all over the place. The smell of fuel and death filled the air. Fires still burned fiercely. These scenes will remain in my mind forever. Nothing can prepare you for this. Even after a lifetime of rescues, it was hard to accept what I saw and felt. We located the main wreckage, which gave us vital information to guide our search areas the following morning.

'The plan was prioritised into a casualty count and a map of all the wreckage and main aircraft parts. The RAF teams had done this many times before, but never on this scale. By now, based on reports and what we had seen, we reckoned the chances of live casualties being found were extremely limited. The brief to the troops was one of the most difficult ever given. We made sure they worked in pairs with an old head alongside a newer troop member and explained what horrors they might expect to find. In the days to come, the RAF, civilian rescue teams and SARDA handlers were all to do a magnificent job in the face of the untold death and destruction. I will never forget their efforts. After the brief we gave each team specific areas to search. We explained the importance of looking for the aircraft's

black box, which was found very quickly by a Stafford team member. This impressed the police and especially the 'men in suits' who had arrived in the middle of the night.

'By now it was common knowledge this wasn't a normal crash and that terrorism was the probable cause of all the death and destruction. The teams worked together in shifts listing wreckage and casualties on the 'crash map'. The debriefings with team members were harrowing but all worked very professionally, gathering information, reporting to base and going out to another area for more of the same. The casualties were left where they fell but mountain rescue personnel covered the bodies with fleeces and clothing and a policeman guarded each casualty, once located. As the list grew, the enormity of what had taken place began to sink in. Everything was now being treated as a scene of crime. There were countless members of the press present, desperate for information. To make matters worse, some mindless individuals had entered the area, removing possessions from some casualties.

'At times of great tragedy, the basic things in life come to the fore. And heroes emerge. The WRVS established a base in the school kitchen and produced meals 24 hours a day for several weeks. These ladies brought a touch of sanity to the scene and they worked tirelessly throughout. Helicopters carrying experienced mountain rescue team members flew across the area to plot the wreckage from low-level photographs. Casualties were found in the main town and in the fields across a vast area. By the end of a long first day the troops were tired

and very stressed, but had located three quarters of the casualties. We tried to relax by going into the village but the town had been thrown into mayhem. Many local people had been killed, several streets had been demolished and wreckage was everywhere. However, some of the pubs were open. The locals, who knew we had been working very hard in a difficult task, made us very welcome. We all felt guilty drinking and trying to relax but it was what we all needed because it served as a safety valve. Very few slept that night. Many had nightmares and were aware that it was going to continue the next day.

'Within a short period of time things took on a degree of order. The police, other emergency services and teams had risen to the challenge and knew exactly what to do. Troops flew out with the helicopters locating casualties and wreckage. Everything was plotted — casualties, belongings, parts of the aircraft were found and marked. Additional resources were mobilised, making life better for us all. Members of the world's media were ever present, all wanting information and to record how we felt. By the end of the third day, we had accounted for all the casualties. Now, there was little left for us to do and so we pulled out but, before so doing, we submitted all of the 'crash maps' to the police. They highlighted the enormity of the tragedy. Each life a tragedy to their families and friends; lives lost because of evil. The local mountain rescue teams worked with the search dogs for weeks after we left, searching for human remains and other items.

'On my return to Leuchars, I was tasked with reporting on the event and, most importantly, identifying the lessons learned.

Many members of the team came to see me, disturbed at what they had seen and done. In those days, there was no training in post-traumatic stress — all counselling was carried out off the cuff. Little did I realise how this would affect me later on in a fairly serious way. It took a long time to go back to Lockerbie but I did. The Garden of Remembrance and the Memorial are impressive. The village is back to normal and life goes on, but I found it easy to visualise what had happened on that dark night and will never forget it.'

Dave Whalley was a key player in helping coordinate the military and civilian MRTs as well as other emergency services. One of these was SARDA. Dogs and their handlers played a vital role in this incident and they were involved within hours of the crash. In fact, Bill Parr, a member of SARDA Southern Scotland who lived in Lockerbie was the first emergency person on scene. He played a seminal role throughout and received the MBE for his work. The contribution of dog teams to the search for casualties continued for almost two weeks. Because of the enormity of the incident, events quickly began to follow a well-recorded timeline. Within two hours of the explosion a local dog team and two police dog teams had been deployed to search the main impact area and the ruins of domestic properties, and to ensure that the immediate area had been cleared of all non-essential personnel. At this time, it was thought some occupants were missing from houses in the immediate impact area and also from vehicles on the A74. During the search, fires were still burning and the streets were littered with glass and rubble. Members of the fire service assisted by damping down localised fires and moving

difficult or awkward obstacles. The whole area was contaminated with aviation fuel. No survivors were located although dogs indicated several bodies, other human parts, personal effects and aircraft wreckage.

On completion of the initial search, the first dog team was dispatched in police transport to follow up a report of possible survivors. The report turned out to be incorrect but, during searches of country roads, several large pieces of aircraft wreckage were located. A chance meeting with a farmer resulted in a quick search of debris on open moorland in sleety conditions. Compass bearings of the general debris trail were taken at known grid references and reported to police control. Human remains, personal effects, additional wreckage and cargo were also located in this area.

By 12.30am on 22 December, additional dog teams had arrived having travelled up to 150 miles from their homes. After consultation with police it was decided that dog teams working in groups and in combination with local and RAF MRTs would search the urban area immediately outside the fire zone and the rural areas indicated by the aircraft debris trail.

By 8.00am these groups had located in excess of 120 bodies but no survivors. After a short break, eighteen search dog teams were redeployed to cover forest and wooded areas with ground search teams and helicopters covering the open ground to determine the location of bodies, personal effects, mail and aircraft wreckage. Dog team searches were terminated one hour after darkness. On Friday 23 December the search took on what turned out to be the general trend until

1 January 1989, comprising open moorland and forestry searches, searches in the area of the explosion and searches in rubble and fuselage wreckage located in the urban area remote from the rural areas indicated by the debris trail. After this, searches became less frequent and of shorter duration. These were, generally, responses to specific police requests for assistance and undertaken by local dog handlers, primarily from teams in Northumbria. The last dog team was stood down on 4 January.

Between Wednesday 21 December 1988 and Friday 31 January 1989, a total of 48 dog teams were used on various occasions, peaking at forty teams on Boxing Day, drawn from four branches — SARDA Southern Scotland, England, Wales and Ireland. Some travelled more than 350 miles to attend the incident and then spent up to five days continuous searching. During the call-out, dog teams accounted for over 120 bodies and many pieces of human debris, as well as a vast amount of personal effects, luggage and aircraft wreckage. Overall, they searched a total area of around 100 square kilometres, over something in the order of 2,800 hours. In addition, a three/four-man planning team on administrative duties took up a further 380 hours.

The incident was not without injury to the dogs themselves. Seven dogs and four handlers suffered injuries whilst searching amongst ruins and many others suffered from exposure to aviation fuel fumes. One of the Irish dogs succumbed to poison thought to have been ingested in a forest area near Langholm and another local dog fell seriously ill. Everybody felt the regular training undertaken by dogs and handlers ensured most dogs adapted with minimum retraining but the obvious stress and tiredness generated by the extremely difficult conditions were important factors in determining handler and dog suitability for certain tasks.

In operational terms, every handler and dog was restricted to a maximum of three seven-hour-days within the impact zone, working up to 20 minutes and resting away from the aviation fumes for at least fifteen minutes. Whilst the aviation fuel restricted dog searches, careful planning of resources meant SARDA was able to provide continuous attendance — day and night — within the areas contaminated with fuel over many days. The most effective technique for searching was to deploy dogs and handlers in extended line searches with a police presence in each line. Members of the Aircraft Accident Investigation Branch were quick to recognise the value of the search and rescue dogs as well as the knowledge of local farmers and members of the then Moffat Hill Rescue Team.

The searches were physically and mentally demanding for all dog handlers. The horrific sight of clumps of bodies and body parts, particularly the night-time finds, were not only stressful at the time but have proved a constant source of anxiety for many in the years since the incident. For one dog handler, Jan Millar, this was no exception.

'After eighteen months of intensive search dog training, I qualified as a Novice Search Dog handler in November 1988 and waited eagerly for my first call-out. And it soon came — on 21 December 1988, around 8.00pm. I'd already seen the newsflash interrupting *This Is Your Life* (a popular TV programme at the time) and anticipated we may be called. I was told to make my way south to Lockerbie. The name would come to haunt me and it probably will for the rest of my life. After being redirected by the police at Moffat, I travelled along an eerily quiet A74. In the distance I could see a red and golden glow: Lockerbie. I made my way to the police station through scenes you might encounter in a disaster movie set. Flames shooting to the sky, the strong scent of kerosene in the air, badly damaged houses and a massive smoking crater with debris all around it. I joined two other dog handlers and we were tasked to search some fields quite far out of Lockerbie. On the way, my headlights lit up my first sight of that nose cone. I can still feel the shock wave I experienced all those years ago — to this day, when I catch sight of it on the TV I still have a reaction.

'The search started. Within minutes our search dogs had indicated on luggage, bundles of cargo and piles of debris all scattered around the field. The dogs were confused at the amount of scent, particularly my dog on her first real search — what to indicate on first? We praised the dogs but continued looking for life. I find it unbelievable now that I was naive enough to think there might still be a living soul waiting to be rescued. It truly didn't occur to me that humans falling over 9,150 metres would have no chance of survival. Or that the impact would leave some bodies in a horrific state. Or that some scenes would be so surreal I still question whether I truly witnessed them.

'Truth to tell, no preparation could have helped me cope with what I experienced over the next twenty hours. The sights encountered are firmly imprinted on my subconscious and rise to the surface in the form of nightmares at times of stress. I am asked why I continue to devote much of my time to mountain rescue as a volunteer search dog handler after that horrific experience all those years ago. It's a difficult question to answer, and I'm not sure I understand why I do it myself. One answer would be that I enjoy the challenge and pleasure of training and working with a dog (my current search dog, Buidhe, is my third search dog). I also thrive on being out in the Scottish countryside experiencing different seasons, the ever-changing scenery and sights and being self-sufficient in fairly remote areas.'

Twenty plus years later, the thoughts and emotions of Jan Millar continue to echo. Those who were there can still recall with great clarity their experiences searching the wreckage-strewn fields around Lockerbie. Once the initial search was drawn to a close, members of SARDA carried out an investigation to ascertain the contribution it had made to the incident and the lessons learned.

It was obvious to everyone that dogs and handlers had played an invaluable and unique role in locating many victims (almost half the total) and other key items of debris. Technically, they experienced some remarkable successes, believing their training to have been highly appropriate to these new and unique circumstances. For instance, the dogs had switched readily from finding bodies on the open hill to those under rubble and little additional training was required to adapt dogs to locate burnt human remains. However, it was considered that future training programmes should be adjusted to include accident scenes where dogs are required to work in unsafe areas. Of great benefit was the excellent liaison some dog handlers had with Dumfries & Galloway Police and the police dog handlers. Previous meetings and joint training had helped establish a useful working relationship with everyone knowing each other's capabilities but there was a feeling that joint training with the other emergency services could be developed further, to allow a greater appreciation of everyone's expertise and needs.

An unexpected consequence of the incident was the huge media attention the dogs generated. This caused some disquiet amongst other rescue team members even though it was made clear to everyone it was the media that had sought out dog handlers and not vice versa. As a safeguard, all contacts with the media were controlled through the police and interviews undertaken in the presence of a police press officer. This went a long way to ensuring a balance between publicising the work of the dog teams and keeping their contribution in perspective. As a cautionary note it was thought that SARDA's leap from relative anonymity was likely to be followed by short bursts of intense activity in non-mountain rescue situations. This was, indeed, the case and it's a trend that has continued unabated with search and rescue dog teams now involved in many hundreds of non-mountaineering incidents every year.

SARDA's review of their involvement in the incident also highlighted a number of operational matters that received further consideration. It revealed the need for closer liaison between area controllers and dog handlers, as well as the need to assign an overall search dog coordinator able to

advise others such as the police on the best use of dogs and handlers in such incidents. It also exposed some inadequacies in equipment. For example, handlers should have been issued with body tags, tapes, safety helmets and so forth, to improve their efficiency on the ground and lessen the risk of personal injury. On this specific matter, it was realised through the course of the incident that, whilst handlers were covered by police insurance, the dogs were not. SARDA felt that in view of the high number of injuries to dogs this matter should be looked into as a matter of urgency. Even today, dogs are not covered by police insurance.

Finally, the review highlighted the extremely stressful nature of the incident, not only to the dogs but also to handlers and their families. There was a genuine feeling amongst handlers that the Samaritans had been extremely useful in easing everyone's minds and inherent tensions. As one handler put it: 'They seemed to have the ability to talk with us rather than to us and didn't utilise 'social work' jargon.'

Thankfully for those involved in mountain rescue, few incidents are as traumatic as Lockerbie. Nor do they involve rescuers coming face to face with the death of their fellow human beings in such numbers. True there are often bruised and battered casualties to deal with — the victims of slips, trips and falls, avalanche burial, hypothermia or medical emergency in the mountain environment. Sometimes there are bodies to respectfully remove from the hills and, frequently, these are suicides. When the police receive information that someone has indicated their intention to

take their own life, potentially in a remote location, mountain rescue team members are frequently called to search for them. Sometimes, despite the immediate mobilisation of resources, the outcome is tragic. Sometimes though, tragedy is averted. Long-serving Lakes handler Mick Guy tells the latter tale.

'The pager goes off at 0146hrs. At first I'm convinced it's the phone, but when it doesn't stop ringing when I pick it up, my befuddled brain realises it must be the pager. By now, my wife Chris is also awake and switches on the light. 'Search at Shap for missing lone man,' read the message, with the call-out coordinator's phone number. I have to say it takes me a minute or two to work out what next. Right now, going back to sleep seems a good option, but a sense of responsibility gets in the way, and I dial the number.

'How many have you got then?' I ask, hoping by this time he'd have half a dozen dogs. 'Three, including you,' comes the reply, as he reels off a grid reference, which I scribble down on an old envelope by the phone. Chris looks at me. 'See you later then!' And she's back asleep by the time I'm dressed. Four minutes later, I'm in the kitchen making up a Thermos and trying to persuade Ginny, the three month old puppy, that she's not going on this particular jaunt. Search dog Mist is already at the door awaiting the moment. Collect the rescue sac and torch from under the stairs, pick up the mobile phone, radio and car keys and we're in the Subaru and rolling within about fifteen minutes of getting the call. Amazing!

'A66 to Penrith, M6 to Shap then A6 to the point designated as the RV: about 25 minutes. As it happens, Mist and I are first on the scene but, within ten minutes, the Kirkby Stephen Land Rover arrives and then Christyne Judge with search dog Skye, and Dave Watt with search dog Dynamite. Chris Francis, the call-out coordinator, also arrives to help plan the operation. Ten minutes later we know the man we're looking for has been missing for about ten hours, in a severely depressed state, and that his car has been found just off the A6 in a quarry entrance. The police have tracked the position of his mobile phone to an area within a kilometre of the quarry.

'We decide the belt of woodland bounding the quarry and road needed clearing first, along with the stream running through it. We also agree who would cover which area. Christyne and I take the south end and I volunteer to work round the end of the wood to the far side. As we cross the fence at the southeast corner, Mist takes off, making the whining half barks I recognise as the same noises she made en route to the last find like this. She shoots off down a ride in the wood and returns to utter a single bark before disappearing again. The blue of her light collar travels maybe 35 metres and stops. A clamour of barking. In the light of the torch, I see a waterproof jacket, covered in blood, a bottle, a Stanley knife, a phone and a watch. 'Search Dog Chris Francis — Priority — I have a blood-stained jacket and other items, 50 metres from south east corner of the wood. Continuing.'

'I send Mist off again and, in what seemed like seconds, she had disappeared and returned, again barking. As she leaps up to tell me, I hear Christyne's dog Skye, barking as well. Alerted by Mist's initial find, Christyne has sent her dog in from the other side of the wood and Skye has also arrived at the casualty. Mist and I crash through the last few trees to find our quarry under some close-planted pine trees. Christyne arrives at the same time. Our man is still alive though only semi-conscious and can only respond to our urgent questions with garbled speech. Chris Francis crashes in from the cars with a first aid kit, at the same time alerting the Kirkby Stephen control vehicle to organise an ambulance. Whipping on latex gloves, we carry out the necessary first aid, whilst trying to tear off low hanging pine branches. Fortunately, a police armed response vehicle, which is passing the incident scene, has an oxygen set on board and the crew make their way down from the forest track to assist.

'Apart from cutting his wrists, the casualty had also taken an unknown number of tablets and drunk the best part of a bottle of malt whisky. From what we could establish from him, he had taken the tablets well before going missing. We control the bleeding from his wrists and monitor his condition. Once the ambulance is on scene, we use a vacuum mattress from the team vehicle as a method of extraction from under the trees and out to the forest road. It takes the four of us, together with the ambulance crew and one of the policemen, to drag/carry him up the slope the 90 metres to the ambulance.

'Our man is just about capable of climbing into the ambulance with support and from that point he is someone else's responsibility. We are left with the task of clearing up his personal effects, all of which are covered in blood. A text message from his wife is still displayed on the screen of his phone. Letters to each of his children and his wife are in the pocket of his jacket. We bag all the items and deliver them to Kendal Police Station.

'We are euphoric that the hours of training with our dogs has paid off. A really positive result: we'd found the man alive and given him a chance. It's my belief he had already changed his mind about what he had done and was trying to crawl back to his car about 150 metres from where he was found. The down side, as we all knew, was that the tablets he had taken would continue to poison his system for some time and they might still kill him — in which case, our efforts would have been in vain. Happily, we later learned he'd made a full recovery.'

Sometimes, as we said, the outcome is not so happy, despite the best efforts of the emergency services. One such incident involved Bill Batson, a dog handler with SARDA England for many years. Bill is well known in mountain rescue circles. For many years he was training officer for all the RAF mountain rescue teams in the UK, and team leader of two of them. In 2002, he was awarded the Distinguished Service Award for his contribution to mountain rescue — an honour bestowed on only a very small number of people.

January 2002. The call from Shropshire Police came as a welcome opportunity to escape my desk at RAF Stafford — not my favourite place, it has to be said. Together with the RAF MRT, I was called out with my first search dog, Kyle, to help search for a suicidal man, missing from home in the Shrewsbury area. Leaving Stafford in a hurry was never a problem (any excuse!), but getting anywhere else can be a different story altogether — particularly if that journey involves travelling via the M6.

Within minutes of passing through the station gates, blue lights flashing and adrenaline pumping, the mountain rescue convoy was brought to a grinding halt as we became embroiled in yet another Junction 14 tailback. The trouble with these situations is: once you're in it, you're in it. No U-turns allowed and blue lights make no difference when you're nose to tail with nowhere to go. There was nothing for it but to chill out while the traffic moved tediously slowly towards the next junction, from where escape was possible. The rest of the journey was, thankfully, uneventful and within an hour or so we arrived at the rendezvous point on Haughmond Hill, a place the missing man was known to frequent.

'I was tasked by the search manager to search a wooded area and paths on the southern edge of the hill, overlooking Shrewsbury. Being the only air-scenting search dog team at the incident I was keen to get going ahead of everyone else and, with another team member as navigator, we were quickly on our way. I began searching along the many paths, pushing Kyle to the left and right into areas of mixed woodland and brambles. Kyle was a dog that loved to range and today was no exception. In the wooded terrain of our search area he was often out of sight, although I could generally hear the bell on his search jacket ringing so was able to maintain a rough idea of his location. He was working well and I was happy for him to quite literally follow his nose as he quartered back and forth across the wind.

'We saw a few walkers as we moved along the paths, and were frequently asked whether it was an exercise or the real thing. None of the walkers we met had seen anything untoward and so we continued. After perhaps an hour of searching Kyle appeared from around a wooded ridge, running directly up to me, and barked two or three times. My navigator immediately asked if he had found something. Not wanting to get too excited I quietly told Kyle to 'Show me!' and he immediately spun round to return in the direction from which he had approached. He was clearly on a mission. Thinking we might be on to something we followed him around the ridge, to be met by a furiously barking Kyle, returning once again to indicate. This time my 'Show me!' command was delivered with a bit more certainty and Kyle was once again on his way to his find.

'Trotting now, we rounded a corner and, to my dismay, were met by the sight of a young couple sitting quietly on a bench, enjoying a flask of coffee while they admired the magnificent view, disturbed only by this strange orange-coated Border Collie running excitedly backwards and forwards from its owner. 'Bugger, he's indicated on these two,' was my first thought, until I realised Kyle was returning to me from a point beyond the couple on the bench.

'With my mind whirling, young couple and navigator temporarily forgotten, I sent Kyle away from me again, watching very carefully where he went. Without even a passing glance, he ran straight past the couple, continuing on for perhaps another fifteen metres or so until, on the very edge of a steep slope, he disappeared under the canopy of a large yew tree. He stopped, looked up... and barked. I realised at that moment that we'd made a find — our first. Under the quizzical gaze of a young couple whose quiet afternoon together was about to be shattered, I bent down to get a better view under the branches of the yew tree. My eyes followed the direction of Kyle's upward stare and there, just in view, I could make out a pair of feet, suspended some eighteen inches off the ground. Ducking quickly under the canopy I was confronted with a middle-age man hanging from a high branch, the blue bailing twine around his neck having clearly done its job. I knew I wouldn't find a pulse, but checked anyway. Life extinct, as they say in the movies. But this was not a movie and we now had to inform the young couple that their quiet corner was about to become a very busy place. Which indeed it did.'

Neill Powell is a stalwart of Irish mountain rescue. His dog Fern is one of the few search and rescue dogs trained to locate drowned victims. Over the years, they have been tasked to assist with many incidents. In March 2009, he was asked to bring Fern to search a section of the River Boyne for a man who had been seen jumping into the water two days before.

'The Garda Dive Unit had already been searching the river, but without success. A local voluntary dive team, from County Meath also dived the river, and like the police, searched along the edges, checking obvious strainers but without finding the man. From our boat, I got Fern to search from the place last seen down to the first weir, about quarter of a mile down stream. She gave no response, so we searched back upstream against the current but again with no indication. I took her half a mile downstream from the weir and searched back towards it. Fifty metres from the weir, in the middle of the river, she gave a very strong indication. The Garda divers were asked to check this but were

ABOVE: SARDA WALES DOG CELYN WITH HANDLER RICHARD BEECH, ON EXERCISE IN SNOWDONIA © RICHARD BEECH.   FACING PAGE: CALUM BLACK OF SARDA SOUTHERN SCOTLAND AND HIS DOG DOCHAS, AVALANCHE TRAINING IN THE CAIRNGORMS WITH GORDONSTOUN SCHOOL MRT.

not interested. They gave a quick bank side check but found nothing.

'We returned the following Sunday and repeated the search, with Fern indicating in exactly the same place. Again the police were invited to check but they gave it only a brief search, finding nothing. Two days later I asked the local dive team, the Lough Rea Sub Aqua Club, to focus on the middle of the river instead of the banks. I asked them to work upstream towards the weir. They located the man metres from the point indicated by Fern. He was being held beneath a large boulder by the pressure of the water. The divers reported that he would not have been found but for Fern.'

When you consider the way dog teams actually carry out their work, and all the operational considerations involved — the search management and planning, the sheer logistics involved in actually getting out there, of training and working with helicopters, the distances involved, the constant pressure of time — the thing that most shines through is the sheer challenge of it all. Then there are the long days and nights spent working in poor weather, the hard, physical grinds across difficult ground, and the knowledge that the outcome may be to find a deceased person — or nobody at all. It takes a very special kind of person to do this, as well as commit to all the rigorous training and ongoing assessment over many years. So who are they, these special people? What makes them tick? One or two of them have been kind — and brave — enough to put pen to paper and reveal what it is about dogs and rescue work that steers their motivation and commitment. We've dedicated a whole chapter to their accounts...

10 In their own words

'Fools wanted for hazardous searches. No wages. Long nights of complete darkness, cold and wet. Two years of monthly training, danger of failing, dog hair all over your fleece, car and home. Pay out of your own pocket until dog on call-out list. Honour and recognition in case of success doubtful.' Tom Gilchrist

Throughout the book, we've retold the experiences of many people and we've done this to give an insight into how things happen for real, but it's those individuals at the sharp end — the handlers, assessors, dogsbodies and casualties themselves — who can best describe the emotions, challenges and pleasures central to working with dogs in search and rescue. We rather suspected there might be a reluctance on their parts to put pen to paper but, how wrong could we be? Quite the opposite! Everyone we approached was more than happy to express their feelings and provide information about themselves, their dogs and their involvement in search and rescue work. We even discovered a number of dogs willing to tell their own story!

But, before we go on, it's worth repeating here the key prerequisites to becoming — and continuing to be — a search dog handler. Most important is the expectation that handlers have all the skills required to be competent in mountain search and rescue work, familiar with a wide range of rescue techniques and able to operate with confidence in potentially hazardous environments. In practice, this means every handler must possess a high degree of mountaineering ability and be competent in all aspects of mountain rescue work such as navigation, first aid, radio communication and technical rescue methods. They must also be mountain fit and capable of working alone, often in challenging terrain in the dark. In fact it could be argued that, because handlers tend to operate independently compared to team colleagues, their self-reliance needs to be especially well developed. Consequent to all of this, all handlers (with few exceptions) are experienced members of mountain rescue.

There are, however, a number of other special qualities required. First and foremost, handlers are dog lovers. Some might say they're 'daft about dogs', and we wouldn't argue with that! Before they embark on a dog handling career, the majority will be familiar with the work of SARDA having worked as a body or with other handlers on actual searches. In fact, experience as a body is mandatory with some associations. Further, the commitment of dog handlers, especially in regard to training, is absolute. Which means they have a lifestyle that permits them to spend huge amounts of time on training and assessment, and a willingness to accept the financial burden associated with, for example, travel, accommodation, dog food, vet fees, clothing and equipment — pretty special, as we said.

FACING PAGE: ANDY FLEMING AND ANGUS © PETER SANDGROUND.
RIGHT: DOG HANDLER DAVE WALMSLEY TAKEN IN THE 1970s © PAUL TOWERS.

The handler's view

John Easton is a long-standing member of SARDA Scotland, having trained and worked three dogs over a period of 25 years. In this time he's been involved in a wide variety of mountain and urban incidents including helping to trace patients who have wandered from hospitals, injured climbers, missing hillwalkers, children hurt in cliff falls and adults threatening suicide in remote areas. He's a former countryside ranger and hails from Aberdeen in the north east of Scotland. He was introduced to SARDA when his own team (Aberdeen MRT) was on a joint exercise with the Tweed Valley MRT in the 1980s. He became interested in their work and very quickly started to train his first dog Cranna. After Cranna came Bran and then Sicoe. He's had his fair share of the ups and downs of dog handling, the challenges and the good times. His words mark the end of a long and satisfying career in search and rescue.

'I always wanted to own a dog but with a childhood spent on a housing scheme in Aberdeen, an adolescence spent on large motorbikes or in the hills and eventually a wife who was more inclined to cats, the opportunity never seemed to present. All this changed in the early 1980s, when I found myself separated from my wife, and about to change jobs and move back from Edinburgh to Aberdeen. I was already a member of the Lothian Search and Rescue Team, a group consisting mainly of outdoor education teachers and was working as a countryside ranger at the time. Although I'd always wanted a dog, I never wanted a dog simply to be a pet. It would have to be a dog with a purpose and a joint exercise with the Tweed Valley team on the Three Brethren, near Galashiels in the Scottish Borders, was my introduction to search and rescue dogs. The team leader, Jim Cochrane, was there with his dog Whin and I was fascinated watching them work. I didn't manage to talk to Jim at that time but I did give my name to another handler who said he would send me further details. Nothing transpired and, in time, I moved back to Aberdeen.

'A couple of years later I finally acquired a cross-collie puppy called Cranna and once again thought about training a search dog. I knew SARDA had been started by Hamish MacInnes and thought it would be useful to speak to him. Hamish put me in touch with Kenny MacKenzie who was Secretary of SARDA Highland at the time. In turn, he put me in touch with Alwyn Jones and Donny Cameron, two local handlers. These contacts marked a turning point and I started training almost immediately.

'No learning experience runs smoothly and I made a few errors along the way. It became apparent very quickly that you must choose the right commands for your dog. I originally taught Cranna to bark when I crossed my arms in front of my body — a big mistake! The first time Cranna encountered someone who was frightened of dogs, they instinctively held their arms in a defensive position in front of their body. Cranna of course was delighted at receiving a command from a new friend and started barking furiously which just exacerbated their plight!

'Secondly, I discovered the importance of keeping a watchful eye on your dog at all times. While walking Cranna on Calton Hill on a visit to Edinburgh, Cranna spotted a man sleeping under a tree. To her, this was obviously a casualty and she ran up to him, stuck her nose in his ear and started barking. Had I been paying attention I would have stopped her before she started but, in the event, I was left with the unenviable task of trying to calm an agitated man the size of Desperate Dan! I made another mistake by teaching Cranna how to get in the car quickly. This seemed a good idea but it proved not to be. At the time, I was working for a Country Park in Aberdeenshire and Cranna accompanied me to work every day. In order that I could get away quickly in an emergency, I trained her to jump on command in through the driver's window of my Ford Fiesta. One day there was an incident and I instructed her to: 'Go to the car!' She ran across the car park and dived for the window of the first red Ford Fiesta she came to. Unfortunately, it wasn't my car and the window was closed! The young lady sitting inside was just taking a bite from a cheese roll when Cranna slammed into the window by her head. The resulting mess and chaos took a long time to explain and it was I, not Cranna who left the scene with their tail between their legs!

'Cranna had her first search in the Central Cairngorms — a missing group of boy scouts on a hike. Our search area was the Braeriach Plateau and the weather was abysmal — wind and sleet all day. At the end of the day, as we were to be picked up by helicopter, I put Cranna's harness on as she was not too fond of the noise and blast generated by helicopters. When the helicopter landed, much to my surprise, she bolted straight for the door, jumped in, and hid under a seat. Obviously, even the big yellow taxi was preferable to the wind and sleet outside.

'A later search with Cranna, in the Pentland hills near Edinburgh, taught me a valuable lesson about a dog's scenting capability. Passing a small lochan, she kept running into the water and then turned to me with a puzzled look on her face. Not a normal indication but certainly not typical behaviour. I eventually decided she was just playing as I did live and work on the shore at the time. After a short time, I called

her off to resume the search. Nothing was found that day, but some days later the casualty surfaced in the lochan where Cranna had been 'playing'. Moral of the story: trust your dog and learn to read its signs!

'Cranna and I were also present at the search following the bombing of the Pan Am jet over Lockerbie, arriving on scene within hours of the plane coming down. The main problem was the vast amount of debris bearing human scent on the ground. At first she tried to take me to any scent source, as she had been trained to do. On-the-job retraining was accomplished quickly and she eventually located three bodies and a number of body parts on the first night. We also returned a week later to search part of Kielder Forest near Newcastleton.

'I retired Cranna from active service after she injured a leg, thinking she may never work again, then started to train Bran, a collie/huntaway cross. In the event, Cranna made a full recovery, which meant I had the choice of two search dogs. One night I was giving Cranna and Bran their last walk of the day when they both suddenly bolted and leapt a fence into a small garden then, to my surprise, indicated a find! Lying in the garden, at the base of a shed, was an elderly man, very drunk indeed. As the temperature was already well below freezing I roused a neighbour and together we dragged the man inside. He lived alone and possibly owed his life to the accident of two trained search dogs passing and catching his scent — he probably never even knew of his luck.

'When Cranna was fifteen-years-old she came to a training session with Bran and me. Sitting in the car she became quite

excited as the other dogs were working their areas. She obviously knew what was going on! I set up a very small area and let her search it. As her hip joints were not in the best of condition, it took her some time to cover the area. Eventually she caught the scent, followed it to the body — and sat down! After a few seconds to catch her breath she indicated a find — proof that, even if they lose the physical ability, search dogs never lose the enthusiasm.

'Interestingly, the lesson I'd learned with Cranna about a dog's ability to scent bodies under water revealed itself on one of Bran's searches. While searching for a missing person along the side of a river, Bran started acting strangely, ranging back and forth along the side of a pool. Slightly further downstream, on the other side of the river, one of the other dogs was acting in the same manner. After taking the wind strength and direction into consideration we told the search organiser we thought there was a high possibility the casualty was in a particular pool. The pool had been searched by police divers, although visibility was such that the search was made entirely by feel and so there was no guarantee of 100% coverage. Nobody was surprised when the casualty surfaced some days later.

'I retired Bran at the annual assessment in 2000 and immediately left for a week's skiing in Chamonix. At the time, *Castaway* was being shown on BBC TV, billed as a social experiment in which 36 residents had to develop a complete infrastructure on the uninhabited Island of Taransay in the Scottish Outer Hebrides. One of the castaways was Patricia Prater who took her Border Collie Fran to Taransay. Early on in the programme, Fran gave birth to six puppies. I was totally unaware of this but, on the way home from Chamonix, my wife Viv picked up a free tabloid as we boarded the plane. Inside was an article about the programme telling of the litter of puppies. Viv suggested one might make a good replacement for Bran as a search dog. As I hadn't seen the parents, and didn't know how the dogs were being raised, I thought this was a rather impractical idea. However, Viv kept returning to it and eventually I wrote to Patricia. Much to my surprise I received a reply saying I could have one — all I had to do was pick it up.

'However, two days later, there was an article in the press saying that the doctor on the island had insisted the pups be removed to the mainland and that the Scottish Society for the Prevention of Cruelty to Animals (SSPCA) had agreed to take them. It also said there'd be a competition to find suitable homes for them. I contacted the SSPCA and explained the situation and, although they said the matter was out of their hands, they said if I was to enter the competition, explaining that I wanted to train the pup as a search dog for mountain rescue, there was a very high likelihood I'd get one. In the event, I was invited to the SSPCA kennels to take my choice of the litter.

'The pup I chose was called Merlin. I wasn't too happy as there was already a dog in SARDA with that name. But, almost immediately, I was approached by our secretary with news that a family had offered to sponsor the training of a dog in memory of their son who had been killed in an accident. It was not a condition of the sponsorship but they would appreciate the dog being named after their son. I agreed to rename Merlin and asked (with some

trepidation) the name of their son. His name was Simon Coe but, as a mark of his adventurous personality, had been known as Sicoe. So, Merlin became Sicoe.

'Sicoe's training had quite a slow start. Almost immediately, foot and mouth disease hit the country, bringing a stop to all mountain training. It took a long time for him to mature, which meant he was almost two before passing his novice assessment. Then another problem become evident.

'Sicoe never looked straight at you and at night exhibited only a single eye shine. It transpired he had a congenital cataract in his right eye. I debated whether to withdraw him from training but decided to keep the information to myself and see how he progressed. This was a good choice as he eventually turned into a good search dog. My friends pointed out that, as Sicoe was blind in his right eye and I was blind in my left, we at least had one pair of good eyes between us!

'Sicoe's first successful search occurred in his novice year. I'd just returned from helping a friend deliver a small yacht on the west coast and was still unpacking when the phone rang. The local police needed a dog to search for a missing person in woods near Aberdeen. I arrived on site to find the police had been there for four hours and had already foot-searched the immediate area. They asked me to cover the area near to the missing person's car again, and then widen the search. We'd only walked about fifty metres along a path when Sicoe burst out of the undergrowth and indicated. The casualty was lying, well tucked in, under some bramble bushes. We reckoned he'd taken about 45 seconds to make the find: all in all, a highly pleasing result.

'I retired Sicoe early in 2010 after seven years on the call-out list. Over this period he was involved in a wide variety of incidents. Together, we searched for patients who had wandered from hospitals, injured climbers, missing hillwalkers, children hurt in cliff falls and adults threatening suicide in remote areas. His ability to scent was quite remarkable. In one incident he actually hit on the scent of a climber lying a quarter of a mile distant, invisible under eighteen inches of snow. He worked long and hard in all weathers and all he asked for at the end of each search was to play with his favourite toy, an old piece of rope.

'It is a shared joy to successfully find a missing person and to track down someone safe and well. Even if you don't find the missing person, there is satisfaction in knowing you have cleared an area and freed up other team members to widen the hunt. At the end of the day though, whilst my three dogs were all operational team members, most important, they were loved members of the family.'

Peter Durst has been actively involved in mountain rescue since 1967. By anyone's standards this is a very long time, which few others in the UK can match. Over this time he's played a significant role at local, regional and national levels. He was a founder member of the Rossendale Fell Rescue Team (now Rossendale and Pendle MRT) in Lancashire and has served as team leader, deputy team leader, chairman and president, as well as ordinary member.

Within SARDA England he has been a body, handler, secretary, chairman and training officer. He has also represented the Mid-Pennine Search and Rescue

Organisation and SARDA England on the national body for mountain rescue, Mountain Rescue England and Wales. His contribution to all these organisations is immense and almost without parallel.

'In 1951, when I was twelve years old, my family acquired a dog and I was smitten. I read every book on dog training I could find in the local library and then spent the next dozen years walking the local fells with her at every opportunity. By the time she was long in the tooth, I was married and had become seriously attracted to rock climbing. My resultant lifestyle suppressed any thoughts of a second dog but, in 1967 — when my climbing partner emigrated to South Africa — I drifted into mountain rescue and became stuck!

'My introduction to the use of search dogs came in 1975 when a team member informed me he'd just passed the first assessment with his German Shepherd. On the team's next call-out I deployed him in a rural search and he had a spectacular find, saving the life of an old lady lying unconscious in a stream. She had been missed by two search parties earlier in the incident. I was prompted to find out more about SARDA and search dogs in general, especially volunteering to body. This gave me an insight into what was required and shortly afterwards I acquired my first potential search dog, Jan. We spent the glorious summer of 1976 building a hill partnership and I began training her formally with SARDA at the start of 1977. Exactly one year later, we passed the assessment and Jan became a graded search dog.

'I recall this was a difficult period for SARDA. Apart from a troublesome dose of internal politics there was a general lack of credibility within mountain rescue. For example, records show that dogs were ignored in 70-80% of searches in the Lake District.

'Determined to tackle both of these problems I was canvassed to stand for the office of chairman. I was elected in January 1981 and, after facing somewhat aggressive opposition from some members, I achieved the required objectives by 1986. Harmony within the association had improved and dog teams were being called to help with over 95% of all searches. This was achieved primarily by concentrating on improving training methods and raising performance standards. It also helped to improve communications with the mountain rescue fraternity and make numerous presentations at national conferences and meetings about the value and success of dogs in search and rescue. An unexpected bonus of this was to recruit to the association dog handlers in the south west of the country.

'I remained as chairman for some ten years but, a year after leaving, the association split when SARDA Lakes established itself as a separate association. Through most of the 1990s my involvement at national level waned although I was still involved in regional affairs as an operational handler, call-out organiser and liaison officer with regional police. I also took the opportunity to attend rescue dog events in Italy, Sweden, America and Norway where I gave several presentations about the English approach to searching with dogs.

'In 1999, I was elected to serve as training officer for SARDA England. I was keen to reflect on our achievements over the years and consider how we should progress. I came to the conclusion that, although we had made significant improvements over the original methods of training, there were flaws in our overall approach. I felt this was the reason for the unacceptably high levels of failure to meet our minimum standards. There was a real need to increase the percentage of passes but without diluting standards in any way.

'I found the next few years difficult. Many people do not readily accommodate change, no matter how subtle it may be. Old habits die hard and transitional periods are always hard to manage. The Foot and Mouth problem in 2000 didn't help and this created a very damaging hiatus in national training activity. However, I'm convinced we are making good progress and the past ten years have marked significant developments in training methods, standards and the successful use of search dogs in mountain rescue.'

Neville Sharp has been president of SARDA England since 2004. He first became aware of the work of SARDA in 1979 when he joined the Calder Valley Search and Rescue Team in West Yorkshire. A couple of years later he was invited by Pete Durst to attend the annual SARDA assessment course at Keswick. At this time he was a police sergeant dog handler with West Yorkshire Police with responsibility for firearm tactical search dogs. He was also the trainer and handler of the only human remains detection dog in the north east of England.

His background with police dogs prompted many questions about how search and rescue dogs are trained and worked and he identified a number of key weaknesses. He was particularly concerned that, despite search areas

TOP: NEVILLE SHARP WITH GAYLE © PETER DURST.
ABOVE: PETE DURST IN THE CAIRNGORMS WITH BRAE
AND FERN © PETER DURST

being completed and bodies found, it appeared to be the dogs that largely dictated the search boundaries, with little structured approach to the overall operation by handlers. Obedience training and the importance of controlling dogs also appeared to be weak — in many cases entirely absent. None of which fitted too well with his own philosophy when working with dogs: An obedient dog is a successful dog.

'Whilst conscious that I was relatively new to SARDA I did feel it important to recommend that, if new skills were taught involving a strong element of directional control, handlers could capitalise on their dog's potential and generally extend their ability to range and search. In addition, I raised the whole idea about stock testing. Eventually, my ideas led to a new practice of Initial Registration, which all handlers had to embark on at the start of training. Essentially, this was a more formulated approach to initial work with dogs that focused on basic control (obedience) and stock testing.

'The many farmers we met on the training circuit at this time were very supportive of these ideas and anxious to become involved. Leading figures in the sheepdog world offered guidance and support and Eric Halsell, the well-known presenter of *One Man and His Dog* also registered interest and support for our work. Contacts with people like these helped to provide the association with greater credibility and accountability.

'When I retired from police duties in 1990, I took the opportunity to train and grade my own search dog. Peter Durst, who had been involved with SARDA for over 25 years at the time, was my mentor and revealed to me what it was like at the sharp end. He laboriously ensured that the basic fundamental process of what a search dog does best — locating and finding missing people — was foremost in all we did. Indeed, it's now well established that this process in a dog's training must be secure before the dog progresses to search work and every handler knows very well that the find sequence and indication is paramount to a successful dog team. Once I'd recognised the critical importance of this, the subsequent progression to search work training was relatively easy.'

As president, Neville provides general support within the organisation, assists with the annual assessment each year in the Lake District and also provides guidance and help to members through lectures and presentations associated with training and search management. As a former police officer, he holds gentle sway in ensuring things are carried out in a structured manner and that everyone 'paws' the line.

Today, everyone joining SARDA undertakes the formality of a registration test and, in recent years, this process has been supported and successfully conducted by a professional dog training and behaviour adviser, Jacquie Hall, who is the Honorary Training Adviser to the Association. She brings a wealth of experience to every potential handler starting out with a new dog, and today, all would-be handlers commence training with puppies to recognised standards established by Jacquie. Indeed, today, nearly all dogs currently operational with SARDA England have passed through her early training and development programme. Jacquie's understanding of dog behaviour and associated issues has ensured every handler is well supported at this early milestone in training. But we'll come back to Jacquie later in the chapter.

Neil Powell is a member of SARDA Ireland North. He first became involved in mountain rescue in the early 1970s. Almost immediately he took an interest in training dogs to help in search work, but was unaware of SARDA and the particular contribution of Hamish MacInnes. In an attempt to gain a professional slant on dog training, he contacted the Royal Ulster Constabulary to see if they could help. They were exceptionally supportive and allowed him to work alongside one of their most successful dog handlers, Joe Boyd.

Joe had won the National Police Dog Trials for two consecutive years. He was meticulous in his training and Neil learned a lot in a very short period of time. They continued to work together every week for a whole year but then Neil learned of Hamish and his good friend and SARDA colleague Kenny MacKenzie, who was a police dog handler with the Highland and Islands Police Constabulary. Delighted to hear that dogs were already being trained for mountain search work, Neil made contact immediately. This was to be the true start of his mountain search dog career.

'I was warmly welcomed by SARDA Scotland and travelled over to Scotland as often as I could, keen to absorb all the new information. Twelve months later I qualified my first novice search dog — Kim, a German Shepherd. He was a great dog and, not long after qualifying, we were called out to search for a missing person in the Mourne Mountains. After about an hour Kim found the man, a local doctor who had become lost in very bad weather. When we found him he was exhausted and suffering

from hypothermia. The news of this first find by a dog spread and helped to set the stamp of approval for search dogs in Ireland. We continued through the '70s and then, with the help of colleagues in Scotland, formed SARDA Northern Ireland in 1979. Our name changed to SARDA Ireland in 1983 to embrace all mountain rescue teams throughout Ireland and later, mainly for logistical reasons, we separated into two groups — SARDA Ireland North and SARDA Ireland.

'Not long after qualifying Kim, it struck me that training him to indicate by barking at the casualty wasn't very efficient given the distances and sounds encountered in the mountain environment. I voiced my concerns but it wasn't easy trying to convince our training officer that it would be better practice to have the dog return to the handler, bark and then take him back to the casualty. That was not the way things were done! However, I eventually convinced him to let me try it. It worked and so the 're-find', as it is now called, was born.

'After Kim retired, my next search dog was a Border Collie called Pepper. He was remarkable and in his working lifetime found a total of sixteen people, including one buried just below the surface at the edge of the impact crater in the Lockerbie air disaster. We spent five days in Lockerbie and, like many others who were there at the time, it changed our lives profoundly.

'One of Pepper's best finds was in the mountains of Donegal where he and I and another handler, Mick McCarthy and his dog Dex were flown by the Irish Air Corps to assist in the search for a missing German schoolboy. The child had become separated from his group in very bad weather and had been missing for almost

two days. It wasn't unusual in the early days of SARDA to call out dog teams only as a last resort. After several hours of searching in the dark with Mick in one area and me in another, Mick asked me to check a part of his area, which he hadn't fully covered. I sent Pepper into the area and in minutes he came back, indicated, turned and took me up a slope to a small trench over which was draped a green waterproof sheet. I was disappointed that all he'd found was a tarpaulin dumped by a farmer but, before turning away, I stopped briefly and lifted the corner. To my astonishment, there was the missing child, soaked, cold, hungry, semi-conscious but alive!! What a great feeling, not just for the child but for me too.

'Pepper was an adorable little dog and, to this day, I still miss him. He featured in Angela Locke's book *Search Dog* where she spoke about the distinctive, emerald green search dog coat he wore when working — the colour we favoured at the time.

'As the years have passed, I've had a number of other wonderful dogs. Two of the most outstanding were my Golden Retrievers, Cracker and Dylan. They were both awarded the PDSA Gold Medal 'For Animal Gallantry and Devotion to Duty' for their work and for finds they made in the two big earthquakes in Turkey in 1999. The award also recognised their work in the mountains of Ireland where Dylan found four young people who had been caught out by bad weather, and Cracker for his work in locating a number of drowned victims in the sea, lakes and rivers.

'After appearing on television — where I was interviewed about my feelings on the quarantining of Cracker and Dylan — a well known dog breeder rang me and offered me the pick of a championship litter of labrador puppies he'd just bred. I was delighted and selected Charco who, true to his potential, has been outstanding as a collapsed structure search dog. He and I have assisted in the search for survivors in earthquakes in Algeria and Pakistan, where he helped locate one lucky young man who had been buried under the rubble of his house for almost two days. Charco has also been involved in numerous searches of other collapsed structures with the Northern Ireland Fire and Rescue Service. Like many other dogs used for search and rescue, Charco lives to work.

'As well as Charco, I currently have a springer/cocker cross called Fern. She came to me because her previous owners were unable to control her and about to put her down. She has been trained as a drowned victim search dog and to date has located six victims in the lakes and rivers of Ireland. She also pinpointed the location of two drowned fisherman missing in Loch Awe in Scotland. I have really been very fortunate to have had such wonderful experiences training and working search and rescue dogs and will always be grateful to SARDA for providing me with the opportunity to do this work. In my opinion, SARDA has been one of the great success stories in mountain rescue in the UK and Ireland and we all owe a huge debt of gratitude to Hamish MacInnes for his foresight and dedication in starting everything back in the 1960s.'

Since Neil penned these words he has achieved success in training two black labradors — Lucky and Flo — to search for illegal copies of DVDs. There was initial scepticism as to whether dogs could be trained to detect odour from optical discs but Neil showed that it was possible. Over the next two years, he and his now-qualified dogs were flown around the world: Los Angeles, Washington, New York, Hong Kong, Dubai and Toronto to demonstrate to the various law enforcement agencies how his dogs operated. In one particular operation, both dogs were flown to Malaysia where they located discs and burners worth many millions of pounds sterling and, in so doing, severely upset the pirating operations. Neil has since written a best-selling book about his work with search dogs — *Search Dogs and Me* — details of which are given in the 'Useful References' section on page 230.

Andy Bluefield is a past member of SARDA Scotland. He joined mountain rescue in 1977 when he became a member of the Assynt MRT in Northern Scotland. Shortly afterwards Andy took an interest in SARDA and began to body for various handlers living in the north of Scotland. This led to him acquiring and then training his own dog, a Border Collie called Snap, for search and rescue work.

Over the years, Andy and Snap had numerous adventures together, including one search where they were tasked to locate two men missing in the high mountains of Glen Shiel. Weather conditions were favourable but fresh snow lay to a depth of over a metre. In those early days there wasn't an avalanche forecasting service but Andy remembers vividly that the risks were extremely high. Both he and Snap struggled for a long time to make any kind of useful progress and it didn't help that poor radio reception made radio contact with base difficult. Eventually, contact was made and they descended to base to discover the search had been terminated. It transpired the two men had turned up safe and well several hours earlier!

'I recall a training exercise where Snap and I were tasked to find two members of the RAF who were bodying for the first time. One of them decided to make life a little more complicated by leaving his rucksack in one location whilst hiding somewhere else. Most hillgoers know that one of the golden rules in mountaineering is never to be parted from your own rucksack — it can be a lifesaver. Snap quickly located the rucksack, but instead of indicating her find to me in the normal manner, proceeded to chew it to bits! The owner of the dismembered rucksack was eventually located by Snap, and I had the task of explaining to him what had happened. At least the RAF chap learned that parting company from your rucksack is not to be recommended!

'As the years rolled on, Snap revealed another unusual pastime — this time a rather more positive one. One day I was walking her near our home when she took off suddenly and quickly returned with a piece of paper in her mouth. Eager for me to see what she'd found, she dropped the piece of paper to reveal a £20 note! I reasoned that Snap had picked up human scent on the note and simply treated it as a missing person find. Without any obvious owner in sight, I gave Snap a biscuit, pocketed the money and continued the walk with a happy smile on my face. Interestingly, Snap's find was not a one off. Over the next few years I pocketed many more notes as Snap went about her financial business. The strange thing is she never bought me any coins — only notes!

'Snap played an important role in one

particular rescue in the winter of 1984. It was late one Wednesday evening in February when the telephone rang. It was Russell, a friend and fellow member of SARDA. Russell asked if I'd heard about Adam. He and a friend had been walking along the summit ridge of Beinn Achaladair in Central Scotland when Adam's dog slipped over the edge into the northeast corrie. Although unhurt, it had great difficulty getting back up again. Adam went to help but in an attempt to rescue his dog, he fell crashing into frozen avalanche debris some 200 metres below. He suffered serious injuries including a dislocated femur, fractured clavicle and multiple bruises and lacerations. Several rescue teams were mobilised and eventually carried him to the road and thence to hospital in Fort William.

'Russell explained to me that Adam was relatively comfortable and out of danger, but his dog was missing. The rescue teams hadn't been able to find Moss when they picked up Adam from the bottom of the snow gully. I decided immediately to drive the four hour journey from Lochinver to Beinn Achaladair overnight and spend the next day searching for Moss. I felt it was the least I could do, considering Adam had recently looked after Snap for three months while I'd been away trekking in the Himalayas.

'The weather since the day of Adam's accident had been bitterly cold with an icy east wind. I wondered if there was any chance of finding Moss alive. Four days was a long time to survive in those conditions.

'Other friends including Norman Brett, who had been walking with Adam when he fell, had been out searching for Moss for

TOP: MOSS JUST MOMENTS AFTER SHE WAS FOUND © ANDY BLUEFIELD.
ABOVE: ANDY'S DOG SNAP © ANDY BLUEFIELD.

the last three days but had found no trace of him.

'I met up with Norman and some members of the Doncaster Mountaineering Club who had volunteered to assist in the search, at the bottom of the mountain in the morning. It wasn't a bad day for the time of the year but the cloud was down low over the mountains. When the group reached the coire where the accident had taken place I started searching with Snap. Every few minutes I made Snap stop and bark in the hope that Moss would recognise her voice and respond if he was within earshot. Snap's barking echoed emptily around the bleak snow-covered coire. After a short period, miraculously, a sound came back from the mountain that wasn't an echo. It was Moss!

'Snap threw her head back and howled like a wolf. Norman tried the metal dog whistle which Adam often used. There was another bark in response. We were in business! Moss was found in the gully where the fall had taken place. She was somewhat thinner, but alive and well apart from a tail frozen to the snow. Norman and the club members guided Moss down the icy gully using a rope and makeshift harness. As this was taking place, Snap simply howled in impatience at not being allowed to go and play in the snow with her old friend! But as soon as Moss was on safe ground and released from the harness the two began to play as if nothing untoward had happened.

'But the best was yet to come. Nothing was said to Adam about finding Moss. Instead, my friends and I drove immediately to the hospital to give Adam the good news. We were refused permission to take Moss to Adam's ward

but, needless to say, Adam was utterly overjoyed to hear Moss was safe and well. The reunion with his best friend was an immediate boost to his recovery. Shortly afterwards, Moss was checked over by a vet and I set off home to Lochinver with two tired, contented dogs in the back of the car. Moss had a quiet holiday in Lochinver while Adam spent the next few weeks recuperating in hospital. The two dogs got on very well with each other — so well that a couple of months later Snap and Moss became the proud parents of a litter of four pups!'

Andy Colau began training Border Collies more than 30 years ago. His interest came about almost by accident. At the time he was a keen mountaineer and member of the Clapham-based Cave Rescue Organisation. One day he spotted a notice on the centre's noticeboard, from Bill Jennison and Phil Haig, asking for volunteers to sit on Ingleborough and wait to be found as part of a dog training exercise. It sounded interesting so he went along to find out.

'I didn't think I'd be found, but while sitting there, this collie called Gwen came out of nowhere. I was so surprised and intrigued I decided to try training search and rescue dogs myself and, three weeks later, I acquired my first dog. She was advertised in the Craven Herald as a sheepdog-type bitch with spotted legs and free to a good home.'

Andy christened her Corrie and went on to train and qualify her very quickly. Shortly afterwards, he trained Corrie's daughter, Gael. Their exploits were filmed over two years for the BBC documentary *Search Dogs of the Summits*. Both Corrie and Gael were involved in the search for victims of

the Lockerbie disaster in 1988. This experience was a steep learning curve for everyone and prompted Andy to launch a new organisation — K9 Search and Rescue — dedicated to training dogs specifically for UK disasters. He even set about training another dog, Fionn, to search for people trapped under collapsed buildings. Andy's initiative prompted some opposition from established members of mountain rescue because, up to then, SARDA was the only established organisation for training dogs.

His third mountain rescue dog was Gael's daughter Rhona. One of her searches was to look for a missing tourist on the Island of Ibiza in 2001. Rhona was then involved in numerous other searches but, tragically, she went missing in 2003. Her body was found in quicksands at Helwith Bridge five months later. It was in Rhona's memory that Andy then started training Tara, now an active search and rescue dog with SARDA England at the grand age of nearly ten.

Following the sad experience with Rhona and the effort involved in training Tara, Andy decided Tara would be his last search dog. Perhaps he'd begin to spend more time with his family and less time as a mountain rescue volunteer? But, these thoughts were short lived. He very soon reckoned, as he was still fit and capable, he'd begin again with another dog! So his household now has a new member in Belle, a Border Collie born in the Lake District.

'I may be in my sixties, but I'm very happy being out on the mountainside in the dark, snow and cold. These days I usually have a navigator with me and also an electronic gadget called a Satmap which pinpoints my position to within an inch. Padding about on the hill is much easier than it used to be!'

If Andy succeeds with Belle — and that is at least two years work ahead of him — he will be one of only three handlers in SARDA to have trained and qualified five dogs — or six, in the case of Malcolm Grindrod, in the Lake District.

Children's TV programme *Blue Peter* has a long association with animals, especially dogs. One of its presenters, Matt Baker, (later, a presenter on BBC's *Countryfile* and *The One Show*) had a black and white Border Collie, which became one of the featured pets. Matt decided to breed from her and, in May 2005, Meg gave birth to five pups on Matt's farm near Durham. Matt and the *Blue Peter* team thought it would be good to offer some of the pups for working positions and for *Blue Peter* to then follow Meg and the puppies in their new life. Of the five pups, one stayed with Matt on the farm, one went to work as a trainee hearing dog for the deaf, one to train as a guide dog and one to work as a sheepdog. The remaining pup was offered to SARDA, to train as a search and rescue dog. Shortly afterwards, James Coles of SARDA Southern Scotland became the proud owner of Corrie and arrangements were made with the BBC to follow her search and rescue training.

James made the trip to Durham in July 2005 to see his new dog. She was too young to leave Meg at that stage so James returned a few weeks later for the handover and first filming. James arrived to meet Matt and the *Blue Peter* film crew and quickly learned the unusual conventions of filming and the need for extreme patience — things do not always go as expected! Filming rarely takes place in logical sequence and often many takes are required to gain the perfect shot. Even the simple act of arrival and knocking on the farm door took four takes of driving into the farm entrance! Needless to say, the dogs were unconcerned by all this. Eventually, after a long day, James left for home with his new puppy, ready to begin the process of obedience training and introductions to his other dogs, and training for rescue work proper.

The second filming episode involved a single cameraman taking background footage at a SARDA training day. The cameraman quickly realised the practical difficulties of filming a search dog at work several hundred metres away. However, James and Corrie managed to set up some short finds and the cameraman went home with suitable film in the can. The next occasion was in Durham when everyone returned to film a puppy reunion and to update *Blue Peter* on the training so far. At this point, Corrie was in the midst of the run-out phase of training, where she follows a body who has her toy. To do this successfully, the camera crew, soundman and producer needed to stand in the middle of the run-out area, potentially confusing Corrie's run. However, completely unfazed, she ran straight past them to find Matt and the toy. The sequence was completed to perfection! Indeed, Corrie completed the task successfully on every film take.

Up to this point, all five puppies were involved in filming. But in January 2006 the first filming dedicated to Corrie took place. The crew and Matt Baker visited James in Dumfries for two days of filming. The first day was set up for training with the naval helicopter from HMS Gannet in Prestwick. On cue, the helicopter arrived in the Galloway Hills and, after the usual safety briefings, James, Corrie and the crew began work.

Filming followed previous procedures with multiple takes and discussion about how to take the best shots. Things began slowly but soon sped up once the helicopter rotors started turning! After two hours flying and winching operations, everyone returned to the landing area for interviews. The helicopter crew had to leave for other duties but not before each member was proudly presented with the obligatory *Blue Peter* badges! On the second day, Corrie undertook a stock test at a local farm and then completed a search with Matt acting out the role of missing person.

Once the editing was done, James and Corrie were flown to London to appear live on the show. Following their successful and highly entertaining TV debut, training continued in earnest and, almost two years to the day of the first film shoot, Corrie was ready to be assessed to become a fully qualified search and rescue dog with SARDA Southern Scotland. A serious injury to tendons in Corrie's paw almost put an end to all the hard work put in to get to call-out status. While jumping over a wall, Corrie landed on a discarded piece of broken glass which severed vital tendons but, after a nervous few months with the leg in a splint, she resumed her training and qualified as a search and rescue dog.

Blue Peter returned to film a follow-up piece with Corrie's local mountain rescue team in Moffat, and Dumfries and Galloway Police simulating a real search for a missing child. Of course, Corrie saved the day and, with the assistance of the *Blue Peter* presenter, helped the team evacuate the casualty to safety! To date she has

ABOVE: JAMES COLES LOOKS ON AT THE BLUE PETER SHOOT © PETER SANDGROUND.
FACING PAGE: JAMES AND CORRIE, READY FOR ACTION; JAMES AND CORRIE WITH BLUE PETER PRESENTER MATT BAKER © PETER SANDGROUND.

attended over 40 call-outs and made two successful finds. She continues to serve with SARDA Southern Scotland and lies in front of the fire as the traditional SARDA dog — happy as a family friend but ready to jump in the car at a moment's notice to scour the hills looking for a missing person in trouble.

Without a doubt, these few stories alone reveal something quite definite about the character and motivation of dog handlers, not least an abiding and clear sense of commitment. The large majority of handlers remain involved for a considerable period, often training and working several dogs during their rescue career. Twenty-five years is not uncommon, whilst some members have been involved with the work of SARDA in one form or another for over forty years. It's a commitment that overrides many hardships — being called out regularly at unsociable hours, travelling exceptionally long distances and frequently braving poor weather. There's also the physical endurance required in searching rough terrain for long periods, often in the dark, and the hundreds of hours invested in fundraising, training, assessment and operational work. It's not surprising that, for the vast majority of handlers, search and rescue work is a central feature in their lives. It dictates their lifestyle, family plans, friendships, holidays and leisure pursuits.

Explaining such commitment is not so simple. Every individual has their own story, their own rationale for what they do, how they got there, but there are common threads in what they say. Belonging to a small and unique group of like-minded people is important. So too is the satisfaction in rescuing people, a motive

that applies to everyone involved in mountain rescue, but the 'canine factor' seems to dominate; the joy in working as an independent team with your 'best friend,' one you've trained over several years, has few parallels elsewhere in everyday life. Quite simply, the combination of togetherness and teamwork brings a level of satisfaction that is second to none. Everything else such as bad weather, travelling, financial and time outlay, pales when the unique satisfaction in working together is brought into the equation.

There is something else which stands proud when you listen to others and there isn't a single word to describe it. It's concerned with variety, the successes and the failures, the numerous ups and downs that go with the job, and the capacity to cope with extreme emotions. The satisfaction felt when a dog makes a find or passes an assessment is experienced by all handlers. These experiences are the culmination of all the hard work but they are invariably balanced by those occasions when all the hard work invested in training results in failure or when the outcome of a find is the sight of someone who has died in tragic circumstances. Handlers need to take the rough with the smooth and, of course, they're well up to the task.

The DOGSBODY
A POEM

Terry Blanchard is a long serving body with Lake District dog handlers. **Over many years, she's found herself in a wide variety of cold, wet and windy positions.**

On one particularly dark evening, she was told to hide in the forest above the Whinlatter Visitor Centre, just to the west of Keswick. Midway through the session, she was requested to leave her position and stroll slowly backwards and forwards along a short section of a forest track. The Lake District teams are often requested to look for Alzheimer's sufferers who've gone walkabouts, so her brief on the radio was to imitate someone with such a condition. She says it wasn't the first time she'd been told to act her age! After stumbling around for a while and thinking seriously about what she was actually doing, she felt compelled to describe her feelings in writing. With William Wordsworth's famous poem Daffodils as a backcloth, she penned the following words.

I wandered, lonely, as one should,
When told: 'Be a misper in the wood.'
Mumble, mumble, stumble and sway,
Why aren't other bodies told to act this way?

Of all the people in this mob,
I'm over-qualified for this job.
I get out of breath; I'm old and fat,
And when it's sunny I'm told: 'Wear your hat!'

Because the sun glints on my golden locks,
And gives away my place among the rocks.
To be honest, my hair's gone grey,
Well, most of it's been gone for many a day.

Back to being a wrinklie in the woods.
Make sure the dogs deliver the goods.
It's cold and wet and muddy and dark,
How did I ever get caught up in this lark?

There are compensations, when the stars are bright,
Or an eclipse of the moon on a special night.
The peace is great; I could enjoy this for hours,
And I suppose the rain will produce nice flowers.

My radio startles me, but I'm alert in a tick,
'Body Terry, Body Terry, from Dog Mick,
The next dog's Dottie, have your head torch off.'
I must remember to mumble, maybe even cough.

Now concentrate hard, don't trip over that log.
Blast! My solitude ruined by a flaming dog!
What did they say? What should I do? Good.
The dog is barking, I must be too!

The dogsbody's view

And so to the bodies, dogsbodies, bravos — different associations adopt different names — without them, training and assessment would be an impossible task. From the very start of a dog's training and all the way through to assessment their task is not just to 'be' the person lost on the hillside, ready and waiting and armed with treats, but also to assist with the dog's socialisation. During a typical exercise scenario, the body is directed to a specific place on the hillside unknown to the handler. Once in position and hidden from view, the search area is described to the handler who then has to locate the body. To avoid being seen or heard, bodies have to wear clothes that match the terrain as best as possible and also position themselves out of sight behind a small mound, in a gully or over a rise in the terrain. In winter conditions the person may be 'buried' under the snow. Bodies are always kitted out with gear to keep them safe and warm such as sleeping bags, bivvy bags, hot flasks as well as a radio to keep in communication through the search. Once in position they may have to remain in place for a long time — sometimes in the order of hours — so

patience is clearly a must! They are given clear instructions about what to do once found by the dog — this may involve playing with the dog before it returns to indicate. Needless to say, if a body is not found they would follow instructions and bale out after a given period of time. So, that's the theory. What about the practice?

Jane Brown is a long-serving body, who works with Lake District handlers.

'I'll always remember Christmas 2001 — the magic of a clear, starry sky lighting up a fine dusting of snow on the fields and fells late on Christmas Eve as I took our dog for a late walk. Christmas 2001 also marked my introduction to SARDA and subsequently to my new 'career' as a 'dogsbody'. Having been an avid reader of the various mountain rescue team yearbooks, I was intrigued to find a pile of SARDA yearbooks in the converted barn where we were staying. Later, chatting to the owners, David and Annette Watt, all became clear. David*, a member of Kirkby Stephen MRT, was a search dog handler and his wife Annette, an old hand at dogsbodying. A glass or two of wine later, I found myself volunteering to body at the Loweswater training weekend.'

'Cold, wet and windy — it was fairly typical weather for January. Actually, the first day I was fairly oblivious to the weather; too busy concentrating hard on instructions about where to go, how to react to the dogs, and how to use a two-way radio. The aim of the game — and that's what it is for the dogs — is for them to indicate or bark at the body, then return to the handler and bring him or her back to the body. The bodies are instructed on how much or little encouragement is required, according to which dog is coming in and the level of training they have reached. I was soon experiencing the joys of being trampled on, scrabbled at, licked to death as the many dogs made their finds. In spite of the weather, and rather I think, because of the dogs, I was hooked and already looking forward to the next monthly training weekend.

'The following months took us to Keld, Patterdale, Thirlmere and Langdale allowing the dogs to get used to different conditions. I was also getting used to the individual needs of each dog, and that split-second timing of whether or not to encourage barking. A return trip to Loweswater in the summer provided us

*A dedicated team member and search dog handler for more than thirty years — and an experienced pilot — David tragically died in May 2011, when his plane crashed on landing near his home. His funeral was remarkable for the number of dogs as well as handlers, proudly showing respect, the route to the church lined with two solemn lines of red.

CLOCKWISE FROM ABOVE: CAMOUFLAGE AND FACE PAINT FOR A NORTH WALES BODY, MIKE RANDALL © RICHARD BEECH; BODY DAVE AND SKY © DAVID NICOL; TRAINING ON BEN LAWERS SHOWING SNOW-COVERED BODY, JOHN CHROSTON, WITH DOCHAS, AND HANDLER DARRYL URQUHART-DIXON TO THE FORE WITH RUBY © CALUM BLACK; ROD STODDART (SARDA SCOTLAND) WITH MIDGE © HEATHER MORNING.

with another new experience, a memorable one for me: being winched onto an RAF helicopter. It's an important part of the dog's training, one that many of them seem to take in their stride.

'The most satisfying moments for me, however, have to be when 'my' dogs do exactly what is required of them, whether it's barking at a squeaky toy or indicating spontaneously as I lie 'dead'. I've experienced many of these moments over the years, while continuing my tour of the Lakes, visiting Coniston, Borrowdale, Ennerdale and Wastwater. The weather may not be perfect every time, but I consider myself the lucky one — wrapped up against the elements in my bivvy bag. So, when my friends ask me what I'm doing at the weekend, I always reply: 'Going to the dogs.'

Rod Kelly is a retired paramedic. He's been involved with SARDA England for almost 27 years and, during this time, has worked continuously as a dogsbody. He's probably one of only a handful of people across the UK to have been committed for so long. In fact, to mark his long career he was made an honorary member of the association, a tribute bestowed on only three people.

'I joined mountain rescue in the early 1980s and, honestly, I had little idea what SARDA was all about, but that would change quite dramatically. Every Wednesday, I'd leave home and drive to our team base for regular training evenings. En route I'd often see fellow team member Jim Gardner. Jim started to train his dog Moss in 1987 and my involvement with SARDA began as Jim's local body to supplement his training with SARDA.

'We soon established a good working relationship but things took a dramatic turn one fateful day. Jim had just turned the grand old age of forty when he developed epilepsy, right out of the blue, with no prior warning — nothing. It might have been a knock on the head as a child or a fall, but nobody really knows why it started. Initially this was a big stumbling block for Jim and Moss's training and their possible future with SARDA. Jim had to surrender his driving licence, which meant he couldn't travel to training events. I came up with a solution. As we actually lived within a mile or so of each other, it was possible for me to accompany Jim when he was doing his training. I could be his driver, navigator and medic (I was an ambulance paramedic at the time). So this is what we agreed and here started a long friendship and the beginning of a most enjoyable and often hilarious period of my life.

'Jim and I worked together through the many ups and downs of his training and, some two years later, he was ready for assessment in the Lake District. We both had high expectations but, unfortunately, this turned out a failure. They just weren't good enough. So it was nose back to the grindstone to get things right for the next time. We attended more courses, organised further training days and practised in new locations in preparation for the following year's assessment course.

'This time Jim and Moss passed with flying colours. I was so proud to be involved throughout their training and eventual success. At last, Jim and Moss could wear their bright red jackets with pride! But this was only the beginning. We continued working together for the full working life of Moss — ten years training and assessing in every conceivable type of weather and

TOP: SARDA WALES BODY AND SEARCH DOG © SARDA WALES.   ABOVE: THE BODY'S EYE VIEW OF HAMISH AND JEN © DAVID NICOL.

terrain. There were many miles travelled, many searches — some very funny and others very challenging. Throughout this period, whilst I continued to assist Jim I also served as a body for other members of SARDA and gradually became familiar with all the procedures and protocols. Eventually, I like to think I became a very experienced and knowledgeable member of the association.

'So what's it like to go out in all weathers, day and night in an effort to elude handlers and their dogs? To be honest you need many different qualities. A strong sense of humour doesn't go amiss, lots and lots of patience and a stoical attitude to poor weather. An ability to smile is definitely necessary, especially on wet, cold days when a smelly, soggy doggy jumps on you, barks its head off when you are snuggled down in your cosy bivvy. It's not unusual on these occasions for the dog to be followed by an equally wet and bedraggled handler who asks something like: 'Are you alright in there mate?' You probably reflect on the fact that you were — before the noisy, wet dog appeared!

'On one course in the Peak District, I was asked on the first day to body close to a rock feature called Allport Castle, a tall tower perhaps 50 metres high. The weather was good for once — bright sunshine and no rain. I was determined to find an ideal (difficult to find!) location to hide and quickly spotted a ledge inside a cave. This happened to be a favourite haunt for members of the RSPB when watching nesting peregrine falcons. I found a path up to the cave and made my way inside to find a nice comfortable bench on the ledge to sit on where I could gaze down the valley below. I felt this was a little too open so

fastened my groundsheet across the cave to make me less obvious. No one came to find me for hours and I was thinking I had beaten everyone, but I was wrong!

'I heard a rustling outside the cave. No barking, but there was definitely something there. I cautiously peered round the sheet and could see Moss peering into the cave. She showed interest but wouldn't enter the cave and then, in a trice, she was gone. I waited for ages for Jim or someone to find me, but nothing happened. Then, after what seemed like hours, there was a crashing noise outside and rocks began to fall across the cave's entrance. Could that be Moss or Jim falling? I dared not think. Things went quiet for a while but then I heard rustling outside and all of a sudden Moss appeared with Jim close at hand.

'I heard Jim, saying to Moss: 'Stupid bitch — there's no one in there!' But of course he was wrong. Jim had assumed there was nobody in the cave and failed to respond to Moss's indication. It transpired Jim himself dislodged the rocks. Standing on the top of the rock and peering over to see if he could see Moss, he dislodged the rocks he was standing on. I think we all learned a lesson that day — always trust your dog!' Something of a recurring lesson theme!

'In the early days,' continued Rod, 'I was fortunate to meet a fellow body called Dave Walmsley. We struck up a friendship that lasts to the present day. Over the years he and I have often been teamed together and we've noticed that assessors and handlers seem to do their utmost to find us the hardest, coldest, wettest and most uncomfortable area to body down into — punishment, I suspect, for so frequently outwitting the handlers and dogs!

Assessors seem to have a common strategy when locating us. They cast their keen eyes over the terrain and mutter or chuckle amongst themselves whilst we stand patiently in wait. Then they gather us together and say something like: 'Can you see that big rock half way up? Well never mind that, just keep heading upwards past those trees, through the distant gully and onwards to the skyline. Now, go beyond that for a few hundred metres and you'll find a lovely group of rocks to cuddle up to.' The grin on their faces says much about their motives!

'Of course, when you're given instructions from the roadside you're well able to see your intended location, but it's not easy to recognise it once you're on the hill. The shape of the land changes and all the detailed instructions you were given are lost to the wind. One such location is Langstrath in Borrowdale valley. We still shudder at the name! Langstrath is often recorded as the wettest place in the UK. The valley sides are littered with numerous big boulder fields making it virtually impossible to find a nice comfortable spot to hide. Which means you end up huddled or jammed between jagged, wet, slimy rocks for hours. Even the dogs find it difficult to negotiate. Langstrath was the venue for an assessment course in the late 1980s. I recall it well. The weather was a little unkind to everybody that year. I struggled three-quarters up the hillside and did manage to squeeze into a crack between two rather large boulders. Unable to lie down, I had to endure the whole day wedged in the most uncomfortable position imaginable. The wind was gusting gale force along the valley floor, with sleet and heavy rain pouring all day long.

'I could see the two assessors way down below me in the valley bottom. They had what they thought was a good idea for protection: a tent! The hardiest and most steadfast of the two was Neville Sharp, who persevered all day through all the elements without faltering. The second assessor Dave Riley retired into the tent halfway through the day. As the day progressed the wind picked up speed and the rain changed direction from vertical to horizontal. By this time the tent was flapping about very precariously. Then, all of a sudden, it was gone, taken away to a distant point way down the Borrowdale valley. Notably, Dave Riley remained lying down in his sleeping bag. It's possible he was taking a different view of proceedings, but I rather suspect he was still asleep! We derived some pleasure knowing Dave was now probably wetter than ourselves.

'I may have given the impression there's an unspoken battle going on between assessors and bodies. It's all in good taste and for a good cause but it's surprising how inventive bodies can be to gain a few points when necessary. Frequently, once settled into a nice comfortable, dry spot, the radio crackles into life: 'Rod, Dave — can we move you to a new location? We need to challenge the handlers a bit more and relocate you both.' You get out of your warm hidey-hole, pack everything into your rucksacks — trying to keep everything as dry as possible — and trudge cold, wet and weary, to the new location. Sometimes I wonder if the assessors are just having a laugh out of devilment, although on some occasions it's amazing how, on these occasions — just by coincidence — our radios develop flat batteries making it impossible to communicate!

'When I cast my mind back over the years, I can't help but think of the changes that have taken place. Most bodies on the early courses were members of mountain rescue teams. They used their team radios and supplied their own gear for bodying. People would turn up for a training session and few would know what was going on or who was doing what. These days, things are much more professional. A lot is done to care for us bodies and more people from outside mountain rescue teams play a part. There's no shortage of people wanting to help and I suspect this is because there are so many positives to being a body and helping the association. Courses are held around the country — Dartmoor, the Peak District, mid-Pennines, Wales, Yorkshire, the Lakes, the north east of England and Scotland — providing us with varying types of landscape to investigate and develop our art of evasion. We see the changes from when a handler begins training through to their eventual success and addition to the call-out list. The differences between handlers and between dogs, and especially the changes that occur as a puppy grows into a mature search dog are a joy to behold. We see how new handlers learn to understand their dog's behaviour and think like a dog. And we witness the developing bond that combines dog and handler as a single team. Knowing we have made a small but significant contribution to all this is very rewarding. It was a great pleasure recently when, with two of my fellow bodies — Dave Walmsley and Stuart Saddington — and I were rewarded for our efforts with honorary membership of SARDA. Together, we can boast over seventy years of dogsbodying. Not bad going!

'Today, I'm the point of contact for new body queries for SARDA England. Our website has generated a lot of interest across the UK and an increased desire by people from all walks of life to support and share in our work. The camaraderie within SARDA is second to none. Handlers, bodies and supporting families really are a true 'Band of Sisters and Brothers'. If I could turn the clocks back would I do it all again? The answer is a firm YES. And will I continue to body? Again YES — as long as I'm able and fit enough, then I'll be there!'

As Dawn Lowe began to climb the last few Munros she reflected on how nice it would be, rather than climb to the very top of each mountain, to find a nice sunny spot on the hillside, read a good book and catch up on lost sleep. So, when the Munro challenge was finally behind her, the scene was set to do just that. She also wanted to do something positive with her free weekends and spoke to her good friend Graham Percival, a handler with SARDA Southern Scotland. Little did she know at the time what that conversation would lead to! Indeed, she couldn't have guessed that the activity Graham suggested would not only give her many restful days on the hill but also help others in a very meaningful way. Of course, it had been suggested she try bodying for SARDA and, several years down the line, she now knows she has the prefect disposition to be a body!

'My first day's experience as a body was one September weekend at Kinloch Rannoch in the Central Scottish Highlands. It was one of my dream days — sunny weather, a good book to read, catch-up on sleep and a dog fix. I've always adored dogs and at the time I couldn't work out a way to own a dog and work full time, so going along to body for SARDA satisfied my yearning.

'For the next couple of years I went along as a body when required, but then my friend Graham left SARDA. However, I decided to continue to get my regular dog fix and, over the past five years, I've served as a body but also helped in a variety of other ways including chief cook at training weekends, dog walker and dog feeder. I don't mind a bit of cooking and I do my bit, but the diet of some handlers does leave me somewhat frustrated: 'I don't eat mushrooms'... 'Greens are bad for you'... 'Where's the salt?'...

'I have frequent requests to feed dogs or take them for a walk. On one occasion I'd hardly left the building to take numerous dogs for a walk when I heard the tell-tale noise of my handler colleagues opening another bottle of wine! I've also discovered that bodies are very useful as taxi drivers especially when the handler, suffering from too much drink the night before, has to be taken to their first search area the following day. I've even had a handler request breakfast in bed. A bowl of cornflakes was suitably 'installed' in the appropriate sleeping bag. Not surprisingly, there's been no further requests of this nature. As you can see, it is exhausting being a body. No wonder we have to lie down for six hours on the hill the following day!

'All bodies have a radio so they can listen to the chat between handlers and assessors, but also to respond to requests from assessors. After a while I switch off from all the chat and get on with my book although, occasionally, something slips through to raise an eyebrow. Despite all the good-humoured banter and leg pulling, SARDA bodies are really very much appreciated. Without us, the handlers couldn't train their dogs or be assessed but what do I get out of it? A day out in the hills enjoying the peace, tranquillity and enforced relaxation, knowing the gardening, housework and other tiresome chores are many miles away back home.'

One of Dawn's body colleagues in SARDA Southern Scotland is Joanna Toohey. Like many others, Joanna was persuaded to join a training exercise one day, without fully appreciating what it was all about. She accepted the challenge and ten years on has never looked back.

'My bodying career began one very wet weekend in the Arrochar hills. The first day it rained heavily. I was sodden before the day had really started. Within minutes of getting into my bivvy bag, I was lying in a pool of water, soaked through. I came off the hill with an horrendous headache, feeling utterly miserable. We headed back to the hostel where a hot shower and food awaited us. Did the experience put me off bodying? Not a chance.

'I realised this was a unique opportunity to meet new people and make friends with common interests. Over the years, I've met people from various walks of life and made many new friends who share a common interest in dogs and hill walking. One of the satisfying and enjoyable aspects of SARDA is to be involved in the training of mountain rescue dogs and witnessing their progression to call-out status. There are many times you learn something new or see something unexpected — all of which add to the overall pleasure of bodying.

'I recall a weekend training exercise at Kinloch Rannoch in the Central Highlands where the scenery is spectacular and absolutely vast. On day one, I was asked to position myself on the hillside not far from a small burn. As I lay there I could see someone running towards me alongside the burn with his dogs. Suddenly he stopped, removed all of his clothes and jumped in the burn for a skinny dip. Unable to move, I simply watched proceedings from my undercover position! Had he been aware of my presence I suspect he would have thought twice about the dip. At least my camouflage was well proven!

'I've spent a lot of time rattling a can and enticing people to make a contribution. These events are always worth the effort and a good time is had by all. Well almost! One event involved a sponsored walk along the Southern Upland Way in the Scottish Borders. I was positioned with two handlers on the summit of a small hill called Three Brethren, our task to provide support for any walkers in need. We initiated some impromptu dog training with a trainee dog. While I bodied, the dog began to search for me, but became more interested in a squirrel in the heather. Eventually, I gave up and made my way back to the handler. In the meantime, the dog caught the squirrel and brought it back to his handler. As we attempted to recover the squirrel, which we assumed was dead, it suddenly turned and bit my friend and escaped from the dog's mouth. The squirrel fell to the floor and the next thing I knew it was climbing up my trouser leg! I was convinced it would take a chunk out of my leg so I frantically began to jump up and down. The others ran to my rescue and started to pat my clothes and shout at the squirrel! Eventually, dislodged from my clothes, it ran back into the heather. Just another of the many unique things you experience as a body!

'But, for anyone with inclinations towards

becoming a body — beware! We sometimes have to turn our hands to all manner of tasks but it's nice to feel wanted and know you are serving a very important function. I know, despite the additional demands they place on us from time to time, that dog handlers really appreciate the time and effort we provide.'

It has often been pointed out — with tongues firmly planted in cheeks — that dogsbodies must have a 'screw loose'! Why else would otherwise perfectly sane individuals devote hours of their free time, wrapped up in their warmest clothing for the dubious pleasure of lying in a snow hole or under some unforgiving bracken being eaten alive by midges and gradually becoming wet and hypothermic?

This is what these selfless people do in order to assist their team colleagues in the training of their dogs. Without them, SARDA would not exist. One couple, on retirement, and with no previous experience of search dogs, or even mountain rescue, decided to buy a caravan and offer their services to SARDA. Throughout the year, weekend after weekend, come rain, shine, hail or snow they crisscross the country, hiding in holes for fun, enjoying every minute of it. Other dogsbodies are full team members who like working with the dogs and their handlers. A key factor is that dogsbodies have to be physically fit and, of course, enjoy working with dogs. Working with experienced search dogs gives the opportunity to observe how search dogs locate casualties using their sense of smell. For anyone interested in becoming a dog handler, bodying is an excellent way of experiencing all the hard work that goes into becoming a search dog team.

The assessee's view

Assessment, in any walk of life — whatever the focus of assessment — is stressful. Failing an examination can leave wounds that never heal. Success can bring pleasure beyond words but, the truth is, assessment is a necessary process in many aspects of life and no less so for prospective dog handlers.

What's it like to be assessed? If a simple stock test can reduce a grown man to a quivering wreck, what about the rest? Kaz Frith, handler and assessor with the Lake District dogs, is no stranger to the stresses and strains of the assessment process.

'The wind was atrocious; the TV weatherman was reporting gusts over the hills of 80 to 100mph and Cumbria Police had advised people not to travel unless necessary. And what was I doing at 7.45am on this Thursday morning? I was travelling to the Newlands Valley in the Lake District to undertake a three-day search dog assessment! The car was being rocked all over the road, I had a rotten bruise on my right foot from the week before and, frankly, I was getting nervous about the three days in front of me. Although we had been under assessment since October (and had already passed six elements) the next few days were beginning to look very important. We were

just one step away from qualification. It was finally beginning to dawn on me that we might just do it.

'In the fourteen months since we'd started training there had been the inevitable ups and down. Nobody can imagine the amount of time that's spent by the trainee handler (and their family) in the training of a dog. At the beginning, everyone tells you what a big commitment it is, yet you smile sweetly and think that it'll be no problem — you're already in a mountain rescue team so you know all about commitment! Six months later, when you explain to your husband for the third time in a week that you're off to dog training, would he mind (yet again) not going out climbing as someone has to look after the other two dogs, or do something trivial like the food shopping or washing, you start to think maybe it's beginning to take over your life. At one point, we established a 'dog watershed' where my husband enforced a 'no dog-talking rule' after 8.00pm!

'I've roped in friends, family and complete strangers to run about waving toys, lie in fields, climb trees, hide behind walls and under bracken. I've persuaded farmers to let me walk in their fields to get the dog used to sheep, cows, even llamas!! My dog has been a complete star throughout — in

KAZ FRITH AND DOTTIE DURING A TRAINING WEEK IN SCOTLAND © DARYL GARFIELD.

fact she seemed to be a natural — the problem has always been me.

'Imagine staring at a hillside knowing that up there somewhere are any number of bodies in unknown locations and the only way you're going to find them is if your little collie picks up their scent and barks at you. You start up the hill — trying to work out which way the wind is blowing, where the possible dead areas (where there is no wind) are, how you're going to navigate through the boulder field, up the crag, across the gully or through the scree and all the time trying to keep one eye on the dog so you know what ground she's covered and one eye on where you are putting your feet so you don't fall over. You try to describe your plan of action or reasons for changing your plan over the radio (sometimes laying on the floor to block the wind noise).

'You've been working an hour and just when you've decided you haven't a clue where you are in relation to the area and think the dog's run off somewhere more interesting, she reappears in the distance.

'She starts moving towards you — the thought crosses your mind that her body language seems different — has she found a body? There's a 30-second delay whilst she runs at you — tongue out, tail wagging. As she closes in she begins to bark and immediately turns and runs away. You follow, hardly daring to believe she's worked out where the body is from a good 200 metres away and is taking you there. In the distance you can hear her barking, then she appears again and barks at you. For the next couple of minutes you concentrate on getting across broken ground to the place where the body is. You arrive at a crag face. The dog rushes around at the foot of the crag barking manically. At the bottom, tucked into a bivvy bag, is a body. Dottie is going wild — she knows she'll get to play with her tennis ball now. You could kiss the body because you were beginning to wonder if you'd messed it all up.

'You get on the radio and tell the assessors you've found — then give them the plan for the rest of your area. At the end of two hours you walk out having found no-one else. You think you've covered everything, think you've got the dog in all the right places and now you've got to face the result. It's a pass! Then they tell you to get yourself ready to do another area, and you go through it all again.

'Towards the end of the assessment process, your confidence grows — you start to understand the way to walk round the area, how to avoid choosing difficult routes, but more than anything you learn to trust your dog — because ultimately that faith will be tested on some cold, snowy, dark night on the side of a mountain.

'Now we have graded, I've realised that the assessment process was just the end of the beginning — the learning curve, now we're on the call-out list, is going to be steep but if I can continue to have faith in my little dog we'll do alright.'

Rupert Bonham works for the Forestry Commission and is a dog handler with SARDA Southern Scotland. He was a member of Tweed Valley MRT for ten years and, for the last four, has been a member of Lomond MRT. His first dog was a liver and white Springer Spaniel called Ben who had to be retired as a full search dog after breaking both his front legs. His second dog is a large Munsterlander called Lewis. Rupert chose him for his spaniel looks and long legs.

'Assessment is one of the necessary evils of becoming a dog handler. Love it or hate it you have to undertake assessment to go on the call-out list. I think it's one of the hardest things about being involved in mountain rescue — it reflects two to three years of hard work and is the break point when you find out whether you're good enough to go on the call-out list and become a qualified dog handler.

'On the morning of each day's assessment, the assessors and bodies leave for the search areas about an hour before the handlers. This gives the assessors time to decide on the boundaries of each area, and an opportunity for the bodies to position themselves. It also gives you time to down another nervous cup of coffee and worry about what lies ahead, reflecting on what if? But this period passes very quickly before you're radioed and asked to come to your first area and given the search area boundaries. Your brain goes into overtime! Primarily, you have to consider how to work the area. This involves taking account of the weather conditions, especially the wind, and also the terrain.

'It's helpful to memorise features in the area because once you're on the hill, the shape of the land changes. Some things come into view that were initially out of sight, whilst other features disappear or change shape. It's also vital, before beginning, to rehearse in your mind the key criteria against which you are to be judged — the need to find bodies (obviously), to fully clear the area, avoid missing sections and to avoid duplicating sections. Once you've thought up a suitable plan, you have to explain clearly to the assessors how you intend to work the area.

'As you're about to begin, you radio the assessors to let them know. Normally you start the area on the downwind (scent collecting) boundary — this gives your dog the best chance of picking up a scent from the whole area – then gain height in the area as quickly as possible. It doesn't take long before you begin to relax and focus on watching your dog and forget the binocular-eyes watching you at the bottom of the area. Sometimes, only a short time into the search, your radio crackles to life as one of the other handlers reports a find. This is one of the worst things that can happen and generates all kinds of negative feelings. The last thing you want is for all the other handlers to find bodies, sometimes two or more, when you have nothing in the bag! Then you might start to guess where the bodies are. Self-doubt begins to creep in. Have I missed a section of land? Has my dog run straight past a body? Are the bodies located in a specific area that I should target? Should I change my plan? If you allow yourself to become involved like this, then your searching will become inefficient and will be noted by the assessors. You have to put all these thoughts out of your mind and concentrate on the task in hand.

'You are allowed to ask for some clarification on boundaries and some handlers inform the assessors when the dog has shown interest in certain areas, but I prefer to keep quiet and get on with the job. All the time, I focus on my dog and any changes in his behaviour. For example, does he stop and lift his nose to suggest he's picked up human scent? This may happen several times but nothing comes of it. But then your dog suddenly takes off on a long strike, vanishes out of sight and comes back barking madly. This is a wonderful feeling and I know the dog is onto something. I call out, 'Show Me!' and the dog rushes back to the source. Once we're both with the body, the dog gets to play with their favourite toy — in Lewis's case this is a few nibbles of chicken meat! Once the first find is out of the way you can relax a little because you've just proven to the assessors you know what you're doing, but all is not over. You have to backtrack to your location before the find and resume the original plan; there may be more bodies to find. From time to time my thoughts turn to other handlers and how they're getting on. Because you work closely together on actual searches and you know how much work they've put into training, you want everyone to do well, but a touch of envy still creeps in when other handlers are asked to return to base while you still work.

'Each day ends with a meeting of the assessors where they discuss each of the dog handlers, how they've performed and whether they should continue the following day. These meetings really seem to drag on when you're waiting patiently to discover your fate. Finally, you're called in one by one to be talked through the day's areas, given feedback and tips for the following day. It's a little like being back at school and sent in to see the headmaster for some misdemeanour — but much worse! If you're allowed to continue, that's good news, but it's not until you've finished the fifth search area and been summoned to yet another assessor's meeting you finally know the overall outcome. The best news is to be told you've passed. It's only then the pressure you've been under really strikes home. This is the moment you and your dog have been working towards for two years. All the training, hardships, the struggle with bad weather, organising people to help you and the sheer amount of work come to a final conclusion. For some, the outcome is not as they expect and they have to train and wait another six months for the next opportunity but, for those that pass, the weekend ends with the presentation of a certificate. However, really this is a token; the key thing is that you've met all the criteria and can now join a select group of qualified handlers and begin the task of finding missing people for real.'

Rupert and Lewis qualified as a search dog team in October 2009. As Rupert worked with his dog through the two years of training he says he was struck by the difference in behaviour of both his dogs. Whilst they were different breeds, they also had distinct approaches to training and learning. Initially, he found himself expecting Lewis to behave like Ben and found if difficult when this didn't happen but he soon discovered it was wrong to compare both dogs and that he had to adapt his own style to suit the new dog. He also felt, with his second dog Lewis, the important thing was not just to 'jump through the assessment hurdles' and qualify as quickly as possible but rather, maximise Lewis's potential before he went for assessment. He was determined Lewis should not only qualify, but that he and Lewis should become an excellent search dog team.

Now that Rupert is on the call-out list he has only one remaining worry: when he's asked, 'Where was the person found?' he just hopes they weren't found in an area already 'cleared' by himself and Lewis!

The assessor's view

Experienced handlers who may have trained more than one dog and who have been on many searches, often find themselves in a situation of role reversal — from the assessed to the assessor. As we've already mentioned, the task for those who assess others is multi-dimensional. They need a good understanding of canine and human behaviour, a knowledge about how to devise and manage a good search plan and, above all, a sensitivity to the stresses that handlers undergo and astute observational awareness about how a search is unfolding and what constitutes success and failure. Mike Hadwin, a member of Cockermouth MRT, has been an assessor with LDMRSD for seven years, and training officer for four of these.

'I was happy as a body. All the dog handlers, all the trainees and all the assessors would be really nice to you. Even if you got sent high up into the crags on a foul day or buried four foot under snow, they all loved you. Then I got a dog and thought it didn't look all that hard. The assessors, well, they'd give you lots of encouraging words like: 'The dog's alright but the handler's useless' or 'Stop messing about and get up that hill!' What do they know? I thought.

'Well, quite a lot actually, and so did the graded handlers, other trainees and dogsbodies who, between them, all helped me and my dog get through the process and onto the call-out list.

'And then I thought. well that's me then, on the call-out list now, fireproof, free and clear. Wrong! The real learning comes after you have graded and, if you know anything at all about the people in the Lake District Mountain Rescue Search Dogs, you'll know they don't take anything for granted. They're always striving to develop dog teams to the best of their ability. So this means more work on the hill, day and night exercises, tricky little exercises to test the mettle of handler and dog — and all under the ever-watchful eye of the assessors. Oh, and you get to go on call-outs, usually on foul nights and somewhere high, yippee!

'After a couple of years I was asked if I'd like to spend a bit of time watching some of the other dogs train and be assessed. Then I was asked if I'd like to become a trainee assessor. I felt very honoured but scared as well. Does this mean they trust me? What do I know? Mum! Help! One of the mantras in mountain rescue in the Lakes is 'commitment' and most of us in it are completely into it. There's no doubt that if you want to be a dog handler you have to be committed. This is because it's like a hobby within a hobby. Your primary hobby is mountain rescue, training and attending call-outs and dog handling is next. You've two or more years of hard work training a dog and then attending all the ongoing training, not to mention call-outs. The thing is, Lakes search dogs have a lot to live up to. They have to have the respect of the police and mountain rescue teams if they're going to continue to be used to search for people missing in the hills and mountains. That respect is hard earned and it's because of that we have to ensure our standards of training and assessment are as high as they possibly can be. This is where our assessors come in.

'It's the job of the assessors to train, improve, test and develop the skills of existing and aspirant search dog handlers. It's not an easy job. Although there's a wealth of experience in the SARDA family, we all agree there's no single way of doing it. Dogs and people are all different — what works for one doesn't necessarily work for another. So there we stand, at the bottom of the hill, looking up at some poor individual flogging his or her pan in working the dog in a two-hour area we've set as an assessment, in the rain, hoping, hoping they'll get it right and we've got it right and there's another dog on the call-out list.'

Mike is currently back in training with his dog Fly. It's good to know he'll be going through it all again!!

The dog trainer's view

Jacquie Hall is a training and behaviour adviser at the Northumberland Canine Centre in Alnwick and also the honorary Training Adviser to both SARDA England and Ireland. She has been a dog training instructor and competed in many forms of canine competitions for over 30 years. In the late 1980s she was looking to find other ways to use and develop her dog training skills when she spotted an item in the local newspaper about the Northumberland National Park MRT and their fundraising efforts to train search and rescue dogs. Immediately, she knew this might be the opportunity she was looking for.

'I was instantly on a mission to train a search and rescue dog. However, there were many hoops to jump through! First, I had to become a voluntary warden with the Northumberland National Park prior to joining the team. I questioned the 'voluntary-ness' of this condition but agreed anyway and, in the summer of 1988, joined the team as a probationer, having fulfilled my warden duties. Once I'd been a full team member for a year I was eligible to train a dog with SARDA England and switched my four-year-old Golden Retriever Dilly from working trials competitions to search and rescue. After almost eighteen months, we were very close to being assessed for Novice Grade when Dilly fell lame. The diagnosis was good and bad. The injury was just severe bruising but X-rays showed she had chronic arthritis in a front knee. As she was

almost six years old the prognosis wasn't good, so we retired from SARDA. A year later, I severely damaged my knee on a skiing trip to Chamonix and, whilst I was still a team member, my serious hillwalking days were over. It looked as if my involvement with SARDA was over too.

'In my professional capacity as a dog training instructor, my interest at that time was leaning towards canine behaviour problems, especially aggression. I was also developing an interest in motivational work with competition dogs. Some years later I returned to SARDA to act as a body. It was then I became somewhat concerned at the lack of knowledge within the organisation about canine behaviour issues. It was also obvious that, whilst handlers were being given the best advice they could from other handlers, there was a clear lack of basic groundwork in obedience and all-round dog handling. Training was highly general and prescriptive and failed to take into account the wide variation between each dog and handler. It's commonly assumed that dog handlers are experts in all matters relating to dog training. Sadly, at that time, this was a misconception in many (though not all) cases and expertise was largely limited to those handlers who succeeded in making the grade. Failure rates were very high.

'In an informal way, I began to advise those who were having problems in their training and also address some of the dog aggression issues prevalent within the organisation at that time. My ideas were taken on board, so much so that, in 2004, I was asked by the association to take responsibility for the 'puppy' group. Shortly afterwards I was made honorary training adviser. This was a landmark step for SARDA England as it marked the first time an external training adviser had been used by the association. It clearly showed a new openness and a willingness to broaden training ideas.

'My remit from SARDA was to take new handlers and their young dogs through the required registration test. However, the task I set for myself was to turn mountain rescue personnel into highly proficient dog handlers. I planned to do this not only through practical training but also through lectures and discussion on dog training theory and related aspects of canine behaviour. For example, I planned to encourage handlers to look at their puppies in terms of their temperament and to address issues of too much or too little confidence in the first few months in order to produce confident, sociable dogs. I was also keen to highlight the value of motivation work (toy obsession) and the handler's understanding of how their dog learns. Over the years I have developed these elements to such a degree that, in a way, the registration test has become almost incidental to showing members how to become capable dog handlers. Indeed, some handlers have been held back in this stage through a lack of understanding of dog training even though, with a prevailing wind and a bit of luck, the pair could possibly have scraped through a registration test.

'However, I don't think scraping through is acceptable. If dog teams just meet the assessment requirements this can lead to problems later when training becomes more intense and demanding. There is little room for uncertainty or doubt when the standard is as high as in SARDA assessments, and all dogs and handlers require and deserve a solid foundation to their dog training career. The importance of these principles has now been fully taken on board by the association which demands that all handlers, not just new ones, attend the puppy group before progressing to further training and assessment.

'Many people were suspicious of my involvement in training in the early days. I felt initially that being female — in a male dominated activity — was a problem but the early successes with handlers quickly eliminated that fear. One particular concern was that I hadn't trained my own search dog. My answer to that was simple: behind every successful athlete, Formula One driver, weightlifter and gymnast is a trainer who rarely succeeded competitively in the sport they taught. Search dog training is no different. Indeed, the principles behind dog training are the same whether dogs are being taught agility, to retrieve, herd, dance or search for missing people. The theory is the same; it's just the exercises that are different.

'There were a few raised eyebrows when I used agility equipment and fun games to train search dog puppies. It was argued that search dogs don't do roly-polys and weave through their handler's legs!! My answer was that these are simply tools to teach handlers how to teach their dogs, to highlight the key principles of motivation and learning and help handlers understand how dog training takes place — or not, as the case may be! These techniques provide a valuable opportunity for handlers to learn through error. Those in the puppy group invariably make errors when tackling agility tasks, and this reinforces the principle that learning how not to do something often helps to reinforce the correct way to do it. It is infinitely preferable to make errors and know how to rectify them during training than when on assessment or on the hill during a real search. It quickly became clear to everyone that these techniques also inject a lot of fun into training and are very bonding for dogs and handlers alike!

'Seeing the first fruits of my labours in 2006, when dogs from my initial training group graded as Novice Search Dogs was a very emotional time for me. Whilst I may never be on the hill with a search dog as I had hoped, it's extremely rewarding to know I play a small part in the training and development of those in SARDA England. When I hear reports of dog teams making successful finds, I recall when those dogs were puppies and feel as happy as any proud parent to have helped in their training. The ongoing requests to troubleshoot training problems help to keep my skills and knowledge up to speed and add extra interest to my involvement. I like nothing better than problem solving of the canine kind.

'Life has a habit of throwing up unpleasantness at times but being able to escape to the hills once a month, share a drink or two with some special friends and play with young puppies provides a perfect antidote which I hope will last for a long time to come.'

SOLO © WILLIE FRASER.

The dog's view

Dogs are, of course, the stars of the show. They're the focal point about which everything else revolves. Without dogs there would be no SARDA and certainly this book would not have been written! So, it's only right we hear what they have to say about life in search and rescue. And if you're in any way sceptical that dogs have views about the life they lead, the people they work with and the pleasures involved — or indeed possess the necessary skills to express them — just read on!

In 1994 an incident took place in the Cairngorm mountains, which attracted massive publicity from the national press. Jacqueline Greaves, a 51-year-old school secretary from Lancashire, went climbing in February of that year with two friends. Near the summit of Derry Cairngorm, the snow underfoot gave way and all three walkers slid over a hundred metres into a deep gully. Her two companions were rescued within hours but Jacqueline Greaves survived three nights in temperatures down to -27°C, much of the time in a small snow hole. This incident took the national press by storm, not so much for Greaves's fortitude in surviving for so long but for the large amount of money she was reportedly paid for her story. Indeed, she did receive money for her story, but she donated every penny to SARDA. Also, following one of the first comments she made to her rescuers — 'I'm looking forward to a pint of Guinness' — she received a year's supply of Guinness, donated by the drinks company!

A number of mountain rescue teams, including handlers from SARDA Scotland, were involved in searching for Greaves. Willie Fraser, a National Trust Ranger in Kintail, and his dog Solo (so named because he was the only puppy to survive a difficult birth) played a key role in locating her. Solo takes up the story.

'This search and rescue lark is all just one big game for me. I'll let you into a big secret. When Willie and I go out with the mountain rescue people, I'm not looking for humans at all — I'm looking for my favourite squeaky toy! Forget all the nonsense you see in films about giving Lassie the missing person's clothes to sniff before they head off to hunt them down. That's not how it works for me! When I was a puppy, Willie started hiding my toys and I had to find them. At first he put them in easy, nearby places. Then he started putting them further and further away. These days they can be anywhere — even half way up a mountain. We've been playing this game for some time now and I've got it pretty sussed. I know if I find people during our hide and seek game, I'll find my squeaky toy. And boy, do I bark when I find it!

'Sometimes we go into the mountains looking for missing climbers but other times we help the police look for people missing from their homes or from hospitals. Willie's a ranger with the National Trust for Scotland and whether he's taking visitors on guided walks or working on footpaths on the estate, I'm usually there with him. I love meeting people — even children. And I love it when Clara — she's Willie's nine year old daughter — takes me walkies. But I don't like little yappie dogs. I bark at them as they pass. Can't help myself, but Willie says I scare them AND their owners and that's not polite.

'Willie sometimes makes me have a proper bath — though not very often — but, given half a chance, I'll go charging into the river near our home. If Willie throws sticks for me to catch, so much the better! All the recent attention with me finding the missing walker has been fun. I was even a guest on the TV programme *Blue Peter* but it'll be nice to get back to our quiet family life. And, of course, our hide and seek games with the squeaky toy!'

Helen McNamara is a long serving member of SARDA Ireland and, currently, their training officer. She was introduced to SARDA via a friend and initially interested in acquiring a dog simply as a pet, but then she attended a talk on search and rescue dogs and quickly realised this was what she wanted to do. Her first dog, a Border Collie, proved difficult to train as it was too interested in sheep, so she passed it onto a farmer to work as a sheepdog. Her next dog was Eiger, also a Border Collie.

'Hello there. My name is Eiger and I'm a mountain rescue dog. I've been trained to find people who go missing on the mountains by following their scent to where they're sheltering. Once I pick up their scent, I return to my handler Helen and bark loudly. That tells her I've found the missing person. I then lead her to the casualty.

'It all seems very simple now but there was such a lot to learn — all the well-mannered things like sitting, lying down, staying and walking to heel on and off a lead, and even learning to ignore sheep. I didn't have a problem with this but I know many of my friends found this the most difficult task of all. Then the fun bit started. One of Helen's friends would hide and I'd run after her then we'd play with my favourite toy when I found her. This was a great game. I learned to speak for the toy, eventually going back to Helen to tell her I'd found someone by barking and taking her to the lost person.

'Once I became proficient at this, I had to look for someone who had hidden without me knowing. This meant I had to use my nose, which wasn't a problem as all humans give off a particular scent or smell that's carried by the wind. I can recognise this and follow the scent. Next on the list of things to learn was going up the mountain when I was asked and then to go down the mountain, all the time looking for human scent. It started out as little searches of five to ten minutes but these became longer as I got older and better at finding people. Eventually, I was working areas for two or three hours then I was ready for a big examination in Wales. This is the one that decides whether or not I was ready to go on real searches for real missing persons.

'After three days of searching seven different areas I was declared a Novice Search Dog and my name was added to the list of other dogs on the emergency service list. At last I was ready to serve my country! This took a long time to achieve but it was all good fun. Of course, for me it was just a game of 'hide and seek'. One year later, I was reassessed and graded as

Doggie Tales
MILLIE HAS A DREAM

Dog owners know that dogs dream. The characteristic signs are a dead giveaway – teeth start to chatter, legs begin to 'dig' and unearthly howling sounds add to the picture of a dog deeply disturbed. But what are the dreams about? We questioned one particularly bright search dog, Millie Morning, and this is what she had to say – although an experienced search dog now, at the time of writing, she had no finds to her credit.

'It was mid-January, still dark and cold as I was woken from a deep sleep by the familiar morning sounds about the house. My handler, 'Special Human' Heather Morning, opened the back door to let me out for my morning constitutional and a pile of snow sloughed onto the kitchen floor. Cursing, as time was running short, she brushed it out and noticed that, overnight, the thick blanket of snow covering the garden had grown several more inches.

'Walking to my favourite spot was already becoming a greater challenge by the day — I'd worn a groove through the snow — but overnight this had totally drifted over. The back garden looked magical, a true winter wonderland.

'The day was forecast good: dry and sunny with a strengthening wind. There'd be lots of people enjoying the hills today! We'd had a fantastic winter so far. Snowy times are one of my favourite periods of the year: snow balls to run after, doggie 'snow-angels' to make and frantic digging for toys hidden by Special Human — now that really is my favourite pastime! Mostly, I find my toy, but if I'm really lucky, I find one of those dogsbody humans — they're a strange lot! Actually, it's not too difficult. Small air gaps in the snow allow human smell to percolate up to the surface of the snow pack. What a giveaway! I sniff 'em out, start digging and, seconds later, she's there with a shovel digging beside me (doesn't she know that's a doggie job?) Doesn't matter though, 'cos I just love trying to catch the snow as Special Human shovels it away.

'The usual drive to Glenmore Lodge today was a little more 'exciting' than normal. At the best of times my eyes scan for exciting things to see as we whizz along the tree-lined road. Today the trees were laden, heavy with snow — most unusual and a sure sign of exciting games ahead. But I soon found myself unceremoniously chained to my kennel outside Glenmore Lodge. I watched lazily as the snowflakes became less frequent and, by mid-morning, a weak winter sun had broken through the thinning cloud. Then Thump! Thump! Thump! as the Sea King broke my peaceful world. Within seconds Special Human was putting on my coat and full body harness and across we ran to the big, noisy, yellow bird.

'Within minutes we'd been dropped into Coire an't Sneachda. The weather was clear now but spindrift ripped across the corrie floor. We arrived at the base of the Goat Track, a popular route up and down to the plateau. I'd climbed it many times but today it looked different. A massive slab avalanche had strewn debris in a wide area across the corrie floor. Instinctively I knew this was my opportunity to put into action all I had learned. People were buried and, as the most important asset the rescuers had, it was my job to find them — I knew the chances of survival are very slim so I had to work fast!

'Glancing up towards the rim of the Corrie, I could make out the crown wall extending about half a kilometre in width just below the edge of the plateau. The avalanche debris was blocky, difficult terrain. But whilst blocks are heavy and can injure anyone in their path they leave air pockets for people to breathe and enable smell to escape through to the surface of the snow. I did just as Special Human had trained me, weaving in and out, over and through the massive blocks, some wa-a-ay

bigger than me. Nose down, concentrating hard and sniffing like mad. Then, I had it... I had a smell... no lost it... and then got it again, this time strong and powerful. I could smell the fear, the trauma and the blood. I began digging furiously. Special Human was there in seconds. Shovels out, she and the other rescuers started digging, but far more cautiously than me. Then, there it was, half a metre down. Was it a leg? An arm... a rucksack? Hard to tell at this stage. Special Human was shouting. Other rescuers ran across. They carefully cleared his head — he was breathing... moving... speaking... injured but alive! I moved back and watched in delight...

'...Then I jerked awake as the familiar tones of the BBC Breakfast TV presenter filled the room: Search and rescue dog hailed a hero as she digs victim out of avalanche...

'A big rescue! And a search dog found the buried man. Was it me? No — only a dream but one day my training will all come good, Special Human and I will find our man!'

a Full Search Dog, then regraded every three years to check I was up to standard.

'I've really enjoyed my work and it felt great when I actually saved someone's life! Two years ago I found two walkers on the Galtees Hills and I also found the body of child in the river in Baltinglass. Thanks to me his family could begin their grieving. Best of all was the patient missing from the Mental Hospital in Glanmire. All the staff searched for three days but then I came in and found him within five minutes — right outside the main door of the hospital! The other searchers had probably passed him thirty or forty times over the three days and never spotted him. But he didn't fool my nose!

FACING PAGE: **HEATHER MORNING AND MILLIE** © HEATHER MORNING. ABOVE: **AUTHOR BOB SHARP'S LATE COLLIE ABIE GETS TO WORK IN THE SNOW!** © BOB SHARP. ABOVE RIGHT: **EIGER** © HELEN MCNAMARA.

'I'm thirteen years old now and slowing up a lot. The work has been very enjoyable though sometimes it's hard with searches lasting for three to four days. In April 2003, I applied for my well-earned pension, hung up my search disc and put my paws up to rest. I now look forward to many days in the garden under the shade of the summer trees or by the winter fireside.

'It's quite easy learning the tricks of the trade — any dog could do it. All you need is a good thick coat to withstand the weather, a good nose for smelling and a bit of nous. Put it all together and you might even save a few lives along the way. And now I've hung up my disc, there's definitely a vacancy! I think I've earned a rest, but if you're looking for something different to do, you could do worse than joining us in a game of hide and seek in the mountains. It really is great fun!'

Sadly, Eiger passed away in the middle of 2004. Helen is now working her third collie, a bitch called Scread.

If we've given the impression that dogs are good at the search and rescue business then that's fine. They're actually very good indeed. In fact, we think sometimes they demonstrate acts of absolute brilliance but they can be just as fallible as people too. They've even been known to be on the receiving end of a rescue. A few years ago Drum, a Border Collie, and his owner were out for a stroll. They were walking next to Black Rock Gorge near Evanton on the Cromarty Firth, just north of Inverness. As Drum peered over the edge, he slipped and took a tumble down a steep embankment and into the gorge proper. It was quite impossible for his owner to climb down without the aid of a rope and climbing equipment. So he called the police who, in turn, tasked Dundonnell MRT to see if they could recover Drum.

'There I was, sniffin' about quite happily. Mmm. Hmm. The mellow whiff of rotted leaf, soft and pungent on the nose. And fungus. Mmm… definitely fungus. Crisp snaps of ever so slightly salty air. A subtle lingering dash of coconut…

'I do have a vague recollection of them calling, 'Come here, Drum', but that's one of the delights of reaching a certain… er, maturity. You can just pretend to be deaf and ignore people when you feel like it. Beside, I'd been there lots of times before. Although, once I was back under the safety of my own roof (and taking full advantage of the TLC on offer) I did have to admit that, on reflection, the grass may have been just a little slippery that day.

'Where was I? Oh yes… (They keep saying my memory's going. Can't remember when that started to happen…) Anyway, apparently I was near the path that runs alongside the Black Rock Gorge, near Evanton when I started to slip… 'Dig your heels in, lad,' I yelped, 'dig your heels in!' Well it usually works. But not this time. I just kept moving. Trees and bushes started flashing past. 'Grab 'em with your teeth!' I thought. No good. No teeth!

'Fifteen metres of this and then a fifteen metre jump (well I am a collie) then… wallop! 'Houston. We have splashdown!' But there's life in the old dog yet. A quick paddle then a waterslide (humans pay money for this sort of thing!) and, eventually, some construction of logs and twigs to climb out on to. Well, it was at this point I realised that not one single person had followed me (bloomin' wimps, humans!) so I decided I'd better sit down and wait, which seems to be what a dog's life is all about these days, anyway.

'It was quite some time later when this guy I have never clapped eyes on before pats me on the head and says, in a very familiar way, 'Hello, Drum.' I haven't a clue where he came from but the first thing he did was tie his lead round an upright log. Then — and you are absolutely NOT going to believe this — he started to feel and prod me all over. Right from the tip of my nose to the pads of my feet. In broad daylight!

'Then another one of his breed appeared (same kind of hard red head) and the two of them started to muck about with all kinds of leads. Thick ones. Thin ones. And shiny clanky things. Then, final indignity, they stuck me in this bag thing and I started to levitate.

'Well, really. Even I could have told them it wasn't going to work. Started to brush against the side, so they lowered me back down again. They had obviously never heard of Benji's story. Of course, he wasn't a collie like me, but when he got into trouble, he was zoomed up in a bag on a high wire. But not me. Oh no! I was hoisted onto the second guy's back like a bag of coal and up we went over rock, moss, bushes, branches and trees. It was okay for him. He was in control and obviously finding the whole thing highly amusing because he kept laughing. But nobody thought to tell me why I was swinging about on a human's back being jolted all over the place!

'Then, when we reached the top, this female specimen started to examine me all over again! What is it with these creatures?

'Anyway, I can't complain too much because they did let me go eventually and, a few days later, when I was more settled, some people came round and took photos of me. Fame at last! It made a real splash in the papers — they must have thought canyoning without a rope was a really good game to invent. Who said we oldies can't teach the young 'uns a thing or two?'

It took ten Dundonnell Mountain Rescue Team members three hours to catapult Drum the Border Collie to his fifteen minutes of fame!

And then there was the case of Spikie the Jack Russell. Darkness had been closing in when Spikie's owner Iain Anderson and his three dogs picked their way down the mountain A'Chrois, near Arrochar in Central Scotland. As Iain, a member of Arrochar Mountain Rescue Team, reached the half way point down the mountain, he came to a large clump of heather in the fading light and decided to jump over it. But as he glanced over his shoulder to check where his dogs were, he realised he had just leapt a narrow crevice which ran deep into the mountainside. Before he could react Spikie, a twelve-year-old bitch, had plunged into the abyss. Iain couldn't see her, but he could hear her pitiful yelps far below as he called her.

Iain ran down the mountain with his other two dogs and called his friend Mark Leyland, the Arrochar team leader. At first light next day, Iain, rescue team members and a group of friends set off to climb up the mountain to the fissure down which Spikie had vanished but, despite scrambling 35 metres down the narrow fissure, they could find no trace of the dog. Exhausted, they returned to the top and agreed Spikie must have perished at the bottom of the craggy crevice a hundred metres below.

The following day — almost 48 hours after Spikie had vanished — a disconsolate Iain and his girlfriend Fiona Jones, returned to the scene yet again and once more tried calling Spikie's name. Astonishingly, they heard a slight whimper, then a yelp and finally a full-blown bark. While Fiona stayed watch at the edge of the abyss, Iain returned to Arrochar and alerted once more the rescue team. This time, fully equipped and buoyed with the knowledge Spikie was still alive, the party set up ropes and belays for the hazardous descent into the crevasse. Once again Iain climbed into the deep and narrow fissure squeezing through subterranean rocks. At one point he escaped serious injury when a falling rock missed him by inches. He managed to scramble across a slippery ledge and his torch picked out Spikie trapped on a ledge five metres long on the other side of what appeared to be another deep crevice. Iain's rope wasn't long enough to reach Spikie and a second difficult descent with a longer rope had to be made to rescue the frightened animal.

By this time it was dark and raining heavily. As Iain returned to the spot, 40 metres below the surface, he managed to reach the ledge and lay his hands on the shivering and bedraggled Spikie. Terrified and deep in shock, she refused to come forward even just a few inches so he could grab hold of her but, by inching forwards very slowing, he managed to grab hold of her and stuck her inside the empty rucksack tied to his safety harness. Spikie was then hauled to the surface with Iain.

Iain said after the rescue that even though the odds were stacked up against the dog surviving the fall, he never gave up hope she would somehow still be alive. The

following day, following a check by the local vet she was pronounced fit and well with only a minor cut on her head to show for her ordeal. Then the press photographers arrived and, all of a sudden, Spikie was on all the front pages of the local newspapers. But, not long afterwards, she returned to her day job as a 'ratter'.

We've already heard from Search Dog Millie, laid up for weeks when a snowboard sliced through a major artery in her leg. Millie's fully recovered now — full of beans and back on the call-out list, and she's taken a break from rescues and training to chat to us about how it all began.

'My first memories as a pup were dominated by feeding times, but it was not the milk I remember most. No, it was the humans, lots of them — coach loads in fact — every day. And their smell! Now that was the really big thing! Boy did those humans smell. Now, I know us dogs are famous for their sense of smell, as we should be, but honestly, you could almost taste the smell of some of them before they got out of the coach! The big, hairy, fat ones and the thin, bony, wrinkly ones — they all smelt stronger than old Blaven who lived in the oil drum with me on our farm. And then there were the wee ones, running about excitedly, poking and squealing and wanting to pick me up all the time. Blimey they smelt real good; hands and faces smeared in sticky sweet stuff.

'Now, you may be a little confused with what I'm saying, so let me explain. My brothers, sisters and I were brought up in a field on a farm close to Aviemore. My parents and extended family (there were thirty six of us at the time) are what you humans call working sheep dogs. Some of the lucky ones lived in ram-shackled old

DOG AND HANDLER AT ONE WITH THE WORLD: JOHN COOMBS (EDALE MT) AND FLASH TAKE A MOMENT OUT TO REFLECT © WILLIAM COOMBS.

cars, wooden boxes, out-houses and even an old suitcase. My siblings and I were born in a field early one summer. Mum had a wee wooden box to take us into if we needed shelter, but most of the time we were happy running around the field playing and scrapping with our siblings. Dad — not sure about him. It could have been Corrie the wise old collie/kelpie cross who lived in the battered old Ford Cortina. But it might have been Aonach. He was kind of cute — something about the way he held his nose as he passed by the nursery area on his way to the big field. He seemed to have a vague interest in us, but he was rather standoffish. Anyway, Mum didn't seem to bother. I remember her saying: 'It's typical, the dogs prance around looking all important, but it's the bitches that end up doing all the work.

'There were six of us, three brothers and three sisters. Life in those early days was fun. The smelly humans loved us and often seemed more interested in us pups than the grown-up dogs that did the sheepdog demonstrations in front of the farm. We were lavished with affection, cuddled, mauled, played with and crooned over six days a week — I just loved it! That was the early days... but I knew things were going to change when Mum started getting kind of snappy and grumpy with us. It was time to grow up and move into a bigger world.

'One day, when I was about six weeks old, a blonde haired lady arrived. She picked me up, poked and prodded and asked Farmer Neil lots of questions about me. I somehow knew she was different to the rest. I'm going to call her Special Human from now on, as she seems to have become a big part of my life. I recall she had something in her pocket that squeaked. I heard the other humans call it a 'squeaky toy'. It sounded very exciting! However, my brothers and sisters didn't think so as most of them shot under the nearest shed, then looked out nervously with their tails between their legs. But I've always been a wee bit cocky — Mum regularly growled to put me in my place.

'The excitement of the toy, and the Special Human jumping around excitedly, was a bit too much. Paws akimbo, I was off, chasing the toy which was rolling down the bank, avidly chased by one of my pesky brothers! 'Whey, hey, I got there first... stitch that boy!' I grabbed it with my sharp puppy teeth and braced myself as my brother landed on top of me, trying to grab it. Shaking him off, I proudly ran back to the excited Special Human and dropped it at her feet.

'That's the one!' I heard Special Human say to Farmer Neil. Next thing, I was picked up and carried into a shiny blue car. It wasn't at all like Corrie's Ford Cortina which I'd sneaked into once before. It smelt much better! Wow, I was almost bowled over by the pungent smell of a pair of climbing boots lying on the floor. In fact, the boots were just the start of a multitude of fantastic new human smells which engulfed me as I started to explore every nook and cranny in the car. But then it started to move, slowly at first down the field and then out of the gate and onto the noisy road I'd always been warned to stay away from by Mum.

'Little did I know that the first chapter of my life was over and that I was heading into an exciting new world where I would be without my brothers, sisters and Mum — a world where I would play lots of exciting search and find games. I think humans call it mountain rescue.'

Have we convinced you yet just how smart and versatile search dogs are, how fully up to the job of working in complete harmony with their handler? That the handlers (and let's not forget the bodies) are consummate professionals, prepared to suffer countless hard days and nights of training and assessment, and selflessly engage in searches at any time of the night or day, often in foul weather and hazardous terrain? Add in the qualities required when faced with death and tragedy and the care each handler gives their dog over its lifetime, and you have it — the true, altruistic spirit of volunteering.

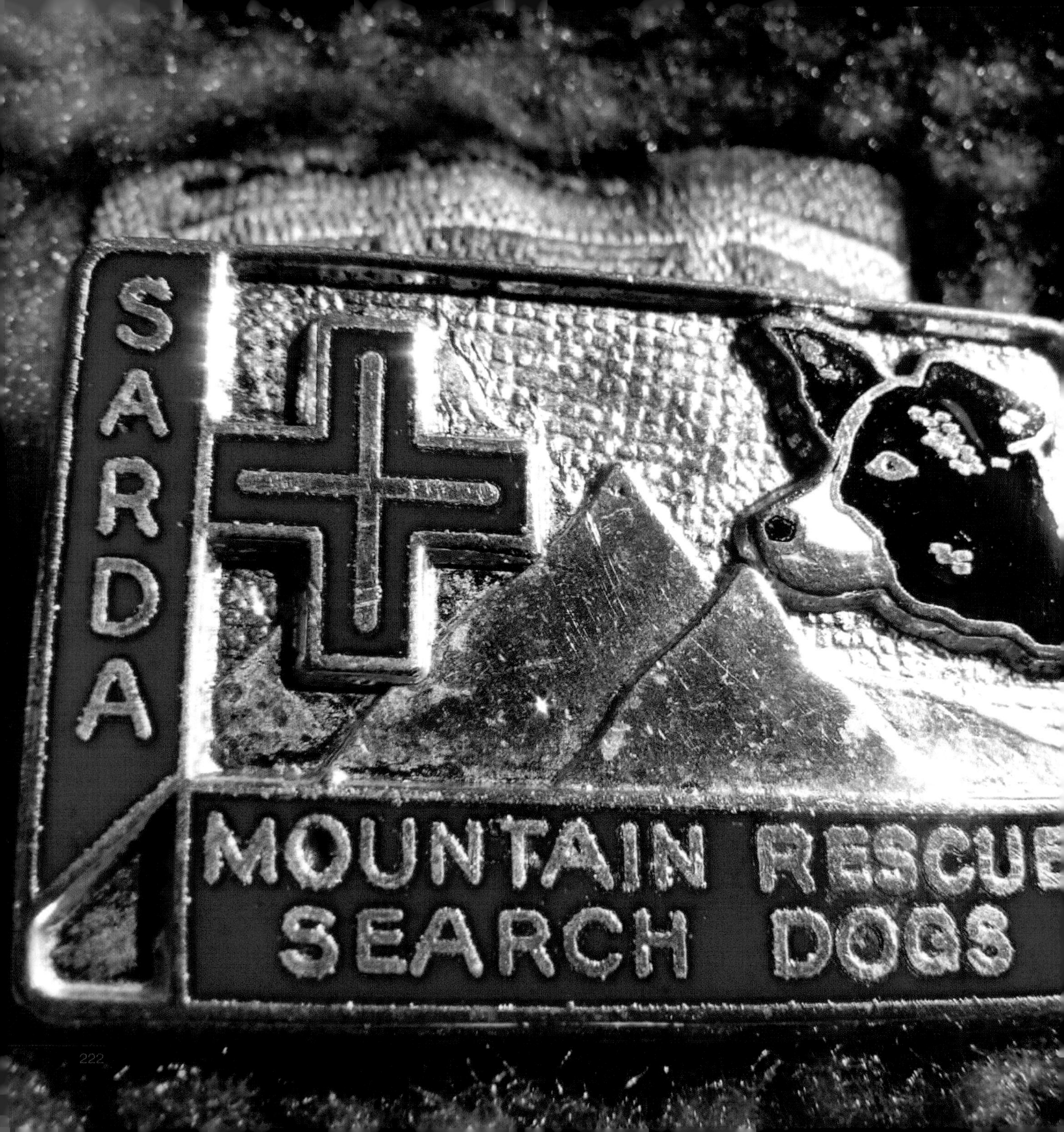
SARDA
MOUNTAIN RESCUE
SEARCH DOGS

11 Paws for thought

'So… when people ask why I'm still involved 25 years on, that's why. It's the look in their eyes, the trust and expectation, the hope beyond hope. All that hope and expectation hangs on us, because we're quite possibly their last and only hope of seeing their loved ones alive.' Joy Grindrod

But what of the future, the next generation — dogs and humans — and the one after that? Where will legislation and the prospect of government funding, the exponential growth of technology and the inexorable change in our society lead mountain rescue and, in its wake, the world of search and rescue dogs — that 'world of exciting search and find games'?

We reckon Millie, in her inimitable, uncomplicated doggie fashion, has it just about summed up. For, despite the tragedy and hardship woven through the fabric of the job, despite the sometimes shocking circumstances they find themselves in, and despite the challenging nature of our British climate and terrain — speak to anyone involved with search and rescue dogs and it's clear they love what they do. There's a buzz about it, a deep sense of satisfaction and joy, a camaraderie quite unlike anything else. The vast majority intend to continue doing it as long as they — and their dogs — are physically able, but summing it up in one word, one sentence, a paragraph even? Now that's hard.

Of course, there are some lighter moments. Many, in fact. Tom Gilchrist recalls a slightly embarrassing incident during a search in Lochaber with his dog (which Tom refers to here as 'Dog'), although we're not quite sure which of the parties was most embarrassed.

'Dawn in the Mamores and we are already on the go looking for a gent who has been out all night. Dog catches a scent down by the riverside and starts to bark and, as I approach the river, I spy a small tent. I realise this isn't who we're looking for, but do as I've been trained to do and follow through on the find. As I get closer I realise that Dog is indicating at a lady standing in the river.

'Dog doesn't like water so stays on the bank. Every time the lady tries to get out of the water the dog get more excited (barks more) because she thinks the lady is going to play with her. The lady is young, attractive, Italian and speaks no English. She is also completely naked, and when she sees me she tries to cover her considerable assets with hands that are way too small. Italian boyfriend emerges from the tent wearing little more than his girlfriend and speaks even less English. He is a lot bigger than I am. I try explaining that we're on a search but give up as I can see the veins sticking out in the Italian man's neck and I suspect I may become the victim of an assault if I continue. We retreat, much to Dog's confusion. I wonder what they told the folks back home…'

The story of SARDA across five decades is an exceptionally positive one. The vision of one man has not only survived the test of time but developed and diversified far beyond his dreams. The numbers of people involved and the related associations have grown and expanded, across all quarters of the UK, into a service fully recognised by the police and other statutory emergency services. All very positive but, nevertheless, there remain issues and concerns which don't just impact on current provision but promise fresh challenges for the future.

A major concern for all involved in mountain rescue is the substantial rise in calls for help — and subsequent demands on willing volunteers — both in the mountains and the urban environment. The

FACING PAGE: **AN EARLY SARDA ENGLAND LAPEL BADGE** © ROD KELLY.

EINICH PICTURED DURING AVALANCHE TRAINING © JOY GRINDROD.

number of call-outs for dog handlers across the UK has trebled in the past ten years. There are variations between associations but the increases for most are still significant. Changes like this, when not matched by corresponding increases in the number of dog teams, put pressure on everyone and cannot be sustained indefinitely. Already there is evidence it is becoming quite difficult for some handlers to attend every incident. The time when handlers (and rescue team members in general), dropped everything when called out, is showing signs of coming to an end. Employers are becoming more critical of the time off work required by handlers and a small number are beginning to question the exact purpose of incidents — they might be happy to release employees to search for a missing hill walker, but not so keen if it's a despondent or person missing from a care home. These are worrying times for everyone — handlers, employers and ultimately, the police.

When the pager or mobile rings 'call-out', most handlers respond immediately but an element of circumspection is beginning to appear — not surprising with greater workloads and increasingly busy lifestyles. When once they'd have done their utmost to attend every call-out, they're starting to consider the nature of the incident first. Are they truly needed? Will they be stood down on — or before — arrival? Is it simply a box-ticking exercise? Okay, this may be an extreme view and a long way from reality, but it does point to a future where, if workload continues to increase, handlers may need to think about their overall commitment in order to maintain a sensible balance in their work, home, social life and rescue commitments.

The number of dog handlers in each association is relatively small compared to the number of members in a mountain rescue team and in some ways it's a very fragile picture. In some cases, numbers are small enough to cause concern about whether the annual workload can be sustained. In some associations, the overall age profile is increasing. Several handlers are quickly approaching the end of their working life. Of course, experience is extremely important, but so too is youth and vitality. Indeed, the future of any organisation lies with new and younger members and the problem is that fewer are stepping forward to become involved. This is a concern for mountain rescue in particular and volunteering in general and may be connected with changes in society and the increasingly busy lives people lead. Dog handlers face many competing pressures — financial costs, the time required for training and call-outs, family and domestic commitments, the demands of work, pressure from employers, commitments to their own rescue team and so on. Training especially has changed in recent years with outside rules and regulations increasing the volume of training, level of intensity and burden of responsibility. Pressure is increasingly placed on team members to attend specialised courses such as casualty care, swiftwater rescue and rigging for rescue and the threat of litigation is ever present.

It's entirely possible that many prospective and current dog handlers are beginning to examine whether they can cope adequately with so many demands on their time and resources. Many, who in the past would have yearned to become associated with mountain rescue are taking a hard-nosed look at what's involved, realising that volunteering now comes with too many strings, and simply moving to something different. What with the proliferation of rules, governance regulations, health and safety issues, it's often said (only half in jest!) that rescue volunteers effectively have two jobs — one paid, one not — the latter being the most demanding!

In the future new recruits may choose to focus their involvement within the arena of urban and semi-urban searches. Every association across the UK is involved in a significant number of these incidents. In 2010, for example, of all the incidents attended by SARDA Scotland, some 50% were non-mountaineering in nature. It doesn't stretch the imagination too far to conclude that it might be more efficient to train dogs solely for this kind of work — as happens in the lowland areas — rather than train all dogs to air scent. Thus any association might comprise some dog teams that are dedicated to wild mountainous terrain, and others who deal purely with urban searches. This has been the case with SARDA Wales for some time, but it could be extended to other associations.

Related to this is the not uncommon view that training a trailing dog is an easy option compared to training an air scenting dog, that it's for ageing people who are perhaps less able to climb the mountains! Neither is true! It takes up to three years to train and qualify a trailing dog and, once operational, handlers do not have an easy time. A trail may start in an urban setting but can quickly lead to semi-urban, moorland and open hillside. Trailing dogs can move quite quickly and handlers have to go where their dog goes — be it through a river, bog, scree slope, boulder field or snow field. Avoiding an area is not an option! It's a fact that more people are beginning to see the advantages of using trailing dogs and search managers may see it as quite advantageous to have at their disposal both trailing and air scenting dogs. We could see a greater proportion of handlers who train only for trailing.

From a financial point of view, current funding doesn't appear to be a major problem for search dog associations. Indeed, one or two are quite wealthy. Both Scotland's associations benefit from government funding and most handlers across the UK receive travel expenses from their local police force, but income streams like this cannot be guaranteed and there is no certainty that funds raised through collecting cans, merchandise, sponsorship and legacies will continue. In short, all associations have to work hard at raising funds and the current financial climate will certainly place increasing pressures on all associations to look hard at how they raise and spend funds and maintain their sponsorship agreements with supporters such as pet food suppliers. Notably, the UK government has recently announced an injection of cash funding to all mountain rescue teams in the UK and it is likely that the various SARDAs will benefit from this initiative.

On the technology front, recent advances in satellite-based navigation aids have had an enormous impact on how hillwalkers find their way across the country and how rescue personnel manage searches. Modern smartphones are equipped with GPS receivers and software that permit accurate location information. A walker lost in the clouds need only switch on their phone, select the GPS app and tell the emergency services where they are located — no need for a search dog! And many walkers have dedicated GPS receivers with built-in mapping software that tells them exactly where they are. The SARLOC system, created by Russ Hore of Ogwen Valley MRO and launched in 2011, is increasingly used by teams across the UK and Ireland. Russ designed the app to help his colleagues deal more quickly with incidents in which a walker needing help was unable to give his or her location. The team sends a text message to the walker's smartphone containing a link to a webpage. Clicking on this link opens a page in the phone's browser which queries the phone to identify its location as a latitude:longitude coordinate. This data is then displayed to the user and automatically added over the internet to the rescue team's database, enabling them to pinpoint the exact location of their missing walker.

Since January 2012, personal locator beacons (PLBs), previously only available for use in the aviation and maritime industries, have been legally permitted for use on land throughout the UK. Now, anyone in distress or lost can inform the emergency services where they are by simply pressing the 'distress' button on their PLB! Again — no need for a search dog.

Navigation aids like this are useful to searchers because they help them identify or confirm their own position. Many dog handlers have mountain rescue radios that are GPS-enabled which means their movement on the ground can be monitored in real time on a digital map at control. This not only adds a measure of security to the handler's movement but also gives the search manager a clear indication of the area being searched. Even better if the dog is wearing a GPS-enabled collar, and these are currently being trialled by one association. But it should always be remembered that even though technology like this can be a blessing and is always improving, it's not infallible; nature invariably finds a way to subvert it. As one handler told us: 'There will always be a case for the Mk 1 human eyeball and the Mk 2 air-scenting dog because you never know when the gadgets are all going to fall apart!'

True, there are a number of issues on the horizon. Technology may have arrived, but for the majority of dog handlers the basics remain in place and the core values are unchanged. We're back to that puzzle: that elusive word, or few, that sums it all up. Of all the handlers we met and interviewed, all the stories we recorded, one struck a chord. It was Joy Grindrod, a Lake District handler.

Joy was introduced to the world of search and rescue dogs by her father, Malcolm, a stalwart from the early days, forty years ago. Between them, they have trained and qualified eight search dogs and attended many hundreds of searches. So, if anyone has the background, passion and experience to best capture the essence of dog handling we reckon it must be Joy.

'One day, when I was a nipper, my Dad asked could I 'just go up on the fell and hide for Spindrift?' And that was it, my introduction to the hills, the world of search dogs and mountain rescue. I'd grown up in a household full of dogs, surrounded by fells. It's no wonder it all became a big part of my life. I'd go so far as to say it was almost feral, our upbringing — me and my sister Kathy and my two brothers Steve and Mike. We'd play outside all day, burrowing through the bracken, making dens and playing travellers on our bikes, somehow carrying a clothes horse and blanket with us to make a tent! We only went home when it was time to eat and sleep. Poor Mum! Our hair would be a wild tangle of knots, bracken and wee beasties, but what an upbringing! I wouldn't swap those childhood experiences for anything. They stood me in good stead for future ventures.

'So when it came to sitting out on the fells waiting for Dad's search dog Spindrift to come and find me, I was already accustomed to spending most of my time in the outdoor environment. Joining the local mountain rescue team and training a search dog was a natural progression, which I thoroughly enjoyed and still do to this day. My first search dog Anna was a lovely natured, very loyal Border Collie bitch I could take anywhere. She was no trouble at all. We never actually had any genuine finds with her because we were rarely given areas to search where the missing person was located. But her potential always revealed itself on training and assessment searches – she never failed to find the bodies. Anna loved people, and finding them was always a big reward. She was a real people dog and loved by everyone. I learned the trade with Anna.

'Training dogs is something I've developed through practice. You grow with your dog, learn from others, make mistakes and, in the process, you become experienced and wiser. Having trained and worked Anna and helped other potential dog handlers, as well as becoming an assessor, I felt I'd accumulated enough knowledge to train another dog with ease.

How wrong I was! Einich was a wilful, lively, alpha collie bitch and she introduced me to a completely new set of challenges! She would often metaphorically raise two fingers at me by sniffing at something on the ground that was much more interesting than responding to my command. I sometimes wondered who was training whom! Basic obedience training was a real contest and that was before we even started search training proper. She was a highly intelligent, instinctive dog that required a different approach; everything had to be set up to enable her to work it out for herself. It was no easy task, but I persevered and eventually we passed the final assessment to become a fully graded dog team. I now feel very confident in her ability and working with her is an absolute pleasure.

'Yes, it's tough at times, turning out in all weathers, taking to the hills when you'd really rather be asleep in bed, the ongoing commitment to training, training and then more training... it's a challenging life. But SARDA isn't just about training dogs. It's about the human beings we set out to search for and the people left waiting and wondering, helpless with fear, hope and expectation — the family and friends, wives, husbands and children, and the difference we can make to their lives.

'I saw it first, one deathly dark night with Anna. By the time I arrived at the offshore rescue base, members of this close knit estuary community were already gathered. They stood silently, clinging to each other for comfort. Their anxious faces, cast stark and white by the floodlights, were reluctant yet to register grief, staring hard into the blackness, willing their loved ones to reappear. It was two of their community —

a father and son — who had gone missing in a small craft whilst out fishing.

'As Anna and I prepared to move away and begin our search, that's when I saw it — that look, etched on each and every face. One by one, they turned towards us and it struck me how critical is this role we play, bringing hope to those in waiting.

'So... when people ask why I'm still involved 25 years on, that's why. It's the look in their eyes, the trust and expectation, the hope beyond hope. All that hope and expectation hangs on us, because we're quite possibly their last and only hope of seeing their loved ones alive.'

Acknowledgments

Searching for missing people is all about dog handlers, rescuers and people from other emergency services helping one another and working towards a common goal. Writing this book has been very similar. We have shared common skills, contributed our own special areas of expertise and worked closely as a team. But we have also benefited greatly from the expertise and experiences of people from many and varied backgrounds both within search and rescue and beyond. All those we have sought help and guidance from have been exceptionally obliging and willing to assist us, in what has been a long and complicated task. We are greatly indebted to the following people for providing gems of insight and permission to use their stories and photographs. A sincere thanks to them and to the many more – too numerous to mention – who have helped us along the way.

Alex Wilson Owner of dog casualty
Alfie Ingram Former chairman MRC of Scotland
Ally Macaskill Wildland ranger John Muir Trust
Andy Bluefield Former handler SARDA Scotland
Andy Colau Handler SARDA England
Annabel Williams Communications officer The Guide Dogs Association for the Blind
Bill Batson Handler SARDA England
Bill McLoughlin Syndication department DC Thomson & Co Ltd
Caitriona Lucas Secretary and handler SARDA Ireland
Caroline Morton Handler SARDA South Wales
Caroline Duce Secretary SARDA Wales
Catherine Kelly Handler SARDA Ireland
Charlotte Thomson Reporter Newsline Scotland

Chris Francis Call-out coordinator and handler LDMRSD
Chris Lloyd Chairman and press officer Ogwen Valley MRO
Chris Nixon Member Kintail MRT
Craig Coady Secretary BADA-UK
Craig Pieroway Police officer Central Scotland Police Underwater Unit
Daryl Garfield Handler LDMRSD
David Allan Chairman MREW and member of Duddon & Furness MRT
Dave (Heavy) Whalley Former chairman MRC of S
Dave Watt Handler (late) LDMRSD
David Benson Handler SARDA Scotland
David Marsh Secretary NSARDA
Dawn Lowe Dogsbody SARDA Southern Scotland
Daz Steatham Handler SARDA Scotland
Darryl Urquhart-Dixon Call-out coordinator SARDA Southern Scotland

Don Murphy Handler and assessor SARDA Ireland
Duncan Tripp RAF Winchman Paramedic D Flight, 202 Squadron
Ellie Sherwin Secretary SARDA England
Elly Whiteford Handler LDMRSD
Eryl Crump Reporter The Daily Post
Gordonstoun School MRS
Hamish MacInnes Founder of SARDA and President of SARDA Scotland
Harold Burrows Chairman NSARDA
Heather Morning Mountain Safety Adviser Scotland and handler SARDA Scotland
Helen McNamara Handler SARDA Ireland
Iain Nicolson Handler SARDA Wales
Ian Billings Proprietor Norvic Philatelics
Ian Hurst Team member Buxton MRT
Ian Thompson Handler SARDA England

Iain Swann Retired A&E consultant
Isobel George Senior press officer The PDSA
Jacquie Hall Training adviser SARDA England
Jane Brown Dogsbody LDMRSD
Jan Millar Former handler SARDA Scotland
James Coles Handler SARDA Southern Scotland
Jim MacGregor Handler SARDA IOM
Jim Sudd Statistician MRC of Scotland
Joanna Toohey Dogsbody SARDA Southern Scotland
John Armstrong Former handler SARDA Scotland
John Bell SARDA Southern Scotland
John Coombs Handler SARDA England
John Easton Former handler SARDA Scotland
John Hill Webmaster SARDA England

Joy Grindrod Handler LDMRSD
Kaz Frith Handler LDMRSD
Ken Weatherstone Secretary
SARDA Scotland
Kenny Lang Veterinary surgeon and
handler SARDA Southern Scotland
Kenny MacKenzie Founder member
of SARDA
Kevin Stead Handler
SARDA England
Kevin Waterson Chairman
NSARDA Anglia
Les Telford Handler LDMRSD
Linda Robinson Former Secretary
SARDA Wales
Liz Outram Handler
SARDA Southern Scotland
Lorna Evans Veterinary surgeon
Killearn, Scotland
Lorna Shelbourne Border Collie
breeder
Lt Col D Ross Commandant
Garelochhead Training Camp
Lynne Warden Former handler
SARDA Southern Scotland
Malcolm Grindrod Handler
LDMRSD
Mark Hogarth Handler
SARDA Southern Scotland
Maureen Hennis Chief executive
Pets as Therapy
Mick Guy Training officer and
handler LDMRSD
Mike Hadwin Treasurer and handler
LDMRSD
Mike Walker Handler
SARDA Scotland

Moira Weatherstone Handler
SARDA Scotland
Morag Lindsay News feature writer
The Press & Journal Aberdeen
Neil Hamilton-Bulger Handler
SARDA Southern Scotland
Neil Galligan Artist
Neil Powell Handler SARDA Ireland
North
Netti Collister Veterinary surgeon
and former handler SARDA Wales
Neville Sharp President
SARDA England
Niall MacLean Police dog handler
Northern Constabulary
Nick Smith Handler SARDA England
Nikki Wallis Former handler
SARDA Wales
Nikki Wright Hearing Dogs
Paul Martin Secretary
SARDA Southern Scotland
Paul Smith Head of photographic
The Press and Journal
Paul Tedder Former member of
NSARDA CanTech
Paul Whiting Former development
officer IMRA
Pete Durst Former handler and
chairman SARDA England
Pete Roberts Director Centre for
Search Research
Peter Sandground Professional
photographer
Phil Williams-Jones Former
handler SARDA Wales
Richard Terrell Equipment Officer
MREW

Rita Howson Director of operations
Support Dogs
Robert Farnham Call-out
coordinator and handler
SARDA South Wales
Robert Shearer Dog handler Central
Scotland Police
Roger Pickup Handler LDMRSD
Roger Smith Former handler
SARDA Scotland
Rosanna Wilkinson Research
assistant Imperial War Museum
Richard Beech Handler
SARDA Wales
Rod Kelly Dogsbody
SARDA England
Rupert Bonham Handler
SARDA Southern Scotland
Sandy Seabrook Former handler
SARDA Scotland
Sarah Sculpher Hearing Dogs
Séamus Kearns Chairman LS Dogs
Shelley Carnell Member of ALSAR
Shelley Coyle Secretary
SARDA Wales
Simon James Handler
SARDA South Wales
Simon Woodrow Former handler
LDMRSD
Stephen Austin Handler SARDA
Southern Scotland
Steve Domeney CRO
Steve Penny Former handler
SARDA Southern Scotland
Stuart Fuller-Shapcott Team
member Borders SRT
Stuart Kenny Secretary

NSARDA CanTech
Stuart Male Member Lomond MRT
Sue Layland Handler SARDA Wales
Terry Blanchard Dogsbody
LDMRSD
Tom Gilchrist Handler
SARDA Scotland
Tom Middlemas SAR dogs trainer
Trevor Lynch Fire investigation dog
handler Central Scotland Fire and
Rescue Service
Wendy Fox Director BADA UK Ltd
Willie Fraser Former handler
SARDA Scotland
Yvonne Oliver Sales and licensing
Imperial War Museum

Useful references

BOOKS

Allan, D., & Whiteside, J. (2006). **So you want to join mountain rescue?** Kirkby Stephen: Hayloft Publishing Ltd.

Barton, B., & Wright, B. (2000). **A chance in a million: Scottish avalanches (2nd ed).** Glasgow: The Scottish Mountaineering Trust.

Bradshaw, J. (2011). **In defence of dogs: Why dogs need our understanding.** London: Allen Lane.

Clunes, M. (2008). **A dog's life.** London: Hodder & Stoughton Ltd.

Coren, S. (2006). **The intelligence of dogs.** London: Simon & Schuster UK Ltd.

Dudley, E. (1970). **Rangi – Highland Rescue Dog.** London: Harvill Press.

Fennell. J. (2001) **The dog listener.** London: William Morrow (Harper Collins).

Fogle, B. (1992) **The dog's mind.** London: Pelham Books.

Herriot, J. (1995). **James Herriot's favourite dog stories.** London: Michael Joseph Ltd.

High, K. (2010). **40 years and counting.** Barnard Castle: Teesdale and Weardale Search & Mountain Rescue Team.

Holmes, J., & Holmes, M. (1998). **Reading the dog's mind: Training by understanding.** Gloucester: Ringpress Books Ltd.

Horowitz, A. (2010). **Inside of a dog: What dogs see, smell and know.** London: Simon & Schuster.

Hurst, I., & Bennett, R. (2007). **Mountain rescue history and development in the Peak District.** Stroud: Tempus Publishing.

Locke, A. (1989). **Sam and Co. Heroic search dogs of the fells.** Berkshire: Awesome Books.

Locke, A. (1991). **Search dog.** Concord, St. MA: Paul & Co. Pub Consortium.

Maslen-Jones, B. (1993). **Countdown to rescue.** Glasgow: The Ernest Press.

Most, K. (1954). **Training dogs: A manual.** London: Popular Dogs.

Powell, N. (2011). **Search dogs and me.** Belfast: Blackstaff Press.

Roy, M. (2009). **The dog lover's pocket bible.** Richmond: Crimson Publishing.

Sand, S. H. (2003). **Physiology of domestic animals.** Scandinavian Veterinary Press:

Sharp, B., & Whiteside, J. (2005). **Mountain rescue.** Kirkby Stephen: Hayloft Publishing Ltd.

Sykes, B. (2009). **Understanding border collies.** Marlborough: The Crowood Press.

Syrotuck, W. G. (2000). **Scent and the scenting dog.** Pennsylvania: Barkleigh Productions, Inc.

The monks of New Skete. (2002) **How to be your dog's best friend.** London: Little, Brown and Company.

Whaley, S. (2003). **One hundred ways for a dog to train its human.** London: Hodder & Stoughton.

Wilhide, E. (2011). **Extraordinary dogs.** London: Quadrille Publishing.

Wight, J. (2000). **The real James Herriot.** London: Penguin Books.

WEBSITES
Features

Butler, J. (2011). Dogs. http://joybutler.suite101.com/

Jacob, T. (2008). Smell (Olfaction): A tutorial on the sense of smell. http://tinyurl.com/69nv8u4

Guy, M. & Nicolson, I. (2011). Search and rescue dog association (SARDA). http://tinyurl.com/7jo2da9

Harris, H. (2006). How dog training works. http://tinyurl.com/6l64akc

Rupkalvis, M. (2011). Are dog intelligence tests reliable? http://tinyurl.com/63ajpzu

Wikipedia (2011). Dog intelligence http://tinyurl.com/zju6s

Associations

Borreliosis and Associated Diseases Awareness (BADA) UK.
http://www.bada-uk.org/

SARDA England
www.sardaengland.org.uk

SARDA Wales
www.sardawales.org.uk

Lake District Mountain Rescue Search Dogs
www.lakes-searchdogs.org

SARDA South Wales
www.sardasouthwales.org.uk

SARDA Ireland
www.sardaireland.com

SARDA Ireland North
www.sardairelandnorth.co.uk

SARDA Southern Scotland
www.sarda.org.uk

SARDA Scotland
www.sarda.org

SARDA Isle of Man
www.sardaiom.im

NSARDA
www.nsarda.org.uk/

NSARDA CanTech
www.cantech.org.uk

Lowland Search Dogs
http://lsdogs.org.uk

Irish Mountain Rescue Association
www.mountainrescue.ie

Mountain Rescue England and Wales
www.mountain.rescue.org.uk

Mountain Rescue Committee of Scotland
http://www.mrcofs.org

ARTICLES & MAGAZINES

Cablk, M.E., J.C. Sagebiel, J.S. Heaton, & C. Valentin. (2008). Olfaction-based detection distance: a quantitative analysis of how far away dogs recognise tortoise odour and follow it to a source. **Sensors, 8** 2208-2222.

Katz, J. (2005).
Train in vain. Why dog training fails.
http://www.slate.com/id/2112301/

Mountain Rescue England and Wales. (2011).
Missing person behaviour resources.
http://www.searchresearch.org.uk/www/ukmpbs/

Nuttall, I. (2008).
Urban search and rescue (USAR) canines within the UK Fire Service. www.leicestershire-fire.gov.uk/documents/Canines-Within-the-Fire-and-Rescue-Service.pdf

Perkins, D., Roberts, P., & Middlemas, T. (2001).
The Performance of Air Scenting Search Dogs in the UK.
http://www.searchresearch.org.uk/downloads/papers/dogstudy.pdf

Perkins, D., Roberts, P., & Feeney, G. (2011).
The UK missing person behaviour study.
http://www.searchresearch.org.uk/www/ukmpbs/

White, S., & Tieken, T. (1999).
Scent – K9's reason for being.
www.uspcak9.com/training/scent.pdf

Your Dog Magazine.
www.yourdog.co.uk

Appendix 1: Timeline

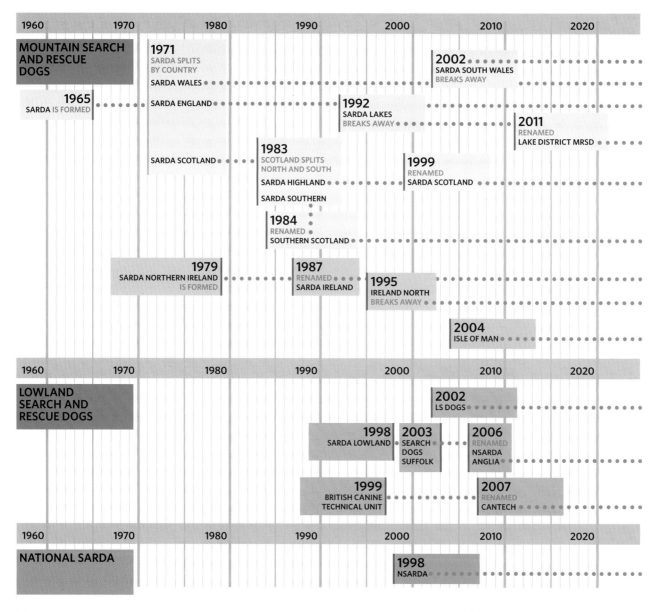

MOUNTAIN SEARCH AND RESCUE DOGS

1960 · 1970 · 1980 · 1990 · 2000 · 2010 · 2020

1971
SARDA SPLITS BY COUNTRY
SARDA WALES

2002
SARDA SOUTH WALES
BREAKS AWAY

1965
SARDA IS FORMED

SARDA ENGLAND

1992
SARDA LAKES
BREAKS AWAY

2011
RENAMED
LAKE DISTRICT MRSD

SARDA SCOTLAND

1983
SCOTLAND SPLITS NORTH AND SOUTH
SARDA HIGHLAND
SARDA SOUTHERN

1999
RENAMED
SARDA SCOTLAND

1984
RENAMED
SOUTHERN SCOTLAND

1979
SARDA NORTHERN IRELAND IS FORMED

1987
RENAMED
SARDA IRELAND

1995
IRELAND NORTH
BREAKS AWAY

2004
ISLE OF MAN

LOWLAND SEARCH AND RESCUE DOGS

1960 · 1970 · 1980 · 1990 · 2000 · 2010 · 2020

2002
LS DOGS

1998
SARDA LOWLAND

2003
SEARCH DOGS SUFFOLK

2006
RENAMED
NSARDA ANGLIA

1999
BRITISH CANINE TECHNICAL UNIT

2007
RENAMED
CANTECH

NATIONAL SARDA

1960 · 1970 · 1980 · 1990 · 2000 · 2010 · 2020

1998
NSARDA

Appendix 2: Call-outs 2001-2011

NUMBER OF DOG CALL-OUTS EACH YEAR FOR EACH ASSOCIATION 2001-2011

ASSOCIATION	2001	2002	2003	2004	2005	2006	2007	2008	2009	2010	2011
ENGLAND	67	97	92	95	64	109	109	169	168	132	128
IRELAND	5	7	8	14	11	16	16	17	22	24	21
IRELAND NORTH	5	10	10	12	7	6	6	14	11	10	23
ISLE OF MAN						13	4	8	9	6	5
LAKES	27	40	33	66	42	49	56	59	73	72	78
CANTECH								36	38	27	46
ANGLIA						17	12	23	19	32	58
SCOTLAND	53	43	55	47	74	64	59	86	81	77	87
SOUTHERN SCOTLAND	39	43	51	33	56	71	71	66	91	55	35
SOUTH WALES			34	34	30	47	50	48	46	35	27
WALES	26	39	38	42	47	51	53	74	71	119	72
TOTAL	222	279	321	343	331	443	436	600	629	589	580

Note: Cells shaded in green indicate that the association had yet to be formed.

By the same author:

The RHP Companion to Outdoor Education by Peter Barnes & Bob Sharp.
Published by Russell House Publishing (2004).

Acquiring Skill in Sport by Bob Sharp.
Published by Sports Dynamics (2004).

Mountain Rescue by Bob Sharp & Judy Whiteside.
Published by Hayloft Publishing (2005)

The Lomond Mountain Rescue Team: All the rescues and more by Bob Sharp.
Published by the University of Strathclyde (2006).

Rescue 2010 by Bob Sharp and Archie Roy.
Published by the Lake District Search and Mountain Rescue Association (2012).